THE
UNITED STATES
OF AMERICA

A SHORT HISTORY

Gateway to America – immigrants at Ellis Island, New York, 1912. (Library of Congress)

THE UNITED STATES OF AMERICA

A SHORT HISTORY

Albert Desbiens

Translated by Julie McPhail

ROBIN BRASS STUDIO
Montreal

Copyright © Les Éditions du Septentrion 2007
Translation copyright © Julie McPhail 2007

All rights reserved. No part of this publication may be stored in a retrieval system, translated or reproduced in any form or by any means, photocopying, electronic or mechanical, without written permission of Robin Brass Studio Inc.

First published 2004 as *Les États-Unis d'Amérique : synthèse historique* by Les Éditions du Septentrion, Sillery, Quebec

English edition published 2007 by Robin Brass Studio Inc.
www.rbstudiobooks.com

Printed and bound in Canada by Marquis Imprimeur, Cap-Saint-Ignace, Quebec

Library and Archives Canada Cataloguing in Publication

Desbiens, Albert, 1939-
    The United States of America : a short history / Albert Desbiens ; Translated by Julie McPhail.

Translation of: Les États-Unis d'Amérique.

Includes bibliographical references and index.
ISBN 978-1-896941-51-6

    1. United States – History. 2. Politics, Practical – United States.
3. United States – Politics and government. I. McPhail, Julie II. Title.

E156.D4813 2007   973
C2007-904600-2

Canada Council   Conseil des Arts
for the Arts   du Canada

Financial support for this translation was provided by the Canada Council for the Arts and the Department of Canadian Heritage through the Book Publishing Industry Development Program.

A Note from the Publisher
We are grateful to Professor Donald R. Hickey, Department of History, Wayne State College, Nebraska, for reading the translated text and making numerous useful suggestions on matters of clarity and historical terminology. Thanks too to Dawn Loewen for editorial work.

À ma fille Véronique
À mon fils Mathieu

Mes meilleurs chapitres

CONTENTS

1 A Successful Colonization   1
    Foundations of English colonization 3
    First settlements: Virginia and Maryland 6
    New England 12
    The Middle Colonies 17
    Turn of the century 19

2 The Colonies within the Empire   21
    The Nine Years' War 22
    The War of the Spanish Succession 23
    Growth and development of the colonies 24
    A new society develops 35
    The Seven Years' War in America (The French and Indian War) 39

3 Separation   41
    The Empire in 1763 and its problems 42
    Root causes of the conflict 45
    Immediate causes 48
    Revolution 55
    War 59

4 Establishing the Republic   64
    A national government 64
    The era of aristocrats 72
    The War of 1812 83
    The "Era of Good Feelings" 86

5 Problematic Growth ~ 1820–1850   89
    A democratic age 89
    Political life 90
    A new age: social changes 98
    The South and slavery 103
    The industrial North 105

6	Trial by Fire ~ 1851–1865	109
	The crisis of the 1850s 109	
	The American Civil War 119	
7	Foundations of the Modern United States ~ 1865–1900	131
	Reconstruction 133	
	The New West 140	
	Industrial Revolution 143	
8	Progressivism and War ~ 1898–1919	155
	Early stages of empire and the Spanish-American War 160	
	The era of progressivism 163	
	The First World War 172	
9	The Roaring Twenties to the New Deal ~ 1920–1939	179
	The Twenties 181	
	The Great Depression 189	
	The New Deal 191	
10	The Second World War and the Rise to Superpower Status	198
	Foreign policy after the First World War 198	
	The Second World War 201	
	The postwar domestic scene 213	
	The Cold War begins 215	
11	High Hopes… and Doubts ~ 1960–1974	223
	JFK: An enduring myth 224	
	Lyndon B. Johnson 235	
	The Nixon years 242	
12	A Turn to the Right ~ 1974–2003	247
	The Carter years 248	
	The Reagan era 253	
	Next in line: George H.W. Bush 259	
	Clinton takes the reins 264	
	2000 election: George W. Bush 269	
	Epilogue	271
	Bibliography	277
	Index	281

MAPS

The American states	x
Colonial America in 1763	43
Borders under the Quebec Act of 1774	53
Expansion of the United States, 1783–1853	96
Allegiance of states in the Civil War	120

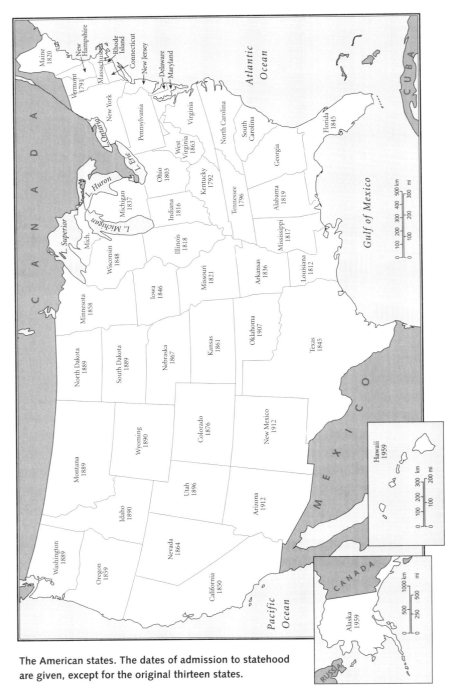

The American states. The dates of admission to statehood are given, except for the original thirteen states.

CHAPTER 1

A SUCCESSFUL COLONIZATION

When America was supposedly discovered by Christopher Columbus in 1492, it had already been occupied for millennia by peoples who had come from Asia in successive waves through the continental northwest. Tens of millions of people lived in indigenous settlements when contact was first made between Native Americans and Europeans. Some estimates even put the total population of the Americas close to Europe's at the time, and up to 10 million people may have lived in America north of the Rio Grande. The conquest and the diseases introduced by Europeans and Africans into the Native American population, who had no immunity to smallpox, mumps, malaria or yellow fever, wreaked unprecedented havoc. Never mind that the New World was no disease-free paradise (an increasingly sedentary and urbanized lifestyle had apparently been undermining pre-Columbian health for centuries); that first contact took an undeniably grim toll. It affected not only health, but also values, customs and relations among American Indian nations.

Some Europeans – Scandinavian explorers, Basque and Breton fishermen – had already established contacts with the continent and its peoples. Columbus's discovery marked the point when Europe and its emerging states were ready to capitalize on those contacts and attempt to settle there in a sustained and permanent way. The Columbus expedition was only one stage in a worldwide process in which the European nations fought over the world's resources, beginning with the Orient's. First to trade with the East were Italian trading cities such as Venice, Genoa and Pisa. Exotic goods, spices, precious stones, carpets and perfumes were imported through Constantinople, Antioch and Alexandria to be distributed by the Italians. The various powers of a newly expansionist

Europe eventually sought to escape the Italian middlemen by looking for an alternate route, especially after the fall of Constantinople to the Turks in 1453.

With the advantage of countless technical advances and innovations in navigation, as well as princes and businessmen to back the costly enterprises, explorers set off to discover the world on behalf of emerging states. Portugal led the way. Since the 14th century the Portuguese had rivalled the Italians on the Mediterranean, and they soon became the leading players in the great explorations. Under Henry the Navigator (1394–1460), they made multiple voyages southward down the coast of Africa then eastward, laying the foundations of an empire out of proportion to the country's small size and population. The Portuguese set up trading posts all along their route, even into India and China, discovered gold in Africa and monopolized the lucrative slave, spice, silk and perfume trades. Lisbon became Europe's distribution centre for Oriental goods. The country grew rich and built a surprisingly long-lived empire.

Spain, reunified by the marriage of Ferdinand of Aragon and Isabelle of Castille and finally free of Moorish occupation (by the end of the Reconquista, 1492), was desperately looking for a new route to the Orient, as the Portuguese had a stranglehold on all known routes. This was the context in which Columbus, a sailor from Genoa by way of Portugal, convinced the Spanish monarchs that it would be possible and profitable to reach the Orient by sailing west. What happened next made history. Spain would go on to build a highly profitable empire based on resources from what became countries such as Mexico and Peru. It found not only gold and silver but populations to work in mines and on sugar and tobacco plantations; when these populations resisted, as often happened, it resorted to slavery. The mother country had the resources to set up the institutions, bureaucracy and military and naval forces to back the endeavour. A century after Columbus's death in 1506, before the English had established a single colony in the New World, Spain controlled almost the entire Atlantic coast of South America (except for Brazil, Portugal's control of which it recognized in the Treaty of Tordesillas, 1494), Central America and Mexico and had pushed northward through what is now American territory into Florida, New Mexico and California, passing through Arkansas, Alabama and Texas.

Spanish predominance in no way meant the other European nations had stepped aside. Far from it – they all wanted a part of the wealth that clearly flowed from colonization. France and England had never accepted the Hispano-Portuguese monopoly over the New World, but the latecomers realized they would have to settle far away from the powerful Spanish. They would go farther north.

King Francis I of France, who had demanded to see the clause in Adam's will dividing the world between the Spanish and the Portuguese, financed an expedition by the Italian Verrazano in 1524 to find a passage to Cathay (China). The explorer sailed up the American coast from North Carolina to Maine, discovering the Hudson River and spending time in New York harbour, but returned to Dieppe empty-handed. He had not found a passage. He was later killed by natives during a second voyage to the West Indies in 1526.

Jacques Cartier took up the challenge of exploring North America for the king of France in 1534, 1535 and 1541. On his first voyage, he discovered no resources, spices, precious metals or passage to Asia, but he brought back useful knowledge of the continent. He left again in 1535 to explore the St. Lawrence, known as the Road to Canada by the Indians. From Stadacona (today's Quebec City) he headed up the river to Hochelaga (Montreal), then turned back to winter in Stadacona, where scurvy added to the miseries of the Quebec winter. He returned to France in 1536. Although empty-handed once again, he had found a way inland. War delayed the next voyage until 1541. This expedition was bigger, and Cartier thought he had discovered gold and diamonds, but disappointingly it was only fool's gold and quartz. The colony was abandoned. France's American ambitions would not re-emerge until Samuel de Champlain began his explorations in 1608. The intervening religious wars distracted France from its colonial enterprise. The French still made a few attempts at settlement on the coasts of Brazil and Florida, but the ever-watchful Spanish and Portuguese wiped them out.

Foundations of English colonization

England, like the rest of Europe at the time, was undergoing radical transformations. It would be reshaped by the combined forces of the "price revolution" (a long period of steady inflation), the Reformation and political turmoil.

The population of England was growing considerably, rising from 3 million to 5 million between 1500 and 1630. Goods were becoming scarce and prices were rising sharply. Inflation was undermining social structure. Noblemen living on fixed incomes saw their wealth shrink considerably and their social and political status follow suit. The middle class and small landowners adapted better to the changes, prospered and began to wield more political influence. The peasantry, three quarters of the population, was also affected by the rise in prices, but even more by the "enclosures" that deprived them of their right to use common land. The enclosures benefited large landowners, who had moved into raising sheep for wool that was then processed and sold on expanding European markets. The dispossessed peasants, often migrating to cities in search of work, made good candidates for emigration.

Colonial expansion would have been impossible if it weren't for a system integrating government aid, legislation, monopolies and subsidies to merchants that encouraged manufacturing, export and, if possible, colonization. Colonial expansion took place within a generally accepted system of mercantilism by which resources from the colonies would be used first and foremost to enrich the mother country, which would use the colonies as markets for the finished products. The English government encouraged national production, curbed imports, increased exports and improved the trade balance. Gold and silver circulated, stimulating the economy. State coffers brimmed as national power grew. While mercantilism took varying forms in Spain, Holland, France and England, every colonial power of the time was determined to set up a trade monopoly with its colonies while competing with the monopolies of rival nations.

In 1497, Giovanni Caboto (John Cabot), a Genoese in the service of the English, explored the coasts of Newfoundland and Nova Scotia, but was not the last to decide the land lacked the resources, and his sailors the determination, to make North American colonization worthwhile. Other expeditions were undertaken to expand English trade to Russia, Turkey, Africa and the Orient, but no settlements resulted. One practice became the norm, however: the expeditions were financed by companies that pooled the resources of shareholders who individually would have lacked the clout.

Despite the interest in exploration, piracy and commercial profits; despite the capital deployed and the advances made; despite the growing conviction that England needed colonies to succeed, nothing concrete and permanent came out of the reign of Elizabeth I. Humphrey Gilbert and Walter Raleigh had failed to settle in Newfoundland or Virginia after several attempts. Raiding Spanish galleons for gold was more attractive to English adventurers in the late 1500s. Famous buccaneers like John Hawkins and Francis Drake brought back fortunes to England, enriching their shareholders, including the Crown, and paved the way for a formidable naval tradition. But by the late 16th century England had more freedom to act in the colonial arena. Ireland had been subjugated and Philip II of Spain's invincible Armada (1588) had failed miserably to conquer England, where the sociopolitical situation brought about by the Reformation and its associated political and religious quarrels was a major factor in creating the final conditions necessary for colonial expansion.

The Wars of the Roses, which had brought the Tudors to the throne, had ended in 1485. The conflict had dealt a severe blow to English feudalism. Henry VII (who reigned 1485–1509) and Henry VIII (1509–1547) were determined to restrict the nobility's powers even further by relying on the support of the new merchant middle class. Henry VIII, a Renaissance humanist prince, had at first sided with Rome in the struggle pitting the Catholic Church against reformers such as Luther and Calvin and their growing numbers of European disciples. The reformers denounced the practices of the Catholic Church, questioned its doctrine and condemned its ostentatious wealth. When the pope refused to annul Henry VIII's marriage to Catherine of Aragon, which had not produced a male heir, the king broke with Rome, declared himself the head of a separate Church of England and looted monasteries, selling the land off to wealthy merchants to consolidate his power.

The change was earth-shaking. While Anglicanism remained close to Catholicism in practice, the breach allowed new religious beliefs to spread throughout England. Some were not content with the English Reformation and pushed for more radical separation (the Puritans) while the majority of the population remained faithful to Rome. The country became a pressure cooker set to explode.

Under Henry VIII's successors, religious turmoil continued to buffet the nation, eventually leading to civil war and forcing large communities wanting to practise their religion freely to look to America. Mary Tudor, eldest daughter of Henry VIII, had tried to return the country to Catholicism but managed only to fan the flames of discord. When Elizabeth I succeeded her in 1558, pressure in favour of the Protestant Reformation was overwhelming. Elizabeth re-established the Anglican Church, yet she did not depart enough from Catholicism to satisfy the Puritans, whose teachings were spreading throughout England, while the Catholics maintained their resistance. Persecution and political agitation spread. Under James I (who reigned 1603–1625) and Charles I (1625–1649), thousands of Puritans set out for a "new England" that would embody their vision of a reformed Christian society. Not to be outdone, the persecuted Catholics left in turn. More so than other colonial powers, England populated its colonies as well as exploiting their resources. The ranks of the emigrants were filled by persecuted religious groups, economic malcontents, political dissenters and adventurers.

First settlements: Virginia and Maryland

The English first settled around Chesapeake Bay in Virginia. Like colonizers from other nations – Portugal, Spain, France, Holland or Sweden – they were looking for gold, furs and other marketable products. In Virginia they found instead fertile soil, a coveted product – tobacco – and enough manpower in indentured workers (and eventually slaves) to establish a settlers' colony.

In 1606, the shareholders (fifty-six busniesses and 659 individual investors) of the London branch of the Virginia Company were granted a charter by James I. The charter conferred resource rights over a huge tract stretching between what is now New York and North Carolina. All American land belonged to the king, and only the king could grant a charter to colonial entrepreneurs outlining their rights and obligations. In addition to the land surrounding the settlements, which companies would control, the king gave them rights over mineral resources (with royalties paid to the king) and all other resources in the territory. The company had to govern in accordance with English law. Colonists and their children would benefit from all the "liberties, franchises and immunities" granted English citizens.

The expedition mounted by the Virginia Company of London (also known as the London Company) in 1607 founded the first permanent English settlement in North America at Jamestown. Forming a settlers' colony was not a priority for the English conquistadors. They were there not to work but to reap gold. The beginnings were hard. The colonists had to rely on the natives for food, and disease struck the population, already weakened by malnutrition. Early relations with the natives had been good but quickly deteriorated, given the Europeans were there as invaders. The company, however, stayed the course and kept fresh influxes coming. Between 1607 and 1610, 1,200 people settled in Jamestown, but fewer than half remained. The colony found a coveted commodity in 1612, however, when John Rolfe discovered that tobacco could be grown there. First brought to Europe from the New World by the Spanish, tobacco was already popular in England. In a few years, shipments from Virginia to the mother country increased dramatically, and as early as 1618, 14,000 kilograms (30,000 pounds) were being exported annually. To attract more colonists, the company established the right to private property (1617), as well as authorizing a representative assembly and allowing women to settle (1619). Between 1619 and 1624, 4,500 colonists settled in Jamestown. A land grant to all new arrivals or whoever transported them to America (the "headright" of fifty acres or about twenty hectares of land) increased the colony's appeal.

The colony needed more people, but also more land, as tobacco cultivation rapidly depleted the thin local soil. More land meant more pressure on neighbouring tribes. English policy became one of exclusion: it wasn't necessary to incorporate the natives into the population, but instead to push them constantly to the outskirts of the settlements by seizing their land. In 1622, the colonists were surprised by an attack that left over 350 dead. Still, the colony held out. The natives were now the aggressors and a "just" war could be mounted against them. The colony, however, was almost bankrupt and in 1624 the king made Virginia a royal colony, the first in a series with governors appointed by the king. Assemblies maintained their legislative power even if bills still had to be approved by the Privy Council. The Anglican Church was also "established" in the colonies, with the citizens required to contribute to parish costs.

Between 1625 and 1640, the population increased considerably to ten thousand inhabitants despite disease, war and famine. There was less pressure from the depopulated Indian tribes; by 1670 only two thousand of the two hundred thousand Algonquin originally living in the Jamestown area remained. Demand for tobacco drove production from 1.4

million kilograms (3 million pounds) in 1640 to 4.5 million kilograms (10 million pounds) in 1660. Chesapeake Bay's economy revolved around tobacco farming, and thrived.

Neighbouring Maryland developed on a similar economic model. Two characteristics set it apart, however. Not only was Maryland a proprietary colony, but its Catholic proprietors would attempt to create a haven there for Catholics persecuted in England. In 1632, Charles I granted Cecilius Calvert, second Lord Baltimore and heir to a family close to the Crown, a 10-million-acre (4-million-hectare) concession on northern Chesapeake Bay. All lands belonged to the proprietor to use as he saw fit. He had the power to appoint the governor and all public office holders. He could even found churches and name pastors. It amounted to a palatinate, meaning the lord/proprietor enjoyed the same privileges as the king in his domain. However, he owed obedience and allegiance to the king. The charter also specified that the landowner had to govern with the "advice, assent and approbation of the freemen" of the colony.

Land was distributed to large landowners, primarily Catholic, in the form of plantations of 1,000 to 3,000 acres (400 to 1,200 hectares). The large landowner then distributed plots to smaller farmers. All paid a quit-rent as well as a poll tax. Pressure exerted by the tobacco-farming economy to expand the domain and the demand for labour quickly led to a relaxing of the rules. Maryland adopted the headright and land distribution became more democratic. The arrival of many non-Catholic colonists forced the Calvert family to revise its plans. The settlement's success took precedence over setting up a haven for Catholics. In 1638, the right to initiate legislation was granted to the assembly, which was divided into two houses in 1650. The lower house represented the interests of ordinary colonists while the upper house remained under the influence of the large Catholic landowners. From the outset, Cecilius Calvert had instructed his brother, Leonard, the colony's appointed governor, to be careful not to scare away Protestants and to downplay Catholic presence in order to ensure social peace and the colony's survival. Lord Baltimore also approved the Toleration Act of 1634, granting religious freedom to all Christians, Catholic and Protestant. Founded in 1634, the only English colony with a substantial minority of Catholics would be successful along the lines of Virginia, and by 1670 Maryland numbered more than fifteen thousand inhabitants.

Indentured servants

The appeal of tobacco farming lay in its profitability, but most Englishmen drawn to America or forced out of the Kingdom of England had few resources. As the crossing was expensive and the costs of settling were substantial, close to three quarters of the Chesapeake Bay colonists crossed the ocean as indentured servants. It is estimated that at least 200,000 English people tried to settle in America in this way. In return for the price of their crossing, workers committed to work for whoever had paid their passage for periods ranging from two to seven years. Planters benefited from the system because each crossing conferred on them a fifty-acre headright. The large Southern plantations were built in this way. Most indentured servants were young, unskilled men working as field hands. There were few craftsmen, women (outnumbered by men five to one in the 17th century) or children. A few vagrants and ex-convicts completed the labour force. Children often had to serve until their twenty-first birthday, and convicts' terms could be as high as fourteen years. Masters were expected to house, feed and clothe their indentured servants properly. Compliance was uneven.

Once their service was completed, the contract workers were to receive tools, a rifle, clothes and a plot of land so they could settle in their turn. Life was still hard in the colonies, however, and only three out of five indentured servants managed to complete their service. Many went in search of new land for tobacco, settling in primitive conditions in the West with their families. They lived in shacks, huts and even caves. Malaria struck and many women died in childbirth. Early death was commonplace. Families were small, and few parents survived into their children's adulthood. Even planters lived in rudimentary conditions, investing everything in tobacco production. They were isolated and had few schools, churches or other institutions. Community was worth little – the autarchy of the plantation was the norm. Cities were few in the South, and the region's extensive network of navigable rivers meant trade was often carried out directly with England. During the 17th century in particular, colonial life was organized around England, which provided the markets and capital necessary for development.

Beginnings of slavery

The solution to the labour shortage was slavery. Both Virginia and Maryland resorted to it early, but the practice did not become widespread until the last quarter of the 17th century when English migration was dwindling and the colonies needed ever more manpower.

The first Africans were unloaded at Jamestown in 1619. Their status was vague. At first it seems they were considered servants, although they'd come unwillingly. Their status quickly evolved to servants for life. Black became a synonym for slave. Given that they cost more than indentured servants and there was as much risk of losing them to an epidemic as white workers, slaves were used rarely in the first few decades. In 1650 there were only a few hundred blacks in the Chesapeake Bay colonies. Some were freed, in part because of religious conversion, becoming landowners themselves and taking on slaves or indentured servants. Religion seems to have played an important role in these cases as it was likely the main criterion for integrating into 17th-century America.

Beginning in the 1660s, the situation changed substantially. The notion of ownership of one human being by another did not exist in English common law. It had to be invented. In Virginia it gradually was, following the obvious example of English planters in the West Indies. Rules were laid out governing the relations between owners and slaves, whose lives were no longer their own. Lifetime servitude was established by the courts and blacks were forbidden to bear arms or serve in the militia. Slaves could not learn to read or write. They could not serve as witnesses or have recourse to the law. They were denied the possibility of owning property. Being black was now a permanent, hereditary mark of inferiority. Sexual relations between blacks and whites were normally banned, but there was much interbreeding.

In 1705, a Virginian ruling declared that all servants arriving in Virginia who were not Christian in their country of origin were to be considered slaves. The Virginia slave code created a slavery-based society that was emulated by the other colonies. Virginia and Maryland had around 20,000 slaves at that point and the "peculiar institution," as slavery was euphemistically called, was spreading like wildfire throughout the American territory. It was most pronounced in the South, where tobacco, rice and indigo farming were labour-intensive. As the number of indentured servants had dropped considerably in the late 17th century, planters fell back on now lower priced slaves.

The tobacco crisis

After years of prosperity from 1620 to 1660, the tobacco market collapsed. In 1660, tobacco prices dropped to a tenth of 1620 prices, for two reasons. Overproduction was the first: as the population grew and plantations multiplied, production rose. From 1.4 million kilograms (3 million pounds) in 1640, production grew to 4.5 million kilograms (10 million pounds) in 1660 then doubled by 1670 to reach 18 million kilograms (40 million pounds) in 1690. That was more tobacco than Europe could consume. The second cause was English policies. Beginning in 1651, Parliament adopted a series of Trade and Navigation Acts that clearly illustrated English mercantilist policy. Under the mercantile system, the purpose of colonies was to enrich the mother country either by supplying gold or by selling raw materials to English industry at a discount and buying expensive finished products from the mother country. Benefits such as a guaranteed market were available to the colonists. But everything had to go through England, where prices were set by English merchants.

In the mid-17th century the Dutch, who occupied an important place in trade, had to be overcome. First, foreign vessels were prohibited from trading with England's colonies. Then it was resolved that imports and exports could be transported only by English-owned vessels with English captains and crews that were three-quarters English. Ships built in the colonies were considered English. Certain items were also "enumerated" to be sold exclusively to England or another colony. Lastly, English merchants were granted a monopoly over colonial trade. All European merchandise destined for the colonies had to go through England. Tobacco planters could no longer trade with the Dutch, who traditionally paid the best prices, or get supplies from them at lower cost. Adding to the effect of these policies was a tobacco tariff aimed at filling royal coffers but which instead raised tobacco prices, causing demand to fall.

The regional economy stagnated. Small producers were particularly affected, as were indentured servants, whose chances for success looked slim. They could no longer set themselves up. The larger planters fared better. They leased out land, lent money and engaged in commerce, coming to dominate life in the area. Resentment set in and divisions intensified in a climate of corruption and elite privileges.

When war broke out with the natives on the frontier, the conflicting interests of the wealthy planters of the east and the small landowners of the west, who felt neglected and exposed, came to a head. In 1676, after the corrupt governor of Virginia, Sir William Berkeley, proposed an unpopular plan, Nathaniel Bacon led a revolt by people who felt abandoned by the grandees on the coast. Bacon overthrew Berkeley and civil war broke out. Jamestown was razed. After Bacon's death in the conflict, the authorities regained control, but lessons had been learned. Caution would be exercised in future. The interests of the lower classes would be taken into account, but the ruling classes would also seek out less dangerous servile labour. To maintain their social position, the large landowners of Virginia and Maryland turned ever more to a social system based on the exploitation of black slaves.

New England

First contacts
At first sight, the northern Atlantic coast did not seem suited to English settlement in the 17th century. The area was already dominated by the French and the Dutch. Samuel de Champlain had established contacts with Indian tribes as far south as Cape Cod. The Dutch controlled the Hudson River fur trade. The English challenged the French and Dutch stranglehold but never dealt the final blow. John Smith of Jamestown was even captured by the French in the area in 1614.

Nature was on England's side. A deadly epidemic ravaged the area between 1616 and 1618, killing tens of thousands of natives, weakening French–Dutch alliances and reducing any potential resistance to English colonization.

The Plymouth Colony
The Virginia Company's venture did not end with the settlement at Jamestown. The Plymouth branch also tried to settle colonists farther north. The attempt failed. The territory set aside for the company, however, would soon be populated by colonists with strong religious motives.

A group of separatist Puritans from the village of Scrooby, Yorkshire, first emigrated to Leyden in the Netherlands in search of a place to practise their religion freely and found a city of God. After ten years there, they realized that they and their children were being assimilated and risked falling prey to worldly vanities. They decided to emigrate again.

They made contact with the merchants of the London Company and, in September 1620, set sail from Plymouth on the *Mayflower*. Whether by chance or design, the pilgrims landed north of Virginia, in what is today Massachusetts, a territory outside the charter. On November 11, the men of the expedition signed the Mayflower Compact, drafted by William Bradford, who for thirty years was elected governor. The Compact was a commitment to good behaviour under a government chosen by the signatories. It was the first constitution adopted in North America.

Life was hard. Only half the colonists survived the first winter in Plymouth, once again thanks to help from the natives. Unlike the Virginians, the pilgrims, who had come over with their families, lived in good houses and worked the land. The colonists' strict religious discipline helped them to overcome hardship, and in the area's healthy climate the colony's population grew naturally. Progress was less rapid than in southern Virginia without a flagship product like tobacco. Ten years after it was founded, Plymouth numbered some 300 inhabitants and seemed destined to stagnate even while gaining new recruits and spreading into outlying areas.

Massachusetts

The political and religious climate in England deteriorated further after Charles I ascended the throne in 1625. Like his father, James I, he reaffirmed the Crown's allegiance to the Church of England and faced strong opposition from Puritans, increasingly influential in Parliament. In 1629, the king dissolved Parliament to exercise personal rule by the "divine right of kings." Many Puritans became convinced that emigration was the best way to protect themselves.

In 1629, a charter was granted to a joint stock-trading company run by rich Puritans, the Massachusetts Bay Company. They were persuaded to hand over the charter to a group of Puritans wishing to settle in America. This time it was a sizeable venture. In 1630, 900 Puritans under the leadership of John Winthrop packed up and crossed the Atlantic to found a "city on a hill," a beacon of reform. Between 1629 and 1643, some 20,000 colonists settled around Boston. A good half were Puritans, but other colonists included peasants, craftsmen and indentured servants fleeing the poverty that was rife particularly in eastern England. Among the emigrants were many families.

Winthrop, taking advantage of the charter's unusual omission of a location for the company's headquarters, brought the charter with him. He transferred operations to America, turning the company into a civil government. The status of freeman, or voter, was granted to all male heads of households belonging to a Puritan church. Freemen could be named to sit in a representative assembly.

Winthrop was elected governor of the colony and remained so for fifteen years. Power was wielded rigidly by a Puritan oligarchy (1 percent of the population). Having emigrated to preserve their religious practices, the Puritans were little inclined toward tolerance. Like most of their contemporaries, they believed that social stability was impossible without religious uniformity. Puritans were convinced they practised the only true religion, and it had to be allied with civil authority. Many of them believed that collectively they were God's chosen people. Disciples of Calvin, they believed in predestination: an elect people, they were destined for heaven even before they were born. The number of the elect was extremely limited and membership in a congregation of the elect was subject to close examination. Even when recognized as part of the elect by the community, a "saint" could not be guaranteed the same approval by God.

Relations with the Indians

The Puritans' relations with the natives were governed by their certainty that they were the keepers of the true faith in the face of heathens. Like most Europeans, the Puritans considered the natives to be culturally inferior and unworthy of civilized treatment. They looked to the Bible and saw enemies of the chosen people, enemies who had to be wiped out. They felt they had a right to seize land that was unoccupied according to English criteria: undeveloped land belonged to no one. Land that had not been worked or fenced off could be seized. As the Indians lived mainly by hunting, gathering and fishing, farming structures were few.

Epidemics were also ravaging native villages and thinning out the territory's population. In 1633–1634, smallpox devastated the natives. Winthrop interpreted the tragedy as a sign that God supported the Puritan cause. How could God be against us, he reasoned, when He is reducing their number and we are increasing ours? The near-extermination of the Pequot – nearly five hundred men, women and children – in the 1637 Pequot War was also attributed to God. Survivors were hunted down and reduced to slavery. At the same time, the Puritans were capable of caring for the sick during native epidemics and trying to redeem them from the sin that caused their "savage" condition. Conversion efforts by the Puritans were characteristically rigid, however. Natives were required to adopt English customs and know Puritan theology by heart.

A Puritan society

A crucial aspect of the just society the Puritans yearned for was independent communities and churches composed of free property owners living in socially responsible families. The colony's General Court did not grant headrights or favours to the privileged, and title deeds could not be accumulated. A system of townships (usually 6 miles by 6 miles, or 10 by 10 kilometres) was set up in which groups of colonists were authorized to settle and divide the land in freehold. Broader distribution of land did not signify equal condition or status. The Puritans believed in a social and economic hierarchy. Inequality was God's will. In most New England cities, the richest and most influential usually managed to get the better part of the land allocated to themselves. Some people owned no land at all but, despite the inequalities, land ownership was more widespread than in Virginia or Maryland, and the least privileged enjoyed more economic security.

Heads of families participated in town meetings, where all local matters were resolved. They voted to establish taxes, supervised the church and chose its pastors, and delegated members to the General Court. Puritan ministers kept a close watch on the community. Everything from public life to political orientation was scrutinized. Although there was never a true theocracy, since the pastors never actually governed, their deciding influence was felt in every aspect of society. Heresy and democratic zeal were particularly mistrusted. In Massachusetts, religious freedom meant freedom to practise the "true" religion, and Puritan magistrates quickly clamped down on dissidence. In 1635, Roger Williams, a Puritan pastor from Salem, was banished for preaching the separation of church and state, questioning the policy on Indian lands and advocating a total split from the Anglican Church. He went on to found Rhode Island with other dissidents, and in 1644 that colony received a charter from the English Parliament, now controlled by Puritans. Rhode Island put Williams's teachings into practice since no church was established there and everyone could practise freely. Anne Hutchinson, who would also eventually move to Rhode Island, suffered the wrath of pastors annoyed that a woman was expressing ideas contrary to their teachings. Exiled in 1637, Anne Hutchinson paid not only for her religious teachings but also for straying outside her female condition.

The intolerance of Puritan Massachusetts society led to resentment and a number of breakaway colonies. Another case was Thomas Hooker and his followers, who were behind the founding of Connecticut; the Hartford and New Haven colonies were united in 1662, and the largely autonomous colony was sanctioned by royal charter. Based on covenants and the purchase of Indian land, these settlements had faced opposition from Boston and needed royal sanction to gain a solid foothold.

The Puritans had emigrated to a much less fertile region than Chesapeake Bay, with the exception of valleys such as the Connecticut and the Merrimac. Yet the area quickly filled up with subsistence farms clustered around a house of worship and a town hall. The family farm required the joint efforts of husband, wife and children. Field work was reserved for men, while women took care of the house, garden, henhouse and dairy. While independent to a degree, women were subordinate to men. Married women could not own property, vote or sign contracts. Women married young by today's standards (around twenty, on average) and had many children (seven or eight if they survived until forty). On the other hand, they could expect to live to around sixty-five, considerably longer than in England. Some widows managed to establish themselves. Although adultery was considered a crime, the Puritans were not hostile to sex, accepting and even encouraging sexuality within marriage. Childless women or overly independent widows were perceived as a threat, and Puritans tended to see supernatural forces, even demons, at work in them. These suspicions came to a head in the witch hunt hysteria. Scores of witchcraft charges were brought in New England. Most were thrown out of court, but many hangings took place, mainly of women. The most famous episode was the Salem witch hunt of 1692. It all started when some young girls claimed to be possessed. They went into a trance and made accusations against men, women and even a child. When the episode was over, almost two hundred people had been charged and around twenty executed. The community and the authorities reacted, and in 1693 the governor put an end to the affair by setting up a court that quickly threw out the charges.

A SUCCESSFUL COLONIZATION

Justice in Colonial times was little changed since the Middle Ages. Here three miscreants were sentenced to have one ear cut off, to be whipped twenty times at the public whipping post and to spend an hour in the pillory at Charlestown, Massachusetts, for passing counterfeit money. (Broadside, Boston, 1767. Library of Congress)

It appears that social tensions were at the root of the hysteria. Many historians have made the connection between the trials and the changes Puritan society was going through at the time. Some have detected a rivalry between Salem Town, where the political and church elite lived, and the less prosperous Salem Village. Others have exposed the central role played by Pastor Samuel Parris, claiming he was taking revenge on parishioners who objected to his hiring. Perhaps most important, the majority of victims were older women living alone. The Salem trials were a clear indication of Puritan prejudice toward women.

The Middle Colonies

After years of wielding arbitrary power over a country divided by religious quarrels, Charles I was forced to recall Parliament in 1639. A Scottish army marched on England. The Puritans who dominated the House of Commons wanted to limit royal power. Civil war broke out in 1642. The parliamentary forces headed by Oliver Cromwell (1599–1658) were victorious, the king was executed in 1649, and Cromwell assumed dictatorial powers himself from 1653 until his death. At that point the country was longing for calm, and in 1660 Parliament recalled Charles II (1630–1685), the exiled son of Charles I. The Stuarts had been restored to the throne, but the troubles in England had loosened control over the colonies, where the legislatures had asserted their independence.

Charles II set about establishing a new series of proprietary colonies to secure the English presence in America. These Restoration colonies served to repay political debts and were an attempt to increase Crown revenue. The king compensated his aristocratic friends and supporters by granting them millions of acres of land: Carolina in 1663 to eight noblemen and New York, snatched from the Dutch in 1664, to the king's brother, the Duke of York. Over decades, Holland had built a trading empire with help from the Iroquois, who brought them furs from the continent's interior. With the elimination of the Huron, who had supplied furs to the French, and the Swedes, who plied the Delaware, the Dutch made gains – only to lose them in 1664 when the English seized Manhattan. From his huge concession, the Duke of York carved the territory of New Jersey and handed it over to other noblemen as a proprietary colony.

Carolina would eventually be divided in two: North Carolina, populated by colonists from Virginia, and South Carolina, whose pro-slavery colonists originally came from Barbados. The latter colony also took in a large contingent of French Huguenots after the revocation of the Edict of Nantes in 1685.

Pennsylvania

In 1681 William Penn, in repayment of a large sum owed by the king to Penn's father, was granted a huge territory west of the Delaware River. He had converted to Quaker beliefs, based on an "inner light" that brings on a trance or trembling state, hence the name. William Penn had suffered persecution and wanted to make his colony a refuge, a "holy experience." Even before the arrival of any colonists, who were guaranteed religious freedom and political rights, Penn negotiated with the natives to purchase their land.

Pennsylvania was a success. Over ten thousand colonists settled there in the first decade. Lessons had been learned since Jamestown. The site had been chosen before the arrival of the colonists; the main city (Philadelphia) was planned by Penn; and settlers were recruited by advertising in England and Germany. Pennsylvania's economy revolved around grain production and livestock. The city of Philadelphia became one of the major ports of the English colonial world. In 1704 Penn, who owned other territories snatched from the Swedish and the Dutch to the south of his colony, recognized a separate administration for Delaware.

The last English colony to be founded in America was Georgia (1733). Its social-reformer proprietors wanted to make it a colony where the poor of England, often imprisoned for debt, could be settled. However, with the colony threatened by neighbouring Spanish Florida, its development was delayed.

Turn of the century

The English had settled over a quarter million colonists on American soil by the end of the 17th century. Unlike the French, Dutch and Swedish, whose main interest was the fur trade and hence settled few farmers, the English were looking for land to settle individuals as well as families looking to emigrate. The colonies were diverse. During the long English civil war, the colonies had enjoyed considerable leeway, but the Restoration changed everything. In the final years of the century, England clamped down with navigation acts and tried to centralize colonial administration further. Charles II's mercantilist policy followed along the lines of Cromwell's: colonial trade had to be profitable. The king created a branch of the Privy Council, the Lords of Trade and Plantations, to advise him on colonial policy. Navigation acts were tightened and duties imposed on American products. In 1696, the Board of Trade (a chamber of commerce made up of the fifteen top experts in colonial affairs) replaced the Lords of Trade and Plantations and centralized decision-making.

England spent enormous amounts overcoming the Dutch and securing a dominant position in world trade. The new policy succeeded, but at the cost of enormous friction with the colonies. The situation did not improve when James II (1685–1688) acceded to the throne. A new, authoritarian model of colonial administration was created with the Dominion of New England. A huge merger of all colonies from Maine to New York State, the Dominion was administered by Sir Edmund Andros, who attacked nearly all the Puritan-established institutions and the colonies' autonomy. Fortunately for the colonists, James II's rivals were keeping a

Table 1
Approximate population of the American colonies, 1610–1780

Year	Population	Year	Population
1610	350	1700	250,888
1620	2,302	1710	331,771
1630	4,646	1720	466,185
1640	26,634	1730	629,445
1650	50,368	1740	905,563
1660	75,058	1750	1,170,760
1670	111,935	1760	1,593,625
1680	151,507	1770	2,148,076
1690	210,372	1780	2,780,369

The Statistical History of the United States from Colonial Times to the Present, Stamford, 1965, 756.

close watch. The Glorious Revolution forced him into exile and brought to the throne his daughter, Mary II (who reigned 1689–1694), and her husband, William of Orange (1689–1702), who accepted a constitutional monarchy and guaranteed the rights of English citizens under the Bill of Rights (1689). The newly installed monarchs dropped the restrictions imposed on self-government but also took the occasion to turn Massachusetts, New York and Maryland, where there had also been upheaval, into royal colonies. This continuing will to control signalled more unrest to come.

CHAPTER 2

THE COLONIES WITHIN THE EMPIRE

In the early 18th century, the English colonies in America were a motley patchwork with diverse origins, varying makeup and often opposing interests. The British government, driven by its mercantilist policy, was looking to organize and control colonial trade to the advantage of its merchants, manufacturers and shipyards. Mercantilists saw the economy as a zero-sum game. The wealth of nations was a function, they believed, of the share of the gold and silver in circulation they could control. Any gains had to be snatched from others in a constant struggle to come out on top. Britain had already managed to replace the Netherlands as the top Atlantic power. The next step involved a long struggle with France for colonial supremacy, a struggle that would end in the British victory of 1763.

The Caribbean islands were the prize colonies. They were so beautiful and so rich in products such as sugar, tobacco, coffee and vanilla. The profits reaped there by Britain backed up its mercantilist arguments. The islands provided the mother country with products it lacked or could easily sell on international markets. Any study of British imperial policy must take into account the islands and the importance of slavery to the empire. In the 18th century, the West Indies accounted for nearly 65 percent of exports to Britain. When exports from the South are added, fully 95 percent of exports were produced in colonies using slave labour. This is how important slavery and the islands were to the imperial economy. In comparison, exports from New England and the Middle colonies made up only 5 percent of the total despite their having at least half the population. Not only was production from slave colonies central to British interests; the slave trade itself was a source of astronomical profits and so weighed heavily in the balance. The ratchet effect of trade with Africa and America meant Britain could accumulate capital, create jobs and build warehouses and factories. The result was a head start in the Industrial Revolution.

Against this background, competition between nations was fierce, and colonial clashes joined the standard European motives for going to war. Conflicts usually began in Europe around the traditional issues of continental balance of power, but colonies could also be the cause, and the colonization of America had always been contentious. As colonies developed, fighting became increasingly unavoidable and every European conflict was an excuse for the colonials to try to wipe each other out. Raids were frequent, in Acadia, New France, New England or Florida, and no mercy was shown. Furthermore, for most colonists the conflicts were a fight to the finish between Catholicism and Protestantism.

The Nine Years' War

At first glance, France might seem to have been the most likely to build an American empire. New France covered a huge territory, ever expanding in search of new fur supplies. Controlled by a system of forts and small settlements, the territory stretched from Louisiana to Hudson Bay and centred on the St. Lawrence River and the Great Lakes. In addition, the French had a network of Indian alliances based on better relations with the natives than the British or the Spanish enjoyed. Yet France was irredeemably left behind in the colonial race. Although French territory hemmed in the American colonies east of the Appalachians and threatened to cut them off, their vitality was a source of concern to the French. The French trade empire was no match for the well-established settlers' colonies. In 1700, the population of the twelve colonies had reached 250,000 while New France's hovered around 15,000, and the territories' unequal resources led to unequal development.

The Nine Years' War (1689–1697) started in America two years ahead of Europe. The Anglo-Iroquois alliance meant the French had to occupy the Hudson Bay trading post network. In 1686, the Compagnie du Nord and the d'Iberville brothers, including Pierre Le Moyne, began taking over British forts. Wide-scale warfare was triggered by an Iroquois raid on Lachine, gateway to the North Country. The French met atrocity with terror. Deadly, surgical raids came one after another on the border of the American colonies. Back in Britain, colonial conflicts had not yet become pressing, and it was left to the New England authorities to devote their considerable energy and resources to the conflict. In 1690, Sir William Phips, governor of Massachusetts, emboldened by having succeeded in taking Port Royal, Acadia (in present-day Nova Scotia), assembled a force of 34 ships and 2,000 men and advanced up the St. Lawrence River toward Quebec, defended by Governor Frontenac, who had recently been recalled to New France. Simultaneously an overland force advanced from the south. Phips's badly trained force was checked at Quebec and the overland invaders were halted by smallpox and dissension. The Treaty of Ryswick (1697) essentially re-established the status quo in the colonies and entrusted the fate of Hudson Bay to a commission.

The War of the Spanish Succession

The War of the Spanish Succession (1701–1713) gave rise to renewed hostilities in the colonies. Priorities remained the same for New England: re-conquering Acadia and trying to eliminate New France. The British wanted to take back the fur-trading Hudson Bay basin, where the interests of many British merchants were at stake. New France, having partially neutralized the Iroquois with the Great Peace of Montreal (1701), won a stunning series of victories – raids on the New England border, the conquest of Newfoundland – and held on to positions on Hudson Bay. Port Royal had fallen again, but the planned invasion of New France failed miserably once again when Admiral Sir Hovenden Walker lost part of his fleet of 12 battleships, 40 transports and 5,000 troops on the reefs in the Gulf of St. Lawrence. News of the failure turned the overland invasion back once again. There were also skirmishes between the British and Spanish in the area of South Carolina and Florida.

The Treaty of Utrecht (1713) was advantageous to Britain, giving it Gibraltar, Minorca and the *asiento*, the right to ship 4,800 slaves annually to Spanish America for a period of thirty years. The British were also authorized to send one ship per year to the Spanish colonies. France lost the most, and the cost to it in America was very high. Newfoundland, Acadia, Hudson Bay and the West Indian island of St. Kitts were lost. France recognized Britain's authority over the Iroquois and opened the door to British claims on the continental interior. France kept Cape Breton Island, where it fortified Louisbourg, but its colonial holdings had been dealt a severe blow. Its demise would have to wait, however. Peace settled in for the next generation. The American colonies would feel freer to develop their social and political institutions as well as their economic potential.

Growth and development of the colonies

Trade and expanding economies

Although factions in Britain wanted to tighten trade controls through navigation acts and impose production limits on colonial goods that could compete with British goods, the Americans benefited from the British trade system. In spite of having to sell their products in Britain, planters benefited from a protected market and their purchasing power grew over the years. Credit was available, and planters took full advantage. Grains, flour, meat, dairy products, wood and fish could be freely sold as they were not among the enumerated commodities. Markets for these products were found in the West Indies and even the American South, where production focused more on rice, tobacco and indigo.

The majority of trade was carried out with ships from New England, which were considered British. As a result, shipbuilding was given a tremendous boost. At the end of the colonial period, some 30 percent of the 7,700 ships registered in British ports had been built in the colonies. Wood was scarce in Britain while the colonies had plenty. Colonial shipyards also produced a large fishing fleet.

As of 1715, trade with the West Indies accounted for half of all traffic in the port of Boston. Northern ports also quickly specialized in re-export of Southern products to the mother country. The Northern and Southern economies became more and more integrated. Transportation, insurance and credit were just some of the services offered by the merchants of Boston, Philadelphia and New York to colonial producers.

It is safe to say that both the Americans and the British were fairly satisfied with the economic system as it operated in the first half of the 18th century. For one thing, many Americans lived on subsistence farms and were little affected by mercantilism. For another, those who were affected often managed to avoid the effects of regulations that were spottily enforced by Britain. The British government was generally satisfied with the prosperity generated by trade in the leading products of the American economy and practised what might be termed benign neglect. British laws were not applied rigorously and Americans got used to getting around them. The British must also have been pleased that the Dutch had been eliminated from imperial trade. Markets were guaranteed and enjoyed the protection of the British army and navy. However, surplus production from the colonies risked competing with goods from the mother country. To prevent this, London ordered, for example, that beaver pelts must be exported unprocessed and iron must not be manufactured.

It is very difficult to say whether the system ultimately helped or burdened the colonials. A definitive assessment seems impossible. What is certain is that once the mother country was obliged to enforce its rules to improve its finances, the drawbacks overtook the advantages. The Americans' view of the situation would lead to changes.

The population grows

The English colonies in America experienced remarkable population growth. While New France had only one period of rapid growth, the population tripling over the twenty years when Jean Talon was intendant (1665–1668 and 1670–1672), American growth never flagged. It was based on a high birth rate (one new child per family every two years), low mortality and heavy immigration both voluntary and involuntary, since slaves contributed significantly to colonial growth. There were 70,000 blacks in the colonies in 1720, 236,000 in 1750 and 386,000 in 1760. In the same years, whites numbered almost 400,000, then 934,000 and finally 1,207,000. The African slave trade continued to expand. Forty thousand slaves were imported during the decade of 1731–1740, then 58,000 between 1741 and 1750 and 69,000 from 1761 to 1770. Only the decade of 1751–1760 bucked the trend while the colonies were embroiled in the Seven Years' War (1756–1763). In total, some 240,000 slaves were imported during the colonial period. Most of the population was composed of men, with a ratio of two young men between fifteen and thirty for every woman.

The most populous region was the South. In the mid-18th century, it had a population of 514,000 compared to 360,000 in New England and 296,000 in the Middle colonies (New York, New Jersey, Pennsylvania and Delaware). Settlement was unplanned. Every American colony was desperate for settlers, who were drawn by the opportunity to live in greater freedom and less poverty.

They came from everywhere and gradually formed a cosmopolitan society. In 1700, 80 percent of colonists in America were English or Welsh and 11 percent African. Tiny Scottish, Dutch and French minorities made up the rest. In 1775, English descendents were in the minority. Blacks approached 20 percent overall and made up a third of the population of the South. Only New England remained, like New France, ethnically homogenous. The population of the Middle colonies exploded and diversified. Germans, Scots and Irish settled there, particularly in Pennsylvania because of its religious freedom and liberal agrarian policy. In 1749, twenty-four ships unloaded six thousand Germans in Philadelphia. Less than twenty years later, 125,000 Germans and Swiss had settled in the Middle colonies. Some feared that the colonies could not absorb such large influxes, but their fears were unfounded. The immigrants assimilated and integrated mainly through British institutions. On the eve of the Revolution, the vast majority of future Americans spoke English. The British policy of encouraging foreign immigration to the colonies had paid off. Even Huguenots came; between ten and fifteen thousand settled in Boston, Charleston and New Rochelle, where they became highly influential.

The population was unevenly distributed. Coastal regions were more densely populated than the interior, where the latest arrivals would be found. These frontier pioneers, who were often fleeing persecution in their homelands, would struggle against the oppression and domination of elites from more established regions. In turn, they took advantage of the availability and low cost of land, often seizing it from the Indians and defending it against them. Although these pioneers are often presented in a positive light relating them to the progress of democracy in America, it is important to be aware that they were people of the 18th century. They believed in a social hierarchy and the subordination of other human beings and, in many cases, that violence was justified and even necessary. On the other hand the frontier had a certain levelling effect on society.

Growth of cities
Heavy commercial activity meant rapid development for American port cities. Boston had 15,000 inhabitants in 1770, New York 21,000 and Philadelphia, by then the largest city, 28,000. Charleston, with 11,000 residents, was the most populous city in the South, which had few cities. There

were also smaller cities such as Newport, Baltimore and Salem. All relied mainly on trade with Britain, the West Indies, Europe and Africa as well as with other regions in America. Fishing was an important industry concentrated in coastal towns. Fish was used to feed slaves and supply the European market. In 1750, no fewer than 4,000 people on 600 boats were employed in New England fisheries. The logging industry, maritime shipyards and other related industries were also concentrated in port towns.

The bustling, smaller cities of the interior developed as trade moved deeper inland in search of products from increasingly productive farms. Carpenters and coopers set up shop. Roads were needed, and inns to lodge the carters who travelled on them. All these occupations stimulated the economy. In 1750, for example, 370,000 bushels of wheat and corn and 16,000 barrels of flour were exported from the interior of Maryland to the coast. As a rule, roads were sorely lacking. In 1756, it took three days to travel the 150 kilometres (93 miles) between New York and Philadelphia. Yet by the time the War of Independence broke out, roads had been greatly improved: the Seven Years' War had forced the British to link cities by decent roads to facilitate troop movements.

Agriculture

Nine out of ten Americans worked in agriculture in the 18th century. Land was cheap, abundant and fertile in many regions. New England, with its thin, rocky soil, was the exception. The growing season was also shorter there, making farms less productive and profitable. Operations were small in New England, often requiring only one family to run them.

The staple product was corn, which was grown in all the colonies. Tobacco was the lifeblood of Virginia and Maryland. Rice and indigo were predominant in Georgia and the Carolinas. Small amounts of cotton were produced in the South, but nothing substantial until Eli Whitney's cotton gin (1793) made production profitable. There were many large plantations in the South but also many small farms, and agricultural production was varied. Wheat made up 16 percent of total exports from the South shortly before 1776.

All colonies produced some hemp, wheat, oats and buckwheat. But the Middle colonies were the leaders in these crops as well as in livestock. They were the breadbasket colonies. On the eve of independence, their grain exports were valued at £348,000, or 73 percent of their total exports.

And yet colonial agriculture was underdeveloped. Plowing implements were often primitive across the Western world, and the American colonies were no exception. The agrarian revolution did not occur until the second half of the 18th century. Farmers depleted the land, and productivity was not an issue when more land could be acquired so readily. Fertilization and crop rotation were rare to non-existent. Livestock breeds often degenerated and epizootic disease ravaged herds. Fifty thousand head of cattle were lost in 1673 in Virginia, and twenty-five thousand in 1694 in Maryland.

Industries develop

The obstacles to industrial development in America's English colonies were many. There was the chronic shortage of capital in what was then a developing country. The specialized labour required was scarce and expensive. Financial instruments to facilitate trade were few. But even more significant were the predominance of agriculture, which allowed so many people to improve their lot, and the mother country's mercantilist policies.

Still, as early as the mid-17th century, a variety of consumer goods were produced to meet everyday needs. As a rule, only luxury goods or goods requiring a large outlay of capital or a highly specialized workforce to manufacture were imported. A major part of what could be termed industrial production came from farms, where men and women were often craftspeople as well. Farmers were also carpenters, shoemakers, coopers, seamstresses, tanners and soap- and candle-makers.

Cottage production eventually reached such a volume that it exceeded local needs. Markets needed to be found, and therein lay a problem. From 1688 on, London attempted to tighten its policy suppressing possible competition from colonial production that involved processing. The 1699 Wool Act banned export of woollen garments abroad or on the intercolonial market. Under the Hat Act of 1732, the result of pressure from London hatters, the export of beaver hats from one colony to another was banned. Apprenticeship to the hatter's trade was restricted and blacks were excluded. In 1750 and 1757, London passed legislation affecting the iron industry: it became illegal to build rolling mills, forges or furnaces for refining steel. Cast iron and iron bars, however, were allowed into Britain tariff-free. The mother country's iron and steel industry had to be supplied and expansion of the processing industry on colonial soil limited.

One industry that prospered was logging. Colonials took advantage of the quality and density of the forests. Britain, dependent on an outside timber supply, encouraged the industry. Beams and planks were needed for the local and West Indian markets and wood for the barrels used to transport practically everything. It is estimated that around 1750 the colonies were building three to four hundred thousand barrels a year for themselves and the West Indies. Most of the industry was concentrated in New England, whose wood exports, on the eve of the Revolution, made up 32 percent of their total exports. Shipbuilding also contributed to the logging industry's robustness. Production costs were lower in the colonies by about a third despite a scarcity of specialized labour and accordingly high salaries. Around 1750, colonial shipyards were building 300 to 400 ships annually. These vessels of varying tonnages supplied both the fishing and merchant fleets.

The shipyards sustained the growth in production of associated equipment such as rope, tar, resin, oakum, nails, chains and anchors. All these products came out of colonial farms and workshops. Farmers often used the winter months to process raw materials into value-added commodities. This was the case, for example, with potash, an essential ingredient in soap, used in wool manufacturing in Britain. The Northern colonies were exporting 14,000 barrels of soap yearly by the end of the colonial period.

Trade relations

From farms, plantations, mines, foundries, sawmills, forges, flour mills and the sea came products destined to be traded either within the colonies or on outside markets. Yet major obstacles lay in the path of commercial development.

Overall, the trade balance was unfavourable to the colonies throughout the entire colonial period and the situation got worse over the years. Whereas in 1700 the value of imports of British products to the colonies exceeded that of exports by £50,680, in 1760 the trade deficit had reached £754,000. All the colonies except the Carolinas had a trade balance deficit. Prices of American merchandise were often set in Britain and duties were often imposed. The British also controlled the price of their own merchandise.

Credit was introduced by London merchants and the interest paid helped drain the colonies. Financial instruments were lacking. It was illegal to take currency out of Britain, which could not spare any. The colonies resorted to makeshift measures. Barter was used. Foreign coins, of limited usefulness, were acquired. Bills of exchange also filled part of the need. Massachusetts struck coins from 1652 to 1684, but the coins also ended up in Britain. It was then decided to print paper money. Trade was stimulated and other colonies followed Massachusetts' suit, but the currency depreciated and bad money drove good money out of circulation. Inflation hit and disagreements between creditors and debtors grew acrimonious. When in 1751 London tried to limit the issue of paper money secured by land, Britain was accused of taking sides with the American bourgeoisie.

The colonies integrated into the mercantile system to varying degrees. And despite strict laws, planters, merchants and white colonists generally benefited from the system. The South, with its coveted products, integrated well. The Northern and Middle colonies produced grains, flour, fish, meat and dairy products, which, not being enumerated, could be sold on the open market. The most easily accessible market for them was in the West Indies and the South. Colonial merchants were particularly active in the West Indies despite bans by the colonizing powers.

The 1733 Molasses Act imposed a duty on molasses bought from non-British islands. French molasses in particular was less expensive than molasses from British islands (having been excluded from France by wine producers who feared competition from molasses-derived rum), and American merchants continued hiding contraband molasses in cargo legally imported from the British West Indies. Fortunately for the colonials, laws were half-heartedly enforced and customs officials eminently bribable. The sixty or so rum distilleries in New England in 1760 were kept running, producing two million gallons a year of the popular drink so much in demand on international markets.

It is true that by 1715 half the tonnage going through the port of Boston was made up of goods destined for or coming from the West Indies. But it also seems that Northern and Southern economies, thanks to trade, were much more integrated than first appears. Taking descriptions of the differences between the regions too literally, and talking about two models of development and two societies, neglects the fact that they were created and functioned within the same economic system, a system that tended toward integrating the neighbouring partners. For example, between 1730 and 1770, the volume of trade between Charleston and Britain doubled, while trade between Charleston and the Northern ports increased sevenfold. Merchants in Boston, Salem, Newport, Philadelphia and New York traded goods back and forth. Wood, grain and fish went to the West Indies in exchange for tobacco, sugar and indigo, which were then shipped to Great Britain at a profit. And all this trade was on ships built in the North. These transactions allowed New England's merchants to line their pockets even though the region had no commodities in high demand in Europe. Profits from interest on commercial transactions, advances on credit and the sale of insurance meant that the necessary capital could be accumulated for the commercial and industrial development of port cities.

Triangular trade

The so-called triangular trade model is often used to represent British commercial relations in the colonial period. While convenient, the model is simplistic and the trade situation involved more than just trilateral commerce. Trade evolves over time and the merchants, ship owners and captains of the time were aware and profit-motivated enough to find opportunities outside established patterns. That said, it is possible to discern the following broad outlines while keeping in mind that, while some routes were controlled more by the British and some by the colonials, there was never a monopoly.

The British largely controlled the trade of manufactured goods and rum to Africa in exchange for slaves, who were taken to the West Indies and exchanged for sugar and molasses, which was brought back to Britain. The third side of the classic triangle was the direct trade of British manufactured goods for sugar and molasses. Yet there were other triangles superimposed. For example, colonial merchants sent fish and rice to southern Europe in exchange for wine and fruit, which were brought to Britain and exchanged for manufactured goods. Nothing prevented colonial merchants from returning directly from southern Europe carrying salt and wine. Another major route was between America and Africa. In exchange mainly for rum, slaves were bought to be resold on Southern or West Indian plantations or exchanged for exotic goods or sugar products.

Finally, as we have seen, the Northern colonies had well-established trade networks with the West Indies as well as the Southern colonies. Grain, wood and fish bought tobacco, sugar products, indigo and rice, which were either processed on site or sent back to the mother country. To sum up, a model of superimposed triangles better represents the reality of colonial trade.

Political life

Despite wide differences in political arrangements among the British colonies in America, two main characteristics of their development were increasingly widespread autonomous government and improved democratic standards.

In 1775, there were eight royal colonies (Massachusetts, New Jersey, New York, New Hampshire, Virginia, North Carolina, South Carolina, Georgia), three proprietary colonies (Pennsylvania, Delaware, Maryland) and two self-governing colonies (Connecticut and Rhode Island). The governor was the leading figure in the colony. He represented and was appointed by the king in the royal colonies. In the proprietary colonies, he was named by the proprietor, except in Delaware, which shared a governor with Pennsylvania. In the case of Delaware, the king had to approve the choice of the Penn family, which controlled both colonies. The king's approval was also required in the semi-autonomous colonies, where the governor was elected by the assemblies.

The governor was the seat of executive power. He convened and dismissed the houses and exercised veto power on legislation by the elected assembly. He generally received orders from the Board of Trade in London. He was advised by a council, a kind of upper house, of a dozen appointed members representing prominent families.

As a rule, before 1688 (the Glorious Revolution), power was wielded in Anglo-America by authoritarian elites little disposed to sharing power, but the political upheaval in Britain served as a model for change. The Whigs triumphed over the king and forced him to share power and recognize the authority of Parliament, in particular the House of Commons. The colonial assemblies claimed to wield the same powers as the Commons in Britain. They voted on taxes, approved budgets and handled a variety of appointments. As voting rights to elect the assemblies were more widespread in America than Britain or anywhere else at the time, much

Table 2
Status of the colonies in 1775

Royal colonies	Proprietary colonies	Quasi-autonomous colonies
Virginia	Maryland	Rhode Island
Massachusetts	Pennsylvania	Connecticut
New Hampshire	Delaware	
New York		
New Jersey		
South Carolina		
North Carolina		
Georgia		

was made of American democracy. While the right to vote genuinely was more prevalent in America, it was far from universal. In the mid-18th century, the vast majority of adult, property-owning, Protestant men had the right to vote. Yet that left out a large number of people, in some colonies an overwhelming majority of the population. Women, slaves, indentured servants, domestics, Indians, Catholics and Jews could not vote or hold office. Even allowing that the right to vote was more widespread than elsewhere, it is clear that power rested with the local elites, the rich planters, merchants and large property owners who made up 5 percent of the population.

The only aristocracy was defined by wealth. Its authority was recognized and generally acknowledged to be inevitable, flowing from a natural social hierarchy. This was particularly true in the South. Restrictions on voting rights were greater there and the ruling elites more firmly established. Representatives of prominent families, who controlled 60 percent of the wealth and over half the land, regularly elected each other to the assemblies. The civil service was practically hereditary, and magistrates and the functionaries of the colonial administration were drawn from it. This is how veritable dynasties, including the Lees, the Carters and the Randolphs, were built. In 1750, the Lee family had seven representatives from five counties in the Virginia Assembly. The Lees shared common ground with representatives of other prominent families and together they controlled the colony's political life.

While property and the right to vote were more equally distributed in the Northern and the Middle colonies, oligarchies and family dynasties still thrived there. Descendants of the first Puritan colonists along with the descendants of the Dutch made up a large proportion of politicians.

Power became ever more concentrated in the hands of local leaders and the assemblies, which were rivals of those of the mother country and of royal power and its representative, the governor. In the resulting conflicts, the governor generally lacked the political clout to impose his will on an assembly solidly rooted in local power. Occasionally a shrewd governor would manage to pit local families and interests against each other, but usually the governor lost out in these clashes. The assemblies that controlled the purse strings used their power to their ends by delaying or refusing to approve the governor's requests and by denying military allocations requested by the king's representative. The governor lacked the necessary military power to take charge. And local elites knew how to wield the force of numbers and of crowds.

In short, the old arbitrary power structure was being challenged throughout the colonies by political institutions increasingly susceptible to popular pressure and outside British control. These challenges were coupled with intensified disputes between the colonial elite and the people. The disputes were rarely about voting rights, turning instead around problems of land distribution, citizen protection, particularly on the frontier, and supply of paper money – in short, conflicts between the haves and the have-nots. Class conflicts and social tensions were rife. The political situation as it existed in the mid-18th century is best understood from the standpoint of social analysis.

While this confrontational mood existed in America, especially between royal power and that of the assemblies, the British government under the monarchies of George I (reign 1714–1727) and George II (reign 1727–1760) set about loosening control over the colonies to encourage commercial expansion and the defence of the empire. Robert Walpole, leader of the Whig party from 1720 to 1742, instituted a policy of benign neglect that left the colonials with broad autonomy. He felt that decentralizing administration of the empire would bring the nation closer to its economic goals and that satisfied colonies would be less of a thorn in the side.

As years passed, the expansion of British mercantilism butted up against the colonies' economic expansion, which threatened the mother country's financial interests. After 1750, pressure mounted from many financial and political quarters to seize back control of colonial affairs by putting an end to the policy of benign neglect.

A new society develops

There existed in America the idea of a new society, more egalitarian than the European society based on class differences. This was largely explained by the accessibility of land. People could improve their situation, class was more fluid and social mobility greater. Almost all, except slaves, could climb the social ladder through their energy, labour and talent.

Social categories had not been abandoned, however. The three basic social categories in the colonies were sometimes referred to as the better sort, the middling sort and the meaner sort. The social pyramid was capped by a title-less aristocracy of wealth and connections. At the top, then, were the rich planters, prominent businessmen, large landowners, high-ranking civil servants, ministers and professionals who made up approximately 10 percent of society while controlling at least 50 percent of the wealth. They dominated economic, social and political life. Although there was broad social mobility, it is notable that the wealth of most high-ranking families was inherited.

The middle class, about 50 percent of society, included independent farmers, small property owners, master craftsmen, small merchants, professionals and shop owners. Near the bottom of the social ladder were European immigrants, and on the bottom rung slaves and Indians. Domestics, indentured servants, sailors and tenant farmers, 25 percent of the population, lived at a subsistence level.

The family was the basic unit of British colonial society in America. As time went by and mortality rates dropped, large families became the norm as children had a high economic value because of the shortage of labour and manpower. Yet the effects of economic prosperity are well known, and after 1750 families became smaller.

Family life revolved around the male head of the household, whose power rested on the Bible. Women were subbordinate to their husbands, and the goal of marriage was procreation as well as providing men with companionship. Upon marriage, a woman handed all her property to her husband, and at his death the inheritance passed to the children. The widow could benefit from a dower (a third of the inheritance) for the rest of her life, but it all went back to the children if she died or remarried. The mainly Puritan churches made little room for women and contributed to their subjugation. The Quakers, however, allowed women to be called to the ministry. Some Baptists allowed women to vote on community matters. All things considered, colonial women were better off than those in Europe, playing a more active and well-rounded role. Some managed to live independently, usually after their husband's death.

Culture and intellectual life

The 18th century, in both Europe and America, was characterized by the Enlightenment. It was the Age of Reason. In the colonies, time and prosperity had weakened religious fervour. Society became secular and Enlightenment figures emphasized the power of human reason to bring order to the world. People turned away from superstition and, based on the discoveries of Galileo, Copernicus and Newton, became convinced that the universe was governed by laws they could understand and harness to improve the world. Newton (1642–1727) in the realm of mathematics and physics and John Locke (1632–1704) in the realm of philosophy overturned received wisdom. Locke believed in the influence of experience and environment and that political power is not a divine right but rather a social contract drawn up between individuals, who could change it. Governments were responsible. They had to obey natural laws. People accepted a government that protected these rights. If a government showed negligence or abuse, people were entitled to break the contract.

In America, the ideas and spirit of the Enlightenment were embraced mainly by the ruling classes and intellectuals. Many became deists, believing that God was a great engineer who had arranged the universe according to natural laws but did not intervene as the world unfolded. The consummate American Enlightenment figure is without a doubt Benjamin Franklin (1706–1790). A self-taught man, he applied his reason to everything he touched, working as a printer, postmaster, almanac writer, inventor, ambassador/diplomat and physicist. He balked at nothing when it came to improving society.

Education was obviously inspired by the British model as well as being intricately tied to religion and the churches. Over time, the ideal of education as preparation for reading the Bible expanded into the training of well-rounded people. The Enlightenment introduced the idea of education for moral and civic purposes.

Education systems differed according to region and social class. In the South, for example, planters' children were educated by tutors, as planta-

Table 3
Higher education and religious groups

Institution	Religion	Year of foundation
Harvard University	Congregationalist	1636
College of William and Mary	Anglican	1693
Yale University	Congregationalist	1701
College of New Jersey (Princeton)	Presbyterian	1746
Academy of Philadelphia (Pennsylvania)	Non-denominational	1751
King's College (Columbia)	Non-denominational	1754
Rhode Island College (Brown)	Baptist	1764
Queen's College (Rutgers)	Dutch Reform	1766
Dartmouth College	Congregationalist	1769

tions were too spread out to justify setting up schools. Apprenticeship was the primary form of education for the working classes. The situation was different in New England, where there were more population centres and the Puritans' religious fervour was extreme. People needed to be able to read the Bible to study it personally. The family was the first school, but in 1642 Massachusetts imposed fines for neglecting education and, in 1647, required every community of fifty families to hire a primary-school teacher. Communities of a hundred families also had to open a secondary school. The Massachusetts model was copied throughout New England, accounting for the region's high literacy rate. In the Middle colonies efforts were made, but much was left to private charity and the churches. In this respect, the Quakers left their mark on the region.

The proliferation of religious groups was conducive to setting up institutions of higher learning. During the colonial period, nine colleges were founded, most for religious reasons. Every school founded by one religious denomination spurred another to found its own institution to protect its orthodoxy.

The growth of these institutions, geared more towards spreading knowledge than promoting new ideas, was halted by the Revolution, only to resume in force afterwards.

Literature
American literature, mirroring American society, was still developing. There were no important American writers before the second half of the 18th century. Once again, as in the case of the colleges, the emphasis was on the practical and utilitarian. American men of letters were journalists

rather than novelists; pamphleteers and memoirists rather than essayists. People looked to the outside world, especially Britain, for wide-ranging, speculative and fictional works. They read Locke (*Second Treatise of Civil Government*, 1690) and Montesquieu (*Spirit of Laws*, 1748). The essential reading remained the Bible, and theological writers proliferated during the entire colonial period. In 1750, there were twenty-seven editions of the *Bay Psalm Book* (1640), a laboured translation of the *Livre des psaumes*. Tales of settlers, Indian wars and captives abounded.

The most published and widely read locally produced books were almanacs. The first one dates from 1639, and by 1750 they were published in every colony. They contained all kinds of information, ranging from horoscopes, poems and maxims to scientific information, weather predictions and children's exercises. The best and most popular were by Nathaniel Ames (1708–1764) and Benjamin Franklin, whose *Poor Richard's Almanack* (1732–1757) went a long way toward popularizing the teachings of the Age of Reason. Ames was cut from the same cloth as Franklin. An innkeeper, doctor, astronomer and writer, he spread Newtonian ideas and maintained unlimited faith in the future of the united colonies, which he deemed the future of humanity.

Religion

The major phenomenon of the first half of the 18th century was the first Great Awakening. The Enlightenment had made religion more rational. The masses still practised traditional religion, but less fervently than before. European pastors, in an attempt to revive the religious flame, began preaching to people's hearts, to their feelings over their reason. The movement reached America around 1720 and spread throughout the colonies. Jonathan Edwards (1703–1758) and George Whitefield (1715–1770) were the outstanding figures. They wanted to lead young people, in particular, to a devout life focused on prayer. The faith they rekindled expressed itself with startling fervour. The established church felt threatened and a debate broke out between the New Lights and the Old Lights. Ministers' authority was called into question, as the converts valued piety over theology and emotion over dogma. There were more conversions in rural areas, where, in a market that was crushing them, people felt threatened by merchants and speculators. In the South, Baptists were strengthened by the movement and made impressive inroads among slaves and poor whites.

Many historians have emphasized the impact the Great Awakening had, shaking up established authority and allowing ordinary people to participate in a debate that prefigured the struggles to come. Clearly, around the mid-18th century, the inhabitants of the colonies could be considered less and less as simple colonials. They had their interests, their own ideas and a novel way of life. Yet they still needed the mother country in their struggle against the French; the bonds would not be broken right away.

The Seven Years' War in America (The French and Indian War)

A prolonged peace followed the Treaty of Utrecht (1713), and France took the opportunity to reinforce its positions in America for what seemed like an inevitable struggle to the death. The British were also busy, exerting greater and greater pressure on the Ohio Valley, coveted by their trappers, merchants, speculators and pioneers.

War resumed in 1740 over the Austrian succession and eventually involved France, Spain and Britain, traditional enemies that also had opposing interests in America. Operations on American soil amounted to a few raids on the New England and New York frontiers capped by another recapture of Louisbourg by British colonials. Peace was restored in 1748. The war had ended in an impasse and the previous quo was restored. The British handed Louisbourg back to France, to the great distress of the Americans.

No sooner were agreements signed than the tug-of-war resumed. The situation was the most tense in the Ohio Valley. In an attempt to assert British rights, Lieutenant-Governor Robert Dinwiddie of Virginia sent a young Virginian planter to confront the French; the planter was George Washington (1732–1799). Like many Virginians, he had a financial interest in the Ohio Company. To oppose British claims, the French had built a series of forts in the Ohio Country. On Washington's second expedition, things turned sour. The death in an ambush of Joseph Coulon de Jumonville, an officer from New France, was followed by Washington's capture by a French force at Fort Necessity in 1754. Virginia was at war with France in the American hinterland.

While all this was happening on the Ohio frontier, representatives from the colonies of New England, Pennsylvania, New York and Maryland gathered in Albany to discuss a plan of union that would ultimately be rejected by all the colonies. Even in the face of danger, the British colonies could not overcome their differences. The Albany Congress also failed on another level. They could not allay the worries of the Iroquois Confederation about the encroachment of British settlers.

In response to the French threat, London sent General Edward Braddock to America in 1755. He had orders to take and destroy Fort Duquesne (modern Pittsburgh). It was a total disaster. Braddock's troops were mauled and the advantage passed to the French for the next two years. Hostilities had not yet been declared, but a state of war existed.

In 1756, the conflict became widespread. Against the will of the exhausted French and British governments, the colonies dragged the mother countries into war. The first years were a near-catastrophe for the British. Terror reigned on the frontier and the colonies were incapable of taking concerted action. Each colony's militia sprang into action when that colony's territory was threatened. Once the danger had passed, it was time to go home.

When William Pitt (1708–1778) took charge in 1757, the situation turned around. He handed European operations to Frederick II of Prussia to focus efforts even more intensively on the American front. He ensured the colonies' cooperation by guaranteeing that the war would be waged at His Majesty's expense. He managed to gather an army of 50,000 men to invade Canada. In 1758, an agreement was reached that satisfied the Iroquois by promising them that their hunting territory would be protected.

Pitt's achievements changed the course of the war. Louisbourg surrendered in 1758. French forts fell one after another in 1758 and 1759. During the siege of Quebec in the summer of 1759, General James Wolfe burned and devastated the surrounding countryside, and the Battle of the Plains of Abraham eventually secured the British victory on September 13, 1759. Quebec formally surrendered on the eighteenth. Montreal fell in 1760.

French power disappeared from America and the Americans were grateful to England. Yet colonial problems would soon resurface.

CHAPTER 3

SEPARATION

The end of the conflict of 1754–1763 had placed Britain on the threshold of world hegemony. Soon, however, the American branch of the empire would weigh heavily on the shoulders of the new Rome. Along with imperial responsibilities, England inherited considerable duties, and it now had to organize, occupy and administer a far-flung set of colonies and pay for everything as well.

The recent war had dangerously depleted British coffers and the extra burdens further jeopardized Britain's finances. It was necessary to look to the colonies to bear a greater share of the cost of administering the empire. The only way to make this happen was to reinforce centralizing measures that would, among other effects, undermine American autonomy. The next twenty years became the history of Britain attempting and failing to reorganize its colonial system.

The American colonists certainly seemed satisfied with their lot in 1763. The original 1607 settlement had expanded into a group of thirteen colonies populated by nearly two million inhabitants. With most of their political, social and cultural characteristics borrowed from the mother country, they began thriving economically. Yet at the same time, the North American setting, remote from the mother country, favoured the emergence of an American society distinct from the British one. The colonists became accustomed to an autonomy that the mother country could not or would not suppress.

In 1763, relations between the two took a different turn. Freed from European and colonial conflicts and driven by necessity, Britain would attempt to put its American subjects in their place, and over their objections. British intentions to apply a series of mainly fiscal measures brought to the surface the latent dissatisfaction of many colonists, who, overcoming the reluctance of some of their neighbours, dragged America into an armed conflict with the mother country: the American Revolution, or the War of American Independence (1775–1783). At first the conflict was a civil war within the empire with no decisive result. But when France and Spain declared war in 1778 and 1779 on the side of the insurgents, the conflict became international and the victory of the former colonies was almost assured.

By 1781, the Declaration of Independence (1776) was no longer simply a justification for the struggle against England but a reality for the American people, whose hopes were realized by the 1783 Treaty of Paris. The struggle had galvanized the Western world; its repercussions were vast and it transformed the world stage.

The Empire in 1763 and its problems

The Treaty of Paris (1763) confirmed British colonial power beyond a doubt. The French presence was greatly reduced in India and practically erased in America. While France retained its most valuable West Indian possessions – Martinique, Guadalupe and Santo Domingo – as well as fishing rights in the Gulf of St. Lawrence and around the islands of St. Pierre and Miquelon off the coast of Newfoundland, it had lost the centre of the North American continent to the British and had ceded Louisiana to Spain to compensate for its loss of Florida. The French empire in North America was no more.

Despite the immense territory it gained in America with the acquisition of Louisiana, Spain was a spent force. France's defeat was also Spain's: it could not re-conquer Gibraltar, it had lost Florida and its British neighbours in America were an increasingly troublesome threat. British supremacy extended not only to America. Britain also dominated Europe from a commercial standpoint with its solid outposts in the North Sea, the Baltic and the Mediterranean, and it also had strong ties in Asia.

Yet British hegemony was not accepted by all. France and Spain contested it. In central and eastern Europe, the growing Prussian and Russian powers had aspirations of their own. All eyes were peeled for the new giant's first stumble. But the giant was impressive, with a population of over ten million, a stable political system, a dynamic economy, the most powerful fleet in history, thirty colonies in the Americas (eighteen continental, twelve West Indian) and a feeling of common freedom combined with a feeling of security, all sources of pride in belonging to the empire.

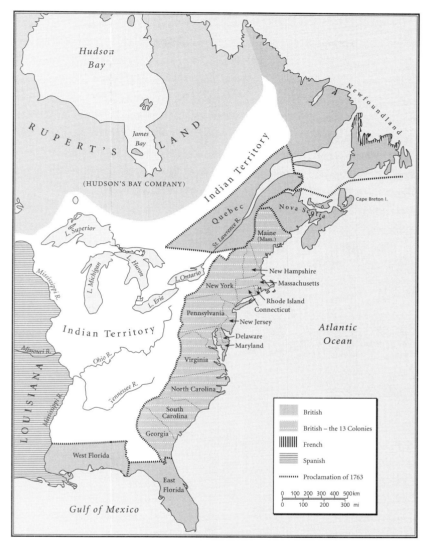

Colonial America in 1763.

What was more, British civilization was dazzling. Its philosophers, jurists, economists, writers and inventors were proof.

Britain's first troubles arose within the empire. For a long time, a large number of American colonial problems had remained unresolved; add to that the burdens of victory. The French threat had until then reined in the colonies' penchant for autonomy but with New France crushed,

Table 4
Trade between England and its American colonies, 1700–1776, in £1000s (E = exports, I = imports)

Year Origin	1700 E/I	1710 E/I	1720 E/I	1730 E/I	1740 E/I	1750 E/I	1760 E/I	1776 E/I
New England	41/91	31/106	48/128	54/208	72/171	48/343	37/599	0.7/55
New York	17/49	8/31	16/37	8/64	21/118	35/267	21/480	2/–
Pennsylvania	4/18	1/8	7/24	10/48	15/56	28/217	22/707	1/0.3
Virginia & Maryland	317/173	188/127	331/110	346/150	341/281	508/349	504/605	75/–
The Carolinas	14/11	20/19	62/18	151/64	266/181	191/133	162/218	13/–
Georgia	–	–	–	–	0.9/3	1/2	12/–	12/–
TOTAL (rounded)	393/342	248/291	465/317	569/534	716/810	911/1311	758/2609	102/55

The Statistical History of the United States from Colonial Times to the Present, Stamford, 1965, 757.

their demands quickly became increasingly threatening. Britain, also free of the French threat, had to ensure the cooperation of all members of the empire to avoid collapse.

The cost of the war had been almost ruinous. British national debt in 1763 had risen to £130,000,000 from £70,000,000 in 1748. A large garrison had to be maintained in North America and officials at all levels had to be paid. British property owners were already heavily taxed, paying up to a third of their income. It became imperative that the colonists share the burden. While mercantilist Britain was still profiting, earnings could have been higher if operations by New England merchants, in particular, were better controlled.

These financial and commercial problems were compounded by the dilemma of the West and its inhabitants, the Indians. What should be done with the huge territories situated between the Appalachians and

Table 5
Revenue to England under various acts, 1765–1774, pounds sterling

Year	Sugar Act	Stamp Act	Townshend Act	Total
1765	14,091	3,292	–	17,383
1766	26,696	–	–	26,696
1767	33,844	–	197	34,041
1768	24,659	–	13,202	37,861
1769	39,938	–	5,561	45,499
1770	30,910	–	2,727	33,637
1771	27,086	–	4,675	31,761
1772	42,570	–	3,300	45,870
1773	39,531	–	2,572	42,103
1774	27,074	–	921	27,995

the Mississippi? Fur traders and speculators had conflicting interests. The former wanted the land reserved for fur trading and Indians; the latter wanted it opened up to white colonization. The Indian presence complicated the problem further in that they had been mostly allied with the French cause during the previous wars. They had to be pacified, and even allied tribes became increasingly dissatisfied.

The political imbroglio made matters worse. Where did the colonies stand within the empire and what degree of decision-making power should they have? The colonies had taken advantage of the mother country's often involuntary neglect to wrest a degree of political autonomy. Britain had to quickly reassert its authority if it intended to reorganize its imperial holdings to its advantage. Relations between the two sides appeared set to change.

Root causes of the conflict

The rebellion of the American colonies against Great Britain started well before the first shots were fired at Lexington and Concord, well before the disputes over the Stamp Act and the "Intolerable Acts" and well before the inflammatory speeches of James Otis and Patrick Henry. Separation had been looming for a long time. "The Revolution was effected before the War commenced. The Revolution was in the minds and the hearts of the people," declared John Adams (1735–1826), future president of the United States.

Social factors
Since the early 17th century, thousands of Europeans had flocked to the American continent in the hope of starting a new life. The life that awaited them in North America was almost entirely foreign to these men and women. Instead of the narrow constraints of their densely populated European homelands with their cultivated land, they were confronted by a largely unsettled world of apparently unlimited vastness, crisscrossed by broad rivers and inhabited by people with strange customs, baffled by their presence. Their lives were inevitably transformed by their new surroundings; the harsh life on the frontier, contact with the Indians and relations with other immigrants all contributed to forging a new people, the American people.

> **Letters from an American Farmer**
> … whence came all these people? They are a mixture of English, Scotch, Irish, French, Dutch, Germans, and Swedes. From this promiscuous breed, that race now called Americans have arisen….
> What attachment can a poor European emigrant have for a country where he had nothing? The knowledge of the language, the love of a few kindred as poor as himself, were the only cords that tied him: his country is now that which gives him land, bread, protection, and consequence: *Ubi panis ibi patria* [Where my bread is, there is my country], is the motto of all emigrants.
> Hector St. John de Crèvecoeur, *Letters from an American Farmer*, London, 1782.

Far from the mother country, in a world that was theirs for the taking, the colonists had learned to be self-reliant. Most had received no help from the mother country to settle in America. A very large number had fled religious or political persecution in Europe – Puritans, Irish, Huguenots – and, in many cases, economic disadvantage and famine.

As the colonies' economic situation improved over the 17th and 18th centuries, their population gradually developed a sense of independence especially in the realms of politics and economics. While American society remained a colonial society with all that entailed (economic dependence, inferior political status, cultural subjection), unconsciously the future nation was straining to sever ties. The lack of a coherent imperial policy encouraged these initiatives, and distance from the mother country had a calming effect on any fear of reprisals for disobeying England.

The Seven Years' War furthered estrangement between the British and the Americans. British soldiers frequently showed contempt toward colonial militias, who on their side were stunned by British violence and brutality. The war brought together colonials who had had few occasions to meet each other and fellowships were forged.

Economic factors

The great European powers of the 17th and 18th centuries practised mercantilism, which ignited national rivalries. Britain was no exception, and its American settlements developed in the mercantile framework it imposed on them. To make sure the colonies played their part, the British government passed navigation acts at regular intervals. Over time, imperial decrees made trade between the colonies and Britain more and more exclusive.

The system had its advantages. Colonial producers enjoyed guaranteed markets in England as well as credit advantages. Americans also made sure to counterbalance laws they viewed as excessive, disobeying them by smuggling and by buying off the officials in charge of enforcing them.

Finally, while British regulations struck the most industrious, wealthy and influential sectors of the population, almost 90 percent of people still lived on subsistence farms and were largely unaffected by these matters.

There are reasons for the incredible development of the British colonies in America: they were quickly populated, mainly with farmers, and they relied on bold entrepreneurs who benefited as much as possible from the advantages accorded by Britain while ignoring the drawbacks of belonging to the empire. While the colonies suffered a trade deficit of £20 million with Britain between 1700 and 1773, they made up the difference through illegal trade. Problems arose only when the Crown, pushed by necessity and finally free to take action, decided to enforce its own rules to the letter.

Political factors

Fundamentally, the American Revolution resulted from the problem of power distribution within the British Empire. From the beginning of British settlement in America, the imperial government had allowed local autonomy to take root in the colonies. The colonists, guaranteed the same rights as British citizens and in the tradition of the long struggle for political power in Britain, did not take long to set up their own institutions. The diversity of the colonies and their distance from the mother country removed any possibility of a unitary government.

Each colony was considered a separate entity with certain specific powers. This situation gradually led to a feeling of independence as each colony snatched a measure of authority from the mother country. No one claims the process was cordial, but the colonies benefited greatly from the circumstances that prevented the British government from clamping down before 1763.

The mother country's incursion after 1763 on what the Americans considered to be established political rights triggered the conflict. The thirteen colonies had representative assemblies that intended to play the same role in the colonies as Parliament did in England. Some even claimed that the colonies embodied the British democratic tradition better than the mother country. In America, it was believed that the revolutionary ideals of 1688 had been betrayed by British authorities.

Immediate causes

In 1763, Britain, beset by imperial problems of all kinds, needed to find solutions. As the previous section explains, several factors in the American part of the empire would, despite the colony's attachment to the mother country, make the medicine hard to administer. It would have taken tact, patience and understanding on the part of the imperial authorities, skills that George III and his colleagues had not been blessed with.

The first grumblings
In the final years of the Seven Years' War, the British government tried to put a stop to smuggling by American merchants, especially in the West Indies. One weapon used in the struggle was the writ of assistance authorizing a constable to help customs officials search the warehouses of American merchants suspected of smuggling. The problem was real; New England, for example, was a bustling hub of illegal trade. In 1761, James Otis, attorney for several merchants, went before the Massachusetts court to argue against the validity of certain writs. He expounded forcefully the colonials' arguments against arbitrary measures by the British government. British officials were allowed to continue using the writs, but the Americans had found in the fiery Otis's speech the principles underlying their opposition to British rule.

Immediately after the treaty of 1763, one of the most pressing problems facing Lord Grenville (prime minister, 1763–1765) in America concerned the West and the Indians. Speculators and fur traders, as mentioned previously, were fighting over the territories between the Appalachians and the Mississippi, and the British probably could not satisfy all the interests involved. While the government sought a solution, the Indians, who wanted neither the British fur traders, who shamelessly robbed them, nor the American colonists, who dispossessed them of their land, decided in May 1763 to take up arms. Pontiac's Rebellion ensued. Quickly crushed (September 1764), the uprising nonetheless caused general alarm. In

October 1763 Parliament adopted the Royal Proclamation setting aside the Western territories for the Indians and establishing three new colonies in America: Quebec, East Florida and West Florida.

George III's American subjects naturally protested vehemently and, worse, continued moving into the interior despite the British ban. In the end, while not repealing the Royal Proclamation, the British government was forced to sign treaties with the Indians to make room for the colonists.

More serious still were the repercussions of Britain's new fiscal policy. Grenville had noticed the poor returns from American customs, whose operating costs were £8000 a year versus £2000 in revenue. By tightening the mercantilist system further, the government could increase revenue while easing the mother country's financial burden. To replace the old Molasses Act of 1733, which brought in practically nothing, Grenville's government enacted the Revenue Act of 1764 (the Sugar Act).

Unlike the old act, the act of 1764 had teeth. Granted, the tariff on molasses and sugar imported from the foreign West Indies had been cut in half, but everything indicated the government intended to collect. The customs service was overhauled and the navy put on the alert. Anyone caught smuggling had to appear before the courts of admiralty without a jury. The act also expanded the list of enumerated items.

Most colonials were opposed to the prohibitive duty and accused the government of wanting to strangle American trade. Rum, manufactured from molasses, was one of the colonies' main export commodities and a means to reduce their trade deficit. Molasses from the British West Indies was not taxed, but producers there could not meet demand; it had to be bought from the foreign West Indies. The newly enforced tax hit the North the hardest, but opposition was so badly organized that, despite protests, the act was enforced. In 1765, Britain took in £14,091 under the Sugar Act. Only a few people had raised the constitutional argument that would later form the basis for opposition to the mother country. However, in Massachusetts an effective weapon had been discovered – the boycott of British goods.

After this controversial act, the Grenville government went on in the same year to pass the Currency Act prohibiting the printing of paper money throughout the colonies. It was the South's turn to be hit and the protest movement intensified.

Beginning in early 1765, Lord Grenville seemed to go out of his way to stoke tensions. His government enacted the Quartering Act, requiring the colonies' civil authorities to house and maintain troops, then the Stamp Act, which taxed colonials directly for the first time. Britain hoped to net £60,000 under the Stamp Act. This amount combined with the anticipated proceeds from the Sugar Act would cover a third of the military expenses incurred for the ten thousand men required to protect America.

Under the Stamp Act, all legal documents, newspapers, pamphlets, permits, contracts and even playing cards and dice had to carry a tax stamp. This time Parliament had struck at the most influential groups – lawyers, businessmen and journalists in every colony. The public was galvanized to resist by any means necessary. The British side also dug in. The Stamp Act was passed by 205 votes to 49.

Early resistance and Parliament's retreat
The Stamp Act united all the malcontents. The boycotts already in effect were coupled with constitutional protests, not to mention violence. The Stamp Act was gutted as a result. Patriots recruited by a resistance organization called the Sons of Liberty burned the hated stamps and the houses of tax collectors and forced officials to resign. The act also forced the colonials to frame a constitutional theory to back up their opposition. The Virginia Assembly, spurred on by Patrick Henry (1736–1799), denounced taxation without representation, and Massachusetts, to avoid having it imposed, convened a congress in October 1765 to discuss the issue. Delegates from nine colonies attended and condemned the Stamp Act as a threat to the colonies' freedom, but still petitioned the "best of kings" under the "most perfect form of government" to rescind the law.

Despite the reluctance of British members of Parliament to lose face, the merchants of Great Britain, hit by the boycotts, managed to have the Stamp Act rescinded in 1766 and the Sugar Act modified after the fall of Grenville. At the same time, however, Parliament reasserted its right to tax the colonies in the Declaratory Act.

In the euphoria triggered by the repeal of the Stamp Act, the colonials hardly noticed that their victory was not as complete as it first appeared. The Sugar Act and the Royal Proclamation both remained in effect, and Britain had just announced that it could start taxing its subjects directly again. Yet business resumed, the Sons of Liberty were pacified and the Americans proclaimed their loyalty and put up statues of Pitt and the king. All seemed for the best in the best of all worlds.

A new offensive

Parliament had recognized the poor timing of the tax but had not abandoned any claim to tax. The Americans were simply given a respite. In 1767, the whole process resumed when Charles Townshend, chancellor of the exchequer, had to prepare a new fiscal plan. He did not make the mistake of imposing an internal tax, instead reinforcing the customs service and taxing glass, paper, lead and tea exported from Great Britain to the colonies. The proceeds (£35,000) were to go toward the salaries of judges, governors and customs officials to shield them from financial dependence on the colonials.

The backlash was less violent. The Americans had been taken by surprise and had trouble finding reasons to oppose Parliament. Nevertheless, they resorted once again to non-importation: they stopped drinking British tea and painting their houses and wore local cloth. In Boston, probably the most active hotbed of resistance, customs officers were harassed and the imperial authorities had to resign themselves to stationing troops in October 1768.

The presence of troops in Boston was a recipe for unrest, especially since in July the governor had suspended the Massachusetts Assembly for refusing to withdraw a circular letter denouncing the Townshend Acts. For over a year, resistance remained passive despite agitation by Samuel Adams (1722–1803), the Boston revolutionary leader. Violence broke out on March 5, 1770, during a confrontation between the populace and troops. The customs house guards, bombarded by various objects from the crowd, opened fire, leaving eleven dead. The agitators, led by Samuel Adams, labelled it the Boston Massacre, clear proof of British tyranny and cruelty. The soldiers were nonetheless defended by John Adams, who blamed "saucy boys, Negroes and mulattos, Irish teagues and outlandish jack tars" for the incident. Six soldiers were acquitted and two released.

Already a movement to repeal the Townshend Acts had arisen in Britain, where non-importation was doing damage. Between 1768 and 1769, trade between the mother country and the colonies had diminished by a third; at the same time, British merchants realized that the taxes were encouraging colonial industry to develop, thereby contradicting imperial policy. Bowing to pressure, the new chancellor of the exchequer, Lord North, urged the repeal of the Townshend Acts, which had brought in nothing, but kept a symbolic duty on tea. This was a new strategic retreat, avoiding extremes but maintaining the mother country's privileges.

North's policy was undeniably astute. Back home, it quelled critics in Parliament and the business sector. In the colonies, it incited a new wave of sympathy for the mother country. Tensions dropped substantially, trade resumed and even the embargo called for by the Sons of Liberty was only spottily observed. The British benefited most from the lull and only a few enlightened souls realized it. The moderate majority gratefully welcomed the renewed calm and prosperity.

The radicals needed a spectacular incident to revive their movement. They found it in the Boston Tea Party.

The final blow

The powerful East India Company was in critical condition in 1773 and called in the government. To save the company from bankruptcy, Parliament granted it a monopoly over direct sales of tea in the colonies as well as exempting it from all British taxes. Since 1770, 90 percent of the tea consumed in the colonies had been imported from abroad and thus was illegal. The privileges granted the company allowed it to sell its tea at a markedly lower price than on the black market. In one move, Britain eliminated the honest merchants and made smuggling unprofitable.

During the lull following the repeal of the Townshend Acts, British leaders, seeing the disputes that still split the colonists, had decided that American union was impossible. But once again, the mother country had underestimated potential colonial reactions to its policies. Not only did the sidelined American merchants protest, the general population refused to buy the tea imposed on them. Worse, the committees of correspondence set up in Massachusetts in 1772 encouraged resistance throughout the colonies. Everywhere measures were taken to undermine the company's plans.

In Boston, however, the authorities were intent on unloading the tea. They were met with violence. On the night of December 16, 1773, the cargo of three tea-laden ships was dumped into the harbour by Patriots disguised as Indians.

In Britain, it was unanimous. Boston had to be punished as an example. Through a series of four acts – the Boston Port Act, the Administration of Justice Act, the Quartering Act and the Massachusetts Government Act – passed over the following year, Parliament intended to tighten imperial control over Boston and Massachusetts, thereby inspiring respect in the other colonies. These became known as the Intolerable Acts, and Boston became a martyr to the American cause. From all over the colonial territory, expressions of admiration and sympathy and even gifts flowed into the Puritan city. The correspondence committees got to work convening the First Continental Congress in 1774 to plan opposition to the Intolerable Acts, to the list of which the Americans added the Quebec Act passed by Britain the same year.

The dramatic expansion of the province of Quebec, the protection given to Catholicism and the recognition of French civil law offended the

Borders in colonial America under the Quebec Act of 1774.

colonials, who saw it as another British provocation. Washington, on his way to the First Continental Congress, declared that "the crisis is arrived when we must assert our rights or submit to every imposition that can be heaped on us till custom and use shall make us as tame and abject slaves as the blacks we rule over with such arbitrary sway."

When the First Continental Congress opened in Philadelphia in September 1774, fifty-five delegates from twelve colonies attended. Georgia was absent. Despite the diverse opinions represented at the congress, all parties agreed that the punishment meted out to Boston was out of proportion to the offence. Their goal was not yet independence so much as protecting the freedom already enjoyed by the colonists:

DECLARATION OF RIGHTS, 1774

That the inhabitants of the English colonies in North-America, by the immutable laws of nature, the principles of the English constitution, and the several charters or compacts, have the following RIGHTS:

That they are entitled to life, liberty and property: and they have never ceded to any foreign power whatever, a right to dispose of either without their consent.

That our ancestors, who first settled these colonies, were at the time of their emigration from the mother country, entitled to all the rights, liberties, and immunities of free and natural-born subjects, within the realm of England.

That by such emigration they by no means forfeited, surrendered, or lost any of those rights, but that they were, and their descendants now are, entitled to the exercise and enjoyment of all such of them, as their local and other circumstances enable them to exercise and enjoy.

That the foundation of English liberty, and of all free government, is a right in the people to participate in their legislative council: and as the English colonists are not represented, and from their local and other circumstances, cannot properly be represented in the British parliament, they are entitled to a free and exclusive power of legislation in their several provincial legislatures, where their right of representation can alone be preserved, in all cases of taxation and internal polity, subject only to the negative of their sovereign, in such manner as has been heretofore used and accustomed: But, from the necessity of the case, and a regard to the mutual interest of both countries, we cheerfully consent to the operation of such acts of the British parliament, as are bona fide, restrained to the regulation of our external commerce, for the purpose of securing the commercial advantages of the whole empire to the mother country, and the commercial benefits of its respective members; excluding every idea of taxation internal or external, for raising a revenue on the subjects, in America, without their consent.

Excerpt from Declaration and Resolves of the First Continental Congress, October 14, 1774.

Overall, the First Continental Congress was a victory for moderates: to satisfy conservatives, ties were not severed with the mother country but it was dealt with firmly enough to please the radicals. The Suffolk Resolves were adopted, advocating military preparedness and ordering trade with the mother country and the British West Indies suspended. At the end of the meeting, the delegates decided to found the Association, which would enforce the boycott of all trade with Britain. Along with the committees of correspondence, the Association introduced revolutionary elements into the American dispute.

There were many conservatives, and the king could have united them by making a few timely concessions. But the mood in Britain was not conciliatory. The king and Parliament were determined to subdue the colonies at any cost. When all hope for settling differences amicably evaporated, the equally large group of moderates threw their support behind the Patriots. From that point on, the king's friends in America were ripe for tarring and feathering.

Revolution

General Thomas Gage, commander of the approximately 3,500-strong Boston garrison, was ill at ease. He saw the Patriots preparing, but he lacked the forces for wide-scale operations. On April 14, 1775, he received orders from Britain to bring the rebels under control. On the eighteenth, he dispatched a column of 700 men to Concord (25 kilometres or 15 miles from Boston) to seize the munitions and food stockpiled by the

Patriots. The entire countryside had been alerted by messengers from Boston and elsewhere in Massachusetts, and British troops engaged in combat first in Lexington then in Concord, where they managed to destroy some supplies. But on the road back, Americans entrenched behind houses and trees mowed down the redcoats, and that very night, after the British reinforcements had returned to Boston, the city was besieged by thousands of Patriots.

The first gunshots had barely subsided when the Second Continental Congress convened in Philadelphia on May 10, 1775, this time dominated by radicals. The question of open warfare had to be addressed. The Congress established the Continental Army and appointed George Washington commander. To support the army, the foundations were laid for a monetary system and negotiations with foreign nations were begun. While the American representatives were taking on the powers of an independent government, they did not go so far as to sever all ties. Although insisting that Parliament had no power over them, they retained their allegiance to Britain and the king. The king was the one they appealed to for justice in July 1775, and even in the Declaration on the Causes and Necessity of Taking up Arms they claimed to have no ambitions to separate from Britain. The Congress and the fledgling American nation could not maintain such ambivalence for long.

The Congress sent a message to the French Canadians of Quebec inviting them to join the revolutionary cause, and an invasion of that British colony was planned in secret. A force led by Richard Montgomery eventually invaded in September 1775, but the invaders were held up for weeks at Saint-Jean-sur-Richelieu. Montreal fell to the Americans but the city of Quebec held out. Montgomery joined up with another force led by Benedict Arnold and led an assault on Quebec on December 31, too late in the season. The attack failed and the Americans dug in for the winter. In spring, 9,000 British soldiers arrived to help drive out the invaders. The population had ignored American appeals to join their cause.

Toward independence
Over a year went by between the first meeting of the Second Continental Congress and the Declaration of Independence. It became increasingly obvious that no compromise was possible. A clean break had to be made with the support of the greatest number of people, but Americans were

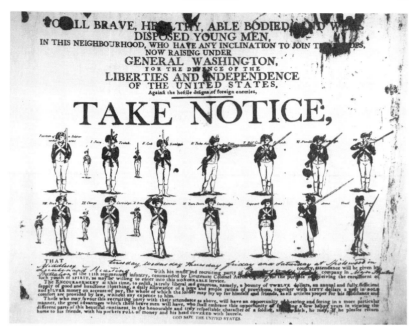

"To all brave, healthy, able bodied, and well disposed young men…" This recruiting poster, often associated with the Revolutionary War, is believed more likely to date from the war scare with France in 1799. (Library of Congress)

divided. John Adams was to claim that one third of his fellow citizens were for independence, one third against and one third indifferent, although the actual number of Loyalists was probably less than 18 percent. Divergent political views and varying economic interests were tearing the nascent country apart. The gap was wide; there was even a majority of Loyalists in New York, New Jersey and Georgia, while the Patriots clearly predominated in Virginia, Massachusetts and Maryland.

Even after the Battle of Bunker Hill, fought on June 17, 1775, just across the Charles River from Boston, the conservatives managed to get the Congress to send the Olive Branch Petition to the king, but it was followed the next day by the Declaration on the Causes and Necessity of Taking up Arms. George III responded by declaring his American subjects rebels and outlawing all relations with them. The radicals took heart. In January 1776 Thomas Paine published his pamphlet *Common Sense*, inflaming the Patriots by the force of its arguments, founded, as were those

> **Common Sense**
> Society in every state is a blessing, but government even in its best state is but a necessary evil; in its worst state an intolerable one....
> Arms, as the last resource, decide the contest; the appeal was the choice of the king, and the continent hath accepted the challenge.
>
> Thomas Paine, *Common Sense; Addressed to the Inhabitants of America* (pamphlet), Philadelphia, 1776.

of the Declaration of Independence, on the philosophy of natural rights. It would be read by hundreds of thousands of Americans.

In the first months of 1776, the pace of events picked up. Between March and May, the Congress embarked firmly on the road to independence by ordering the states to set up new governments, sending representatives abroad for assistance, disarming the Loyalists, opening American ports to all foreigners but the British, and sending privateers to attack British ships. Some were still dissatisfied, feeling that the Congress lacked bold leadership.

On June 7, 1776, Richard Henry Lee submitted a resolution to the Congress in favour of independence, foreign alliances and a federation of the former colonies. The delegates entrusted the task of drafting a declaration to a committee headed by Thomas Jefferson (1743–1826). The delegates unanimously approved it in principle on July 2. On July 4, the Congress approved Jefferson's amended version and the Declaration of Independence was complete.

The Declaration was intended to announce and justify secession and was grounded in the people's right to rise up against a government that had not fulfilled its obligations and to change the form of that government. To the declaration in principle, Jefferson added a long bill of indictment against the king of England; George III became the scapegoat as he represented the last link still uniting the colonies to England. By singling out a personal, flesh-and-blood enemy, the Revolution took on the force of popular emotion. The new philosophy of human freedom set forth in the Declaration would be a powerful force in America and throughout the Western world. To those who faulted him for disregarding historical fact in his charges against the Crown, Jefferson replied that in drafting the Declaration of Independence, he was not writing history, he was trying to change it.

Any hesitations had vanished. There had been many, but they illustrate one of the paradoxes of American independence, that in the end the Americans actually had little reason to rise up. Another paradox is that independence was won not against the British constitution and traditions, but in their name.

War

Had the Americans been as united as the Patriots claimed or as the Declaration of Independence implied, they might have achieved their goal more quickly.

They controlled the bulk of the country, and the English were unenthusiastic and disadvantaged by distance. While the radicals now had the advantage, there were still many conservatives and neutral parties. The Americans were split – the coming confrontation pitted not only American against Englishman but also American against American. Predictably enough, the cause of independence inspired little enthusiasm in the enslaved blacks. The revolutionary rhetoric, spiced with calls for struggle against tyranny in the name of freedom and human dignity, led a large number of slaves to question their own oppression while being aware that emancipation would not come from the masters. Many took advantage of the conflict to gain their freedom either by escaping behind British lines, sometimes serving in the ranks of the British army, or by taking refuge in the hinterland with Indian tribes. In the end, more blacks served on the British side than with the Patriots and quite a few emigrated to Nova Scotia at the end of the conflict. But for the vast majority, Revolution did not lead to emancipation.

Independence did not provoke wild enthusiasm among natives either. Early in the hostilities, they were pressured by the British and the Americans to remain neutral. However, a large number opted to support the British. The West was terrorized by joint Loyalist/Indian campaigns. In 1778, Washington would be forced to send in 4,000 troops to lay waste to Iroquois territory. These confrontations were indicative of the subsequent approach to the Indian "problem."

The conditions of the struggle for independence were harsh: an extended war against a great power of the time, with the Americans divided and their army ill-trained, undersupplied and badly led. There was no denying British superiority. Britain had a population of 11 million compared to 2.5 million Americans, 20 percent of whom were slaves. The British navy was the most powerful in the world. Add to that a regular army of 48,000 men who could count on help from the Loyalists and the Indians. The British strategy from the beginning was to employ the overwhelming superiority of British power to put down the rebels. On the American side, Washington relied not on a professional army but on badly equipped recruits with little experience. Congress could never supply Washington with more than 18,000 troops. The farmers and craftsmen already trained for the militia preferred to serve locally, close to their farms and their families. Soldiers were often paid in depreciated currency and the Continental Army had to beg to survive. Washington was lucky not to suffer any major defeats during the war's initial phase.

Prime Minister North decided to pour resources into an ambitious military mobilization. The Howe brothers, General William and Admiral Richard, commanded the British forces. William Howe was the commander-in-chief. He had orders to isolate the New England Patriots by taking New York and controlling the Hudson River. In August 1776, he had 32,000 men, 30 warships and 10,000 sailors at his disposal. His forces were seasoned, disciplined and well armed.

The British accumulated victories. In September, Howe occupied the city of New York, abandoned by Washington under Howe's relentless pursuit. The retreat ended when Congress was forced to leave Philadelphia for Baltimore under British pressure. Washington surprised the British at Trenton and Princeton. It was already apparent that British unwieldiness was a handicap. They did not capitalize on their victories or take the time to plan operations that could ensure a final, decisive victory. Washington's strategy was quite the opposite: digging in, mounting small-scale attacks and avoiding the crucial confrontation. In spring 1777, the American strategy seemed to be working, even though there were more defeats than victories.

Howe resumed his offensive. General John Burgoyne would come down from the north via Quebec and Lake Champlain, Barry St. Leger would sweep down on Albany from the west and a contingent from New York would join up with Burgoyne. Howe wanted to hem Washington in and seize Philadelphia at all costs. He sailed up Chesapeake Bay, disembarked and captured Philadelphia, but Washington escaped. Much time had been wasted, there were no more reinforcements available, and in the north St. Leger was retreating. Burgoyne was immobilized, then surrounded by American forces. He surrendered at Saratoga on October 17, 1777, with 5,000 regulars and 600 Indians and Loyalists.

It was the turning point of the war. The American victory boosted morale and raised hopes of diplomatic success in Paris to gain French support. Then came the dreadful ordeal of winter 1777–1778. While Howe went into winter quarters in Philadelphia, Washington retreated to Valley Forge, 30 kilometres (19 miles) from Philadelphia, with 12,000 men suffering from malnutrition, fatigue, cold and infections. Washington, fearing perhaps the British propensity for biological warfare, had his soldiers inoculated to protect them against smallpox. Almost 3,000 of them did not survive and a thousand deserted. The neighbouring population was split and even Patriot farmers could not resist the profit motive, selling to the British, who paid in gold, rather than to the Continental Army, which had only depreciated paper currency to offer.

Congress's finances were in a pitiful state. After exhausting its credit in France and Holland and with rich Patriots, Congress printed money (a nominal value of $191 million) but had little revenue. The currency depreciated and galloping inflation took hold. The situation improved greatly after the French alliance was negotiated in Paris on February 6, 1778. France wanted revenge for the humiliating defeat of 1763. At first, it supported the Americans secretly, waiting for serious proof of their chances of winning. After the Patriot victory at Saratoga, everything happened at once. Vergennes, minister of foreign affairs under Louis XVI, fearing a reconciliation between the rebels and Britain, proposed an agreement to the American delegates. His fears were justified; the British prime minister, Lord North, made overtures and even offered to repeal all the acts adopted since 1763, but his delegates could not recognize American independence and the mission failed. America's treaty with France specified that France would go to war with Britain to ensure American independence and that neither signatory would sign a separate peace without prior consultation or agreement. Both parties also pledged to protect their respective possessions. France renounced claims to Canada, though the American government would recognize French conquests in the West Indies.

The conflict spread. Britain declared war on France. In 1779, Spain allied itself with France in the hope of re-conquering Gibraltar and Florida.

France formed the core of the alliance since Spain did not recognize the confederation now calling itself the United States. Once again, France promised not to sign a separate peace and vowed to fight until Gibraltar was Spanish again. In 1780, the League of Armed Neutrality, led by Russia, threatened the British blockade against France and Spain, and Britain declared war on Holland. The war became international, isolating Britain and diluting the British advantage.

British strategy changed after Saratoga. Instead of maintaining control of the thirteen colonies, they would try to keep the essential part, the South. They would re-conquer Virginia, the Carolinas and Georgia, relying on the many Loyalists to hold the re-conquered territory. The South was divided. Racial tensions ran high and black support was not a given. The inhabitants of the interior, long-time opponents of the eastern planters, often fought for the British cause since the planters were Patriots. Henry Clinton was now in command of the British forces. The occupation of Philadelphia over, they headed south, retaking Georgia then South Carolina, but the arrival of the French turned things around. In July 1780, General Rochambeau landed 5,500 soldiers at Newport, Rhode Island, and threatened New York City. In the South, the Patriots won a few victories. Lord Cornwallis, now in command, refocused operations on Virginia. He was surrounded in Yorktown with his 9,500 men. The combined forces of Washington, Lafayette and Rochambeau numbered over twice as many, and Admiral de Grasse cut off retreat and the arrival of reinforcements by sea. Cornwallis surrendered on October 9, 1781. Britain had lost the war.

The British tried to limit the damage by concluding a treaty as quickly as possible with the Americans, who were happy to oblige and negotiated secretly with them. The Treaty of Paris (September 3, 1783) favoured the Americans. Britain recognized their independence, handed over the land between the Appalachians and the Mississippi and between the Great Lakes and Florida, and granted them the right to fish the Grand Banks off Newfoundland. In turn, Congress agreed not to stand in the way of British creditors collecting on private debts and agreed to recommend returning property confiscated from Loyalists. Britain was more generous than it needed to be, but the majority at home was hostile to the conflict and wanted it resolved at any cost. Certain interests also wanted to protect their future.

The Treaty of Versailles, signed at the same time, established peace between France, Spain and England. Spain received Florida but not Gibraltar. France received Tobago and was left with a deficit that was among the causes of the French Revolution.

Peace opened the centre of the continent to American expansion and paved the way for building a powerful nation. As the Americans busied themselves making their government functional, they were the focus of attention for millions of rapt spectators around the world. The consequences of American independence went beyond a simple cutting of colonial ties. Through all the debates and the questioning, and founded on the great principles of freedom and equality, the conviction was forged that the new American society represented something better than the old, monarchist, decadent and corrupt Europe.

CHAPTER 4

ESTABLISHING THE REPUBLIC

Independence was far from the solution to all problems. A choice had to be made between union and disunity. A new legal entity had been created but it remained to define the contents. The matter of home rule, now resolved, was replaced by the question of, as one historian put it, who should rule at home.

The constitution would define the balance of powers, but the path to it was long and arduous. The first experiment was with the Articles of Confederation, which set up a decentralized system that was unsatisfactory to the most influential groups, who wanted more centralization, stability and room to manoeuvre. A climate of dissatisfaction set in, the economic crisis of early independence caused unease and physical safety was threatened. The first constitution needed amending.

When the Founding Fathers met in May 1787 and decided to draft a new constitution that enshrined the new values, it was practically a coup d'état. The battle, for it was a battle, would be won when nine states out of thirteen signed on. The new country could function with a new constitution, but the practicalities needed defining. The state had to be financed. Individual interests were expressed through political parties, which disrupted plans. Before people even had time to assimilate all these changes, President Jefferson had doubled the national territory. Debate now raged around territorial policy. The gap between free states and slave-owning states widened. A new phase in American history had begun.

A national government

While Americans were united enough behind Congress to declare independence, the fact remains that during the revolutionary period most of them identified politically and socially with their states and local communities rather than with the nation under construction. The first instinct of many Patriot leaders was to return quickly to their respective states to serve in the government that was most important to them.

The period's political unrest widened the debate over democratic participation. The new state legislatures included more farmers and craftsmen than before, who radicalized the debate by advocating more democracy. Their grassroots idea of democracy contrasted with that of the colonial elites who, mindful of their own power, sought a balance of power between the upper and lower houses in the legislature. They were still mistrustful of democracy and fearful of the tyranny of legislative majorities.

Starting in May 1775, Congress, choosing the path of conflict, had recommended that the Patriots overthrow royal power and adopt new forms of government based on the power of the people. Most states followed the recommendation. In late 1776, eight states adopted new republican constitutions that eliminated all mention of the king. The definition of "people," however, had yet to be clearly established, and most Americans of the time had a relatively narrow conception of the political nation. The right to vote and run for office was considered the province of white, property-owning men, excluding women, blacks, Indians and non-property-owning whites. The more conservative Patriots wanted nothing to do with a wider popular sovereignty. The radical Patriots saw it otherwise. In a few cases, they managed to be heard. Pennsylvania, for example, granted the right to vote to all tax-paying men, who could also be elected to an assembly.

Pennsylvania's constitution was an exception, and alarmed even some Patriots by its excessive democracy. Most states preferred the model put forward by John Adams in his *Thoughts on Government* (1776). He proposed a bicameral legislature with an elected executive and a judiciary appointed to review laws. His proposal had the advantage of being familiar ground. The former colonies usually had two houses, one elected, and a governor with the right of veto. With mistrust for the executive level running high, only three states granted the governor the right of veto. Many states also continued to make the right to vote and hold office subject to property conditions. The constitution of New York allowed only 40 percent of white men to vote in elections for the upper house. Georgia allowed all property owners to vote, but neighbouring South Carolina imposed the strictest conditions: owning property valued at £10,000 to be governor, £2,000 to be a senator and £1,000 to be a representative.

In spite of these limitations, the political system was opening up. There were more voters and they could hold seats in the legislatures. Farmers and craftsmen of modest backgrounds went on to hold a majority, or at least a strong minority, of these seats in a large number of states. All states outlawed importing slaves, but there was no question of emancipation. Progress was made in the North, but Southerners opposed freeing all the slaves and throwing the economy and society into turmoil. Even though many were convinced that slavery was immoral and violated the principles of the American Revolution, they justified it as a necessary evil – especially once cotton growing began making the system profitable.

The Articles of Confederation

At the same time as local governments were being set up, Congress realized that a formal union was needed and in June 1776 set up a committee to draft a bill. The Articles of Confederation, primarily the work of John Dickenson of Pennsylvania, was finally approved by Congress in November 1777. It had to be ratified by all the states before taking effect and becoming the first national constitution.

The proposed confederation was a weak one in which every state kept its sovereignty, independence and all powers not expressly delegated to the new national government. It was to be nothing more than a "firm league of friendship." In 1779, twelve states approved the new constitution, short of the required unanimity. Maryland refused to sign as long as the states with land in the West under the old charters had not granted the land to Congress. Once Maryland got its wish in March 1781, the Articles went into effect.

The United States' war effort would be led by the Continental Congress in the absence of a true national government. Before the Articles, Congress handled the war well enough given its powers and the nation's resources. Congress was not allowed to tax; it asked the states to do it, just as it transmitted to them Washington's requests for men and equipment. The Articles of Confederation, as of 1781, did not fundamentally change the balance of power between Congress and the states. Each state delegated and paid its representatives, who were allowed one vote per state. The approval of two thirds of the states was necessary for major acts and unanimity was required for constitutional changes. Congress had no tax-collecting powers, and no real executive or authority over trade. Its powers related essentially to war and diplomacy as well as arbitrating disputes between states. Attempts to increase Congress's powers fell through. In 1781, for example, the constitutional amendment offered by Robert Morris, superintendent of finance, to institute a customs tariff of 5 percent on all foreign goods was rejected because one state was opposed.

The Americans were choosing their path between union and disunity. But all hesitation, trial and error and obstacles aside, the defective constitution maintained continuity between 1781 and 1789. Congress even managed a few successes despite having no power of coercion. Its most striking accomplishment was the adoption of two laws that fostered the development of the Northwest Territory. The Ordinance of 1785 divided the territory into townships. Each township covered 36 square miles (93 square kilometres) divided into 36 sections of 640 acres (259 hectares) each. Sections were reserved for the army, the government and educational purposes. The rest would be auctioned off at a minimum price of $1 per acre. The Northwest Ordinance of 1787 provided for the admission for the three to five new states. These states would enjoy the same powers as the older states, and their citizens the same freedoms. There would be no slavery in the territory.

American historians have had greatly conflicting interpretations of the 1781–1789 period. Some have felt the country was on the road to ruin, so plagued was it by problems both in the interior and on the frontier. Others have seen it as certainly a difficult period but not unduly so for the beginning of such upheavals. These scholars also believe that Congress weathered the worst, maintained continuity and adopted its greatest legislation in the Northwest Ordinance. In any case, they maintain, the danger has been exaggerated to make it appear that the Fathers of the Constitution of 1787 had saved the day.

Whatever the case, it is clearly a matter of assessing a complicated situation. The war undermined trade when traditional ties to Great Britain were severed. Indigo from South Carolina had no more takers. The Americans had lost access to sugar from the British islands. Tobacco no longer had a protected market in Britain. Peace did not bring a return to prewar prosperity. Competition returned in the form of cheaper British goods. American manufacturers were in trouble. Depression hit hard in

1784–1785 and recurred in 1786, and the economy remained sluggish in general.

The governments' financial woes accentuated the situation. The war had forced the states and Congress to commit sums beyond what they could afford. Congress printed quantities of money, so much that in 1781 the currency was being traded 141 to 1 for gold or silver. "It's not worth a continental" came to mean something was worthless. The biggest losers were the farmers, craftsmen and soldiers who were paid in the depreciated currency. Republican virtues were sorely tested, especially since, as some have noted, many valued their private interests above the republic's survival. The states were also in debt and their currencies depreciated.

Tensions ran high between creditors and debtors. Creditors holding state notes wanted governments to raise taxes so they could be reimbursed for money lent. Some creditors refused to be paid in depreciated currency. In several states, under pressure from debtors, terms of debt repayment were granted that prevented farms from being seized. Debtors well knew that they would be the first and primary targets of taxation. War veterans were particularly outraged. In 1783, Congress owed $2 million to veterans. Officers, threatening mutiny, obtained pensions that stretched public finances.

The first armed revolt in the young republic broke out in Massachusetts. As soon as the war ended, merchants and creditors put pressure on the state to increase taxes and limit the printing of paper money. The state's debt to them was quickly repaid, but farmers in the interior were in a tough spot. Seizures, trials and imprisonments for debt were the measures that sparked the crisis. Protests grew more frequent. Courts were prevented from sitting, and debtors were freed from prison. Resistance turned to revolt when hundreds of farmers took up arms under the leadership of the veteran and farmer Daniel Shays. Emotions ran high. With support from eastern merchants, the governor raised a force to crush the uprising in the winter of 1787.

The consequences of Shays' Rebellion were mainly political. Many were upset to see the economic crisis and social unrest threaten the very existence of the republic. The more conservative elements wanted to regain control and set up a government with enough power to establish a national state where order reigned. Two movements combined at this

Paper money issued by the Continental Congress and individual states soon lost its value, leading to pressure to rein in instability by creating a national debt guaranteed by the American government and a central bank to manage the stability of the currency.

point to save the republican government: the first to protect Congress from the states, the second to protect the states from each other.

The situation was no less bleak in foreign relations. There was a dispute with Great Britain over western forts that the mother country was slow in leaving. The matter of American debts also caused friction and the fate of the Loyalists was an irritant. England used the last two matters to justify its inaction on the first. Approximately one hundred thousand Loyalists left the newly formed United States. Their departure helped destabilize the social and economic order, since most of them belonged to the wealthiest and most politically powerful groups in society.

Drawing up the Constitution

Owing partly to economic hardship, partly to unrest and the climate of insecurity, partly to the poverty of the government of the confederation and partly to the shortcomings of state governments, American nationalists arrived at the consensus that the troubles stemmed from the weak central government and that the Articles of Confederation needed to be overhauled. These nationalists all favoured giving the central government the power to regulate trade and impose taxes.

The first meeting, called by Virginia in 1786, was a failure. Only twelve delegates from five states arrived in Annapolis, Maryland. Another meeting was convened in Philadelphia. The nationalists in Congress were deeply disturbed by news of Shays' Rebellion and, in January 1787, passed a resolution favouring a review of the Articles of Confederation.

On May 25, 1787, fifty-five state delegates met in Philadelphia. Only Rhode Island, opposed to any increase in central power, did not attend. The delegates were all members of the upper class – distinguished, wealthy and influential people. They consisted mainly of merchants, slave-owning planters and lawyers, with no craftsmen or farmers from the East or the frontier. It was a lofty gathering whose true leaders were James Madison (1751–1836), Gouverneur Morris (1752–1816) and George Mason (1725–1792). George Washington, known to all as the general who defeated the British, presided over the meeting. Franklin, the grand old man at eighty-one, was also there. He was particularly helpful in the debate between the small and large states. Alexander Hamilton (1755–1804) was an advocate of a strong centralized government that could protect the republic from the "imprudence of democracy" by state legislatures.

From the beginning, the meeting resembled a coup d'état. The delegates decided to draft a new constitution and to go beyond the "sole and express purpose of revising the Articles." The sessions took place behind closed doors and continued until September 17. Americans would know very little about what took place in Philadelphia until notes taken by Madison were discovered, and the Constitution was never submitted directly to the people but it was submitted the next best thing, conventions elected by the people.

The majority of delegates eventually agreed on a number of points: the need for a new constitution, the primacy of a central government, the separation of powers, and the re-balancing of power between large and small states. But debate was fierce and many compromises were necessary before the final draft emerged. The Philadelphia Convention was a success, but the delegates were not overwhelmingly optimistic. Foreseeing that certain states would remain implacably opposed, they decided that approval by nine states out of thirteen was sufficient to make the new Constitution workable. And since the delegates mistrusted excesses of democracy, they decided to submit the Constitution to special conventions rather than the legislatures, and wider consultation was out of the question.

When the work was finished, Franklin acknowledged that the document had not achieved perfection but urged the forty-one delegates still present to sign it anyway as it had come close.

Ratification

Congress agreed to the proposed procedure and sent the text of the Constitution to the states, which organized special conventions to ratify it.

From the beginning, the debate raged between Federalists and Anti-Federalists. The latter represented the old tradition of the autonomy of states, fear of a strong and possibly tyrannical central government and suspicion of the rich and powerful. The Federalists had the advantage of providing a solution to a situation that seemed impossible if no change of course were adopted. They also benefited from better cohesion, while their adversaries were often divided over local interests. The sides were aligned according to positions they had adopted on issues that had been debated since the Revolution. The same alignments – local/debtor/agrarian and cosmopolitan/creditor/commercial – were recreated.

The Federalists would make two winning moves that would determine the outcome of the debate: publishing the Federalist Papers and agreeing to include a bill of rights (the first ten amendments) in the Constitution. The Federalist Papers were a remarkable collection of eighty-five articles published in 1787 and 1788 by Madison, Hamilton and John Jay. They defended the new Constitution as a better vehicle for conducting foreign relations and protecting group interests through a system of balance of powers that prevented factions from taking over and thereby avoided tyranny. The Federalists also brilliantly defended the idea that a large group was more favourable to democracy. By promising to include a bill of rights guaranteeing the fundamental freedoms so dear to the Anti-Federalists, the Federalists stole their opposition's thunder.

At first, ratification went smoothly. In January 1788, five states were on board, including Pennsylvania, where the battle had been hard fought. After five weeks of deliberation, the side for change won by 46 votes to 23. Massachusetts was the next important test. The state had a strong tradition of local autonomy and was an Anti-Federalist stronghold. Heroes of independence such as Sam Adams and John Hancock were opposed. Early on, Anti-Federalist views predominated but the Federalists neatly turned the situation around using a combination of promises and threats. The final vote was close at 187 votes for and 168 against.

When New Hampshire ratified it in June 1788, the nine-state threshold had technically been reached. Yet two significant states remained, Virginia and New York. Without them, the union would fail. The battle was hard fought in both states, but Federalist pressure was stronger. In Virginia, the vote was 89 to 79 and in New York State, 30 to 27. A closer result is hard to imagine.

The era of aristocrats

The Federalist victory changed the course of the United States and brought about a resurgence of the traditional elites that had been temporarily sidelined during the upheaval of the Revolution. These elites controlled a single national political system that claimed to combine and defend the interests of all participating groups and parties.

The elections of 1788 brought the Federalists to power. Washington was elected the first president unanimously and John Adams vice president. There was resistance to political parties, but soon unbridgeable divides would appear and give rise to them. Fortunately, Washington inspired confidence and would have the manoeuvring room he needed to set the gears of the federal state in motion. The economic recovery meant a favourable climate. The fate of the government depended on precedents set early on.

Congress established the posts of secretary of state, secretary of the treasury, secretary of war and attorney general. Washington appointed respectively Thomas Jefferson, Alexander Hamilton, Henry Knox and Edmund Randolph. All were now advocates of the Constitution and had roots in different regions. They were members of Washington's "cabinet," a body not mentioned in the Constitution. Congress then passed the Judiciary Act, creating a federal justice system comprising a Supreme Court (with six judges at first), three circuit courts and thirteen district courts. This authorized the Supreme Court to review cases from lower courts. The work was completed when the first ten amendments were adopted protecting the fundamental freedoms of religion, speech and the press. The final one guaranteed to the states the powers not expressly granted to the central government.

The new government's worst problem was financial. Here, Alexander Hamilton played a decisive role. Born in the West Indies, he was educated in America at King's College in the 1770s. He sided with the Revolution and served as Washington's aide-de-camp. After marrying into the upper class, he became one of New York's most influential lawyers. He attended the Philadelphia Convention and contributed to the Federalist Papers. He believed in a centralized government drawn from the rich and well-born. As treasury secretary, he would come up with policies to overcome the financial problems, naturally with the help of his own kind. His plan involved linking the interests of the wealthy to the government. Hamilton reasoned that if the rich supported the new government, that would improve its chances of succeeding.

He put forth solutions to the nation's problems in three reports: the Report on Public Credit (1790), the Report on a National Bank (1790) and the Report on Manufactures (1791). The United States was faced with a $75 million debt, including a $12 million foreign debt, a $42 million debt inherited from the Confederation and $21 million in state debts. Hamilton proposed that the new government take responsibility for all these debts. He wanted to establish the nation's credit, get the national debt recognized by all and at the same time tie the wealthy to the government. The national debt was readily recognized, but his other two goals posed problems. Hamilton proposed reimbursing the debts of Confederation at par whereas their value had dropped considerably and the original creditors had long given up their promissory notes. Others had bought them up at cut-rate prices and were waiting in the wings to make a profit. Hamilton also proposed replacing the old promissory notes with government bonds at 4 percent interest, handily tying the moneyed classes to the state.

Faced with criticism that Hamilton's cronies were speculating, the secretary stayed the course and proposed that the national government take on all debts of the states. The measure caused a general outcry, especially in the South. People were scandalized not only by the corruption and speculation, but also by how unfair the measure was to the Southern states, which had quickly repaid their debts and now had to pay those of other states. To gain their support, Hamilton conceded the site of the future capital, Washington, to the South. Cracks began to appear in the Federalist structure. Madison, an ardent defender of the Constitution, turned against Hamilton.

Battle lines were drawn around the bank issue. In his report, Hamilton proposed setting up a national bank, one fifth owned by the government, that would ease commercial and credit transactions, issue paper money, secure public funds and act as the government's financial agent. The plan was approved over the objections of Jefferson and Madison, who protested that since the Constitution made no mention of setting up a bank, it could not be done. This was a strict interpretation of the Constitution. Hamilton favoured a looser interpretation that allowed for a bank to be set up because of the "implicit" powers given Congress. Washington backed his treasury secretary.

In his Report on Manufactures, Hamilton recommended industrializing the country to compete with foreign-made goods. He favoured promoting immigration of specialized labour, encouraging inventors and, especially, raising protective tariffs to shield industry while it developed. His policy was aimed at uniting the North and the South, but the lines had already been drawn. The South was for free trade and even Northern merchants were in favour of liberal trade. Everything would, of course, change when the North became industrialized, but in the climate of 1791, Hamilton's call for action was largely ignored.

To bring in revenue to the government for running the state and to service the debt, Congress raised the customs tariffs set in 1789. As trade resumed, customs revenues would regularly increase, providing 90 percent of government revenue between 1790 and 1820. Hamilton's plan was working. Congress also added an excise tax on whisky and other commodities. The tax raised the ire of farmers in the West in particular, who had become used to turning their excess grain into whisky. Value was added, the product had a long shelf life and it could be used as currency. Collecting the tax was difficult, and the law was spottily enforced. Revolt was a possibility. Or at least that was how Hamilton and Washington chose to interpret an uprising in western Pennsylvania known as the Whiskey Rebellion. Hamilton led a 13,000-man army to crush the uprising. The government had shown its strength. There would be order in the republic – except that the Federalist government had alienated the people on the frontier.

The Alexander Hamilton program was good for the rich and powerful. The Federalist Party attracted more and more members in favour of a strong, centralized federal government that kept order and loosely interpreted the Constitution. Northern merchants, financiers and manufacturers led the ranks. Hamilton's foes, identified as Democrat-Republicans or Republicans under the leadership of Jefferson and Madison, defended freedom over order and saw the people as the true wellspring of democracy. Their vision was more agrarian and they advocated a strict interpretation of the Constitution. Southern planters and Western farmers formed the core of the political organization, which was partial to states' rights.

Washington was handily re-elected in 1792 but resistance was brewing. No one dared run a candidate against him, but George Clinton (1739–1812) put up a good fight against John Adams for the vice-presidency and the Democrat-Republicans took control of Congress. Jefferson remained in cabinet until 1793, but the Federalist and Democrat-Republican positions were now irreconcilable and foreign policy problems would further harden party lines.

Foreign entanglements and domestic affairs

Americans for the most part were enthusiastic about the French Revolution at the outset, opposed as they were to royal absolutism. But the execution of Louis XVI, the Terror and the French declaration of war on Spain and England changed all that. In particular, the news aroused the antagonism of the Federalists, who were wary of democratic excesses. The Republicans, continuing to support the revolutionary cause, took solace in their hatred of despotism and in their belief in people's inherent trustworthiness. When war broke out between France and England in 1793, there was the matter of how to respect the treaty of 1778. Washington declared American neutrality on April 22, 1793. The Republicans disputed the constitutionality of Washington's move, maintaining that proclamations of neutrality, like declarations of war, were the province of Congress.

Both Republicans and Federalists realized that the war was profitable to the Americans. Farmers, who supported Jefferson, were doing a roaring business as grain prices rose and Southern commodities were more and more in demand. Federalist merchants also profited handsomely. Prosperity had returned.

The arrival of Citizen Edmond-Charles Genêt in April 1793 further complicated the situation. The French minister plenipotentiary made several blunders. He openly fomented attacks on Florida and Louisiana and commissioned privateers against England in violation of American neutrality. Even the Republicans were embarrassed. In August 1793, Genêt was removed from his position by his government at Washington's request.

Trouble came next from Britain. The Americans profited from their neutrality by expanding trade, in particular to the French West Indies. Britain objected, reasoning that trade that was illegal in peacetime should not be allowed in wartime. Numerous ships were seized, a blow to American honour and commerce. To add insult to injury, the British refused to leave the Western forts until the matter of the pre-Revolutionary War debts had been cleared up.

Congress adopted a policy of trade reprisals and voted for an embargo in 1794. The embargo was painfully detrimental to merchants; when England softened its policy, the Americans rushed toward a diplomatic solution. John Jay (1745–1829), chief justice of the Supreme Court, was sent to

London to negotiate. The results of Jay's Treaty were so disappointing that they were kept quiet and barely ratified by the Senate in 1795. The Republicans protested strenuously. Britain surrendered the Western outposts in 1796 but refused to concede a broad definition of neutral rights or to fully open ports in the British empire to American merchants. On the other hand, the Spanish wanted to settle their differences with the United States. Under the Treaty of San Lorenzo (1795), the Americans won the right to navigate the Mississippi and to use the port of New Orleans. The United States also secured a favourable border with Spanish Florida.

For several years, Washington had wanted to retire. In 1796, nothing could hold him back. He had completed two terms, which became the traditional limit. In his Farewell Address to the nation, he warned his fellow citizens against partisan tendencies and permanent foreign alliances. The outgoing president was well aware of the dangers lurking for his country.

Parties arose nonetheless. Washington had tried to stay above the fray, but his continuing support of Hamilton's positions contributed to the rise of political organizations. During the 1796 elections, the candidates ran not as individuals but as representatives of parties that backed specific policy measures. The Republicans recruited mainly among Southern planters, workers and tradesmen in the cities and small farmers in the West and everywhere else. The Republican base was very solid, but the Federalist Party had wealth, prestige and experience on its side and was also the party in power. In 1796, the Federalists managed once again to stay in power with a majority in Congress and John Adams as president. But internal divisions among the Federalists (Hamilton, as the party's *éminence grise,* held the reins and did not like John Adams) meant that Thomas Jefferson, not Adams's running mate, became vice president. In effect, the electors of the Electoral College voted for two people independent of office. Whoever won an absolute majority of votes cast became president and the person in second place vice president. The administration was split. It did not bode well for Adams.

The foreign policy problems persisted. Trouble came this time from France, which after Jay's Treaty began seizing American merchant vessels around the world. Hundreds of ships were seized. John Adams supported Federalist views that favoured Great Britain, but he managed to resist pressure from the radicals to go to war. He sent envoys to France to try to negotiate with the Directoire. A grave mistake. The minister of foreign affairs, Talleyrand, refused to see the Americans, sending agents instead who demanded a $250,000 bribe. In their report to Adams, the envoys named the perpetrators of the attempted bribery but in his report to Congress, the president substituted the letters XYZ for their names. The XYZ Affair was born. The Republicans were neutralized. The Federalists rose in popularity and Adams had to play the radicals' game. He prepared the country for war. For two years, from 1798 to 1800, the United States was virtually in an undeclared war with France and allied with its former enemy, the mother country.

The Federalists took advantage of the situation to muzzle the opposition. Success went to their heads, and in June and July 1798, on the pretext of the French threat, they passed the Alien and Sedition Acts. For the first time in American history, but not the last, foreign policy problems caused protest and a government clampdown. Among the Republicans were many foreigners, including French and Irish. The acts extended the residency requirement for naturalization from five to fourteen years and authorized the president to deport or imprison foreigners as he saw fit. "He that is not for us is against us," thundered the Federalist-leaning *Gazette of the United States*. The Federalist-controlled Congress resorted to the Sedition Act, which threatened anyone who dared to write, publish or utter anything "false, scandalous and malicious" about the government or its officials with fines or imprisonment. No fewer than twenty-five publishers and writers were tried and imprisoned. Even a member of Congress, Matthew Lyon from Vermont, was imprisoned for libel. Voters returned him to Congress. The Republicans played the martyr.

Republican opposition moved into constitutional territory. Jefferson and Madison succeeded in having resolutions passed in the Kentucky and Virginia legislatures in November 1798 to nullify the acts passed by Congress. They claimed that the states had the right to refuse to apply acts of Congress if they overstepped the powers granted by the Constitution, since the agreement of 1787 was a contract between the states. The foundations of the theory of nullification had been laid. The theory would soon be used for other purposes.

Jefferson ran in the 1800 presidential election by hammering hard on states' rights and the imprisonments. The Federalists criticized Jefferson as a dangerous, pro-French radical and a free thinker with atheist leanings.

Adams, wise enough not to listen to the radical Federalists who wanted war with France, settled the Franco-American dispute.

The Republicans won by a landslide. Voters were protesting the war, increases in taxation and the Alien and Sedition acts. Discord among the Federalists did the rest. Jefferson and Aaron Burr (1796–1836), his running mate, each won seventy-three electoral votes. They were from the same party, and everyone who voted for Jefferson also voted for Burr. In a stalemate, the vote devolved upon the House of Representatives. After thirty-six ballots (with each state casting one vote and nine votes needed for election), Jefferson became president. Once again, Hamilton was instrumental. He paved the way for Jefferson by declaring his opposition to Burr. He would later pay with his life when Burr killed him in a duel in 1804. The twelfth amendment would prevent this type of stalemate from happening again by making the electors vote separately for the president and the vice president.

The Republicans also won control of Congress, which Jefferson referred to as the Revolution of 1800. The election marked the end of the Federalist era and its aristocratic approach, and ushered in a more democratic period. In a sense, the peaceful transfer of power was in itself revolutionary. A change of direction had become inevitable. The Federalist goal of establishing a strong government was attained. No one doubted any longer that the country would survive, but many were dissatisfied with the Federalists' conduct and political philosophy. The government was outwardly more democratic but the legislation it passed was not revolutionary, and people noticed that the goals of the Republican Party and of the Federalist Party tended to converge. While the government was now in the hands of a different elite that had refused to follow Hamilton, it often retreated back to patrician, Federalist positions.

The country now faced new challenges, chief among them a doubling of its population and the attendant problems of rapid growth.

An agrarian republic
In 1800, the population of the United States totalled 5,300,000 inhabitants, almost 94 percent living in rural areas. In 1776, most American lived less than 100 kilometres (about 60 miles) from the coasts. In 1790, around 200,000 of them lived west of the Appalachians. In 1820, out of 9,600,000 Americans, 2,000,000 lived in the nine new states and three territories

established in the West. The birth rate remained high, as did immigration, but internal migration was largely responsible for the changes.

From the North and the South, migrants crossed the Appalachians to reach the fertile soil of Kentucky, Tennessee, western New York and the territories of the Old Northwest. Those from the South were poor farmers fleeing the plantation-dominated East with its overworked soil. Kentucky was admitted to the United States in 1792 and Tennessee in 1796. Over 100,000 Southerners had settled in the two states and the exodus continued. Together the states boasted almost a million inhabitants by 1820.

In the North, internal migration originated in New England. People migrated first to Vermont, admitted in 1791, and Maine, then further inland under demographic pressure. Families who could no longer find land to raise children relocated after selling their small operations at a good price to buy more land at a lower cost. American farmers were also speculators, and migration increased as prices rose. By 1820, 800,000 people lived in western New York between Buffalo and Albany. In the Ohio Valley, the Indians ceded over 40 million hectares (100 million acres) of land between 1800 and 1810.

American agricultural society was expansionist. Farmers did not wait for territories to be opened up before settling there. Ohio (1803) was the first state to be carved out of the Northwest Territory. Indiana and Illinois followed in 1816 and 1818. The Republicans' rise to power made it easier to buy land as they brought about changes to the Federalist policies that had favoured speculators. The minimum plot was reduced from 640 to 320 acres, then to 160, with prices dropping proportionately. Buyers could pay over four years. Most of the land, though, was still purchased in bulk by government-connected speculators, funnelling generous revenues back to the government.

Life on the frontier was far from ideal. Farmers were often in debt for years. It was hard for them to sell their products with the inadequate and expensive transportation system. It cost a Pennsylvania farmer the same amount to send his grain to Philadelphia, a 50-kilometre (30-mile) trip, as to send it from Philadelphia to London by boat. Development necessitated improvements to roads and canals. When the Erie Canal between Buffalo and Albany (580 kilometres or 360 miles) was completed in 1825, the New York–Buffalo journey dropped from twenty days to six. Passengers and merchandise from inland now had reasonably priced access to the port of New York. The success of New York's canal would be copied widely. The fortunes of Western farmers gradually improved and colonists continued flooding in, hoping to improve their situation.

The late 18th century was a good time for American farmers, with the French Revolution throwing Europe into chaos. The Americans took advantage of their neutrality to increase trade. American exports tripled between 1793 and 1807 in spite of all the difficulties caused by the European powers. Furthermore, prices were high. The urban population was growing significantly – from 202,000 to 693,000 between 1790 and 1829 – and had to be fed as well.

A new team

When he took office in 1801, Jefferson was careful to mark the transfer of power to a more democratic team in a symbolic way. He walked through the muddy streets of the new capital, Washington, to the Capitol, still under construction. He refused the military honour guard. He genuinely wanted to encourage an agrarian "republic of virtue" emphasizing simplicity and frugality. He abolished internal taxes, including the hated whisky tax. He reduced the size of the army and navy. Relying on the work of the treasury secretary, Albert Galatin (1761–1849), who believed that the national debt was an evil of the first order, he and his successor shrank the national debt to $45 million between 1801 and 1813. The savings in interest paid to government creditors gave him the necessary room to manoeuvre. Finally, he repealed the Alien and Sedition Acts.

In the final days of his administration, President Adams had appointed many Federalists to judicial posts. The Republicans were scandalized by this "packing" of the courts; they repealed the Judiciary Act of 1801 and rendered the appointments null and void. One justice of the peace whose commission was withheld by the new administration sued the government. The case was heard by John Marshall (1755–1835), chief justice of the Supreme Court, an ardent Federalist appointed by John Adams. Marshall defended judicial independence and the principle of constitutional review by the Supreme Court, but conceded that the court could not force the administration to hand over commissions to judges, even if duly appointed. The seemingly Solomon-like decision *(Marbury v. Madison,* 1803) established the central principle of the federal judiciary's authority over legislative constitutionality.

The Louisiana Purchase

Jefferson would soon have an opportunity to advance the creation of the great agrarian republic he envisioned. Napoleon Bonaparte had ambitions to build a new French empire in America. In a secret 1800 treaty, he recovered Louisiana from Spain. He then set out to regain control of rebellious Haiti. All these incidents caused concern. The Republicans' traditional sympathy toward France was called into question. The closing of New Orleans, an unacceptable impediment to free navigation of the Mississippi, became a possibility, and the Federalists demanded aggressive action; they even toyed with an Anglo-American alliance. Jefferson sent negotiators to Paris in the hopes of buying New Orleans. The deal they were offered was a generous one: Napoleon had abandoned his dream (the situation in Haiti was disastrous) and was offering the Americans the entire Louisiana territory for $15 million (see map, page 95). Even the most visionary Americans had not imagined such a possibility. The United States could not turn it down. The administration immediately accepted the agreement, doubling the nation's size, even though the Constitution did not provide for federal purchase of territory. Expansion was necessary for freedom, it was claimed, and the Constitution could be stretched. The Federalists pointed out the president's contradictions, but had to agree that the offer was too good to refuse. The treaty was ratified by the Senate in October 1803 and the House of Representatives approved the amount required.

As much scientist as politician, Jefferson had long wanted to finance an expedition to the West, of which little was known. The Louisiana Purchase made the task even more imperative. He had already instructed his personal secretary, Meriwether Lewis (1774–1809), and a soldier, William Clark (1770–1838), to survey the region and catalogue its inhabitants, plants and animals. The clear goal was to find the fastest and most direct continental waterway. After two years (1804–1806), the explorers returned with the first maps of the region and the first descriptions of its flora, fauna and Indians.

Jefferson was handily re-elected in 1804. Prosperity, Louisiana and Republican policies gave his party a solid majority in Congress, but foreign policy would again come back to haunt them.

In his inaugural speech of 1801, Jefferson had more or less confirmed Washington's policy of neutrality and, considering how advantageous it was to the Americans, it had to be maintained. But the United States was caught in the crossfire. Napoleon controlled the continent of Europe but England controlled the seas. Napoleon issued decrees excluding British goods from European countries, even if transported by neutral nations. Britain responded with orders-in-council imposing a blockade of the European coasts. The British seized ships and used press gangs to round up British sailors or those presumed to be. Innocent Americans were impressed into British service, a hardship to the victims and an insult to American honour American merchants did not suffer, however, as profits were high and the value of exports even rose from $55 million to $108 million between 1803 and 1807. In desperation, after failed negotiations, Jefferson secured Congress's approval for an embargo in December 1807. The idea was that depriving the world of American goods would force it to recognize the rights of neutral nations. Prohibiting American ships from leaving port meant signing the death warrant of prosperity. Exports fell to $22 million. The embargo was not respected, smuggling was rife and the Federalists fanned the flames of discord by accusing Jefferson of being responsible for the disaster, which hit New England the hardest. His second term ended badly. So unpopular was the embargo that three days before the end of his presidency Jefferson was forced to accept its repeal and the substitution of a more limited trade restriction.

Despite Federalist gains, the Republicans won the presidency in 1808 with James Madison as well as control of Congress. Efforts continued to remain neutral while the dominant European powers clashed, but with little success. Frenetic diplomatic activity brought no results. In the country's heartland, another crisis was brewing that would have an impact on the first: it involved the Ohio Valley Indians.

The War of 1812

Since 1790, the Intercourse Act had stipulated that Indian land had to be ceded by treaty and not simply seized. As a rule, farmers did not wait for territories to be opened up and treaties signed. They occupied land, and if the Indians resisted, they called in troops. Between 1801 and 1809, William H. Harrison, governor of the territory of Indiana, signed fifteen treaties (using any means, including tricks, bribes, liquor and threats, to get signatures) that many Indians did not recognize. Tecumseh, a traditional Shawnee leader who defended the Indian way of life, realized

Washington came under attack in the War of 1812 when, in August 1814, British forces burned the navy yard and public buildings, including the White House, and forced President Madison and the govenrment to flee. As prints of the time often did, this shows many stages of the event at once. (U.S. National Archives and Records Administration)

that the time had come to fight back. He and his brother, the Prophet, preached a sacred Indian union. Every treaty Harrison signed increased Tecumseh's supporters. In 1809, Harrison signed another dubious treaty (3 million acres or 1.2 million hectares in the Wabash Valley) that was denounced by Tecumseh; he claimed that the land belonged to all Indians and he threatened both surveyors and farmers. In November 1811, while Tecumseh tried to expand the Indian alliance toward the south, Harrison marched on the village of Tippecanoe with a thousand men. The Indians tried to surprise them, and the resulting battle claimed more white victims than Indian. But Harrison claimed victory, terror set in on the frontier and Tecumseh formed an alliance with the British. The Indian threat was greater than ever.

It seemed it would take a war with England to settle the Indian problem and get the rights of neutral nations recognized. The United States declared war in June 1812. Madison was bowing to pressure from the War Hawks, young Republican politicians from the West and the South. Most of them had been elected to Congress in the elections of 1810. They were a new breed of Republican, expansionists and extreme, hot-headed nationalists, who dreamed of doing battle with England and seizing Canada and Florida for good measure. The declaration of war was approved by Congress, but the distribution of votes showed to what degree the country was divided. New England was opposed, while most of the Middle, Southern and Western states were in favour. The results of the ensuing elections of 1812 confirmed the split.

It was an unfortunate war, approaching disaster militarily and politically – Mr. Madison's War, it was called in the North to signal opposition. Troops were ill-prepared. The army and navy had been weakened under Jefferson. The Eastern militias were unreliable while those in the West were confident of an easy victory. The Kentucky militia was convinced it could take Canada by itself. The governors of New England refused to call out their militia, ruling out an effective invasion of Canada. Yet the country was the chink in the British armour, as evidenced by the American victories on the Great Lakes and the burning of York (Toronto). The British made the most of their naval superiority and imposed a blockade of the Atlantic coast. They succeeded in sailing up Chesapeake Bay and burning Washington in summer 1814. Boston financiers and bankers refused to lend the government capital, and smuggling thrived all along the border with Canada. The most spectacular American victory was won at the Battle of New Orleans, when Andrew Jackson (1769–1845), the future president, defeated the British on January 8, 1815.

The Treaty of Ghent, putting an end to the conflict, was signed on December 24, 1814, and restored the status quo. The Americans had no reason to rejoice, but Jackson's victory helped salve American wounds. The war's biggest losers were the Indians. The British abandoned them to their fate and they were defeated in the North (Tecumseh died in 1813) and the South (the Creek were defeated in 1814). Expansion could be resumed, and the United States pursued its economic growth with an additional weapon, industrial development that had been fuelled by the war as American factories produced what the British had previously provided.

The "Era of Good Feelings"

In the 1816 elections, the Republicans easily managed to get their candidate, James Monroe (1758–1831), elected over Rufus King, the last Federalist candidate in American history. Monroe, associated with the Virginia Dynasty, was re-elected without opposition in 1820. A single member of the Electoral College voted against him to avoid giving him the same honour that Washington enjoyed. He got a good reception on his tour of the Northeast and West of the country, especially in New England, where Boston's *Columbia Sentinel* coined the expression Era of Good Feelings to describe the climate of the time. The term became associated with Monroe's presidencies. It seemed as though opposition had disappeared.

Granted, the Republicans had adopted some Federalist policies and seemed won over to Hamiltonian nationalism. The second Bank of the United States was established in 1816. The tariff imposed the same year was the first protective tariff in American history. American manufacturers, upset by the reappearance of British competition in 1815, had demanded protection. Support for the measure came from both the North and the South, but consensus was short-lived. The Republicans also came around to supporting the idea of a national system of roads and canals, although they were reluctant to fund strictly local projects.

Reconciliation seemed possible. Expansion and prosperity resumed. Monroe even chose John Quincy Adams (1763–1848), son of John Adams, from Massachusetts for the strategic position of secretary of state and heir apparent. Any good feelings, however, owed more to appearance than reality. Dissent and conflict brewed, and they would steadily worsen until the Civil War.

The North was already industrializing and focusing on trade and finance. The South, after the invention of the cotton gin (1793), stepped up cotton production, producing more and more to supply the textile industry in the North and, especially, in Great Britain. The South increasingly relied on the North for its manufactured goods, financing and trade. The policies advocated by each were greatly at odds. Would the national policy be free trade, as the South increasingly hoped for, or protectionist, as the North wanted? The two regions fought over the West, where many states had been established that would determine the outcome of the political struggle in Washington. The Missouri Compromise (1820) illustrated at once the intensity of regional opposition and the extent of polarization around the issue of slavery, which would complicate all the other problems.

The Missouri Compromise

As the free states of the North and the slave states of the South advanced westward, they readily agreed to maintain a balance between the two as new states were admitted to the Union. The problem arose when Missouri requested admission in 1819. The balance at the time was eleven free states and eleven slave states. Missouri was a pro-slavery region on the boundary between the North and the South. A representative offered a motion to ban slavery in the long term in the state by emancipating all children of slaves when they turned twenty-five and banning the import of other slaves.

Southerners balked at the federal interference. They felt that slavery was a property matter and therefore under state jurisdiction. The controversy raged for a year. A compromise was found when Maine was admitted in 1820, then Missouri in 1821. Balance had been maintained. The 1820 Compromise seemed to settle the slavery dispute for a generation. Missouri was admitted as a slave state on the condition that slavery would henceforth be prohibited north of latitude 36° 30'. It could be only a temporary solution, since the matter of balance between the North and the South had not been resolved. The deal held out until 1850, when slavery was readmitted into the territories where it had been banned.

At his retreat at Monticello, Jefferson sensed how dangerous the issue was, comparing it to a "fire bell in the night."

The Monroe Doctrine

In foreign affairs, the administration observed developments in the post-Napoleonic world with unease. Spain's colonies in South America were breaking free and forming republics, with the possible danger of other European powers stepping in, either to support or to supplant Spain. The Monroe Doctrine, presented by the president in his State of the Union address of 1823, and authored mainly by Adams, essentially said that the United States would remain neutral in European affairs, except where

> **The Monroe Doctrine**
>
> Of events in that quarter of the globe, with which we have so much intercourse and from which we derive our origin, we have always been anxious and interested spectators. The citizens of the United States cherish sentiments the most friendly in favour of the liberty and happiness of their fellowmen on that side of the Atlantic. In the wars of the European powers in matters relating to themselves we have never taken any part, nor does it comport with our policy so to do. It is only when our rights are invaded or seriously menaced that we resent injuries or make preparations for our defence. With the movements in this hemisphere we are of necessity more immediately connected, and by causes which must be obvious to all enlightened and impartial observers. The political system of the allied powers is essentially different in this respect from that of America. This difference proceeds from that which exists in their respective Governments; and to the defence of our own, which has been achieved by the loss of so much blood and treasure, and matured by the wisdom of their most enlightened citizens, and under which we have enjoyed such unexampled felicity, this whole nation is devoted. We owe it, therefore, to candor and the amicable relations existing between the United States and those powers to declare that we should consider any attempt on their part to extend their system to any portion of this hemisphere as dangerous to our peace and safety. With the existing colonies or dependencies of any European power we have not interfered and shall not interfere. But with the Governments who have declared their independence and maintained it, and whose independence we have, on great consideration and on just principles, acknowledged, we could not view any interposition for the purpose of oppressing them, or controlling in any other manner their destiny, by any European power in any other light than as the manifestation of an unfriendly disposition toward the United States.
>
> President James Monroe, State of the Union address to Congress, 1823.

they affected the Americas, and that the United States would not tolerate further colonization in the American hemisphere. The doctrine, with subsequent corollaries and modifications, became a cornerstone of American foreign policy.

CHAPTER 5

PROBLEMATIC GROWTH

1820–1850

The Jacksonian era was a distinct period in American history that marked a break with that of the Patricians. Dominated by the charismatic Andrew Jackson, the period saw changes that had much greater consequences than a simple change of leadership. Jackson was also carried along by these changes, especially the rise of the common man (white, obviously). Until then all political leaders, even those as democratic as Jefferson, shared the conviction that government was the province of an elite. Many of the revolutionaries of 1776 had become conservatives by 1800. Jeffersonian democracy encouraged citizens to vote and increased the number of voters, but Jacksonian democracy would go further by encouraging public participation.

The period would give rise to a large part of the American mythology, as much for the image of the harsh life on the frontier as for the idea that it was possible for everyone to climb the social ladder. The political and social thinking that resulted is an original American contribution.

The country's socioeconomic transformations, fast and intense as they were, built a nation. They took place in a regionalist context that foreshadowed the problems of later years. These problems were often exacerbated by the policies of Jackson and his heirs.

A democratic age

The migration westward begun in 1790 had become a rush by 1830. Between 1800 and 1830, the population of the United States doubled, but during the same period, the population of the West grew tenfold, to almost four million. In 1830, over a third of Americans lived west of the thirteen original states.

Westward expansion upset the political order. As each state joined the Union, it brought its own regional perspective. Although the Southwest had more in common with the South and the Northwest with New England and the Middle states, as a rule the views and positions of the Western regions were fairly similar, a fact that politicians from the two older regions had to take into account.

In the expansion states, the right to vote was extended to all white men over the age of twenty-one. This was the case in Kentucky (1792), Tennessee (1796) and Ohio (1803), where the right to vote was almost universal for white men. From 1791 to 1837, thirteen new states were admitted, doubling the number of the original states. Even the latter were led to expand voting rights. Progress was not equally strong in every state, but it is a fact that by 1840 over 90 percent of white men nationwide could vote. Women and blacks, even free ones (except in some Northern states), could not vote. In 1825, only 68 of the 13,000 blacks in New York City had the right to vote. In the new states, blacks had made no progress. Democracy was the preserve of whites.

Political life

Elections of 1824 and 1828
The expansion of voting rights also brought about changes in the issues citizens were consulted on. Governors as well as members of the Electoral College were now elected. In the 1824 presidential election, 355,000 votes were cast, compared to 1,155,000 in 1828. These elections marked a dramatic end to the Era of Good Feelings and indicated the scope and the strength of the democratic movement fostered by the emerging party system.

In 1824, the election was contested within the Republican Party. Four candidates vied for the presidency. Andrew Jackson, the hero of New Orleans, won the most votes in the Electoral College (99) but not a majority. John Quincy Adams, the heir apparent, followed with 84 votes and William H. Crawford and Henry Clay took respectively 41 and 37. Jackson also won the popular vote with 43 percent of all votes cast. The election result was clearly regional. Adams took only New England and most of New York, Clay won Kentucky, Ohio and Missouri, and Crawford won Virginia, Delaware and Georgia. Only Jackson garnered support outside one region. He still did not have a majority and the election was handed over to the House of Representatives. Clay instructed his supporters to vote for Adams, who was elected. But when Adams chose Clay as secretary of state, there was an uproar over the "corrupt bargain."

Adams's presidency was a debacle. He advocated a strongly national policy of central government when public opinion favoured states' rights. His wide-scale program of public works was not supported by Congress, and he alienated the South by refusing to strip Indians of their land in Georgia. To make matters worse, in 1828 a new protectionist tariff was passed at the request of Northeastern manufacturers. The South called it the "tariff of abominations," as its pro-free-trade position had hardened. Goods from the South had to be sold on the open market, and American protectionism would lead to protectionism abroad.

This was the context of the 1828 election. The Republican schism was formalized with the establishment of the National Republicans behind Adams and the Democrats behind Jackson. Jackson had the advantage of a better political machine. Well-organized mass political parties had appeared. Parades and large political rallies maintained partisan loyalty toward clearly defined programs. Jackson embodied democracy versus the privilege represented by Adams. Accusations flew from both sides via party members, as any hands-on involvement by the candidates themselves would have been considered undignified.

Both sides pulled out all the stops to slander the opposing candidate. Adams became a narrow-minded, hypocritical puritan who had bought billiard and gaming tables with public funds. Jackson was described as a boor, a murderer and an adulterer; unwittingly, he had married a divorcee whose divorce had not been legally finalized.

Jackson said that a democracy should be led by Democrats. The people understood: power should be taken away from family dynasties and elites. When the mid-term elections of 1826 were held, a remarkable coalition had been set up in support of Jackson. It took control of Congress but was a motley assortment of opponents and supporters of the Bank of the United States, of protectionists and of free-traders. The appearance of John C. Calhoun (1782–1850) on the Democratic ticket illustrates the ever-changing politics of the time. Calhoun had been vice president under John Q. Adams and rallied to Jackson, bringing him Southern votes. Although an alliance with the man who most embodied the interests of slavers eventually caused a problem, Jackson created unity, brought people together and was everything to everybody. His party was the first to create and maintain a truly national coalition.

Jackson took 56 percent of the popular vote and 173 Electoral College votes to Adams's 83. At his inauguration ceremony, it seemed as though the people had genuinely taken over the government. Ten thousand people invaded Washington, raising fears of what conservatives called "mob rule." It quickly became clear that Jackson was not the common man he claimed to be. He was a military hero, a lawyer who had become a wealthy slave owner, and an authoritarian, and most definitely not a democrat. On the other hand, he came from a humble background and was associated with a sense of egalitarianism and class pride. He fulfilled the needs of voters. He was the symbol of democracy and would have a profound effect on American life. His era would provide the momentum for economic individualism, enterprise and the self-made man. This was the period when an American society, as distinct from European society, began to take shape, including its excesses.

Jackson began his mandate by rewarding his loyal supporters with civil service posts. He brought the spoils system, already widespread at the state level, to the national stage. Jackson had ties to the West but was a nationalist by temperament. He was much more interested in promoting a strong national leadership than in protecting himself from possible disunity by advocating regional compromises. As president, the embodiment of the popular will, he was accountable only to the people. He imposed his style: many called him Old Hickory for his toughness or King Andrew the First for his authoritarianism. He did not share power and ignored his official cabinet in favour of his informal or "kitchen" cabinet. He used his veto liberally, more often than all previous presidents combined, and forced Congress to consider his views. During his presidency, Jackson did not shy away from taking strong positions. He often caused controversy and his term led to the formation of a new opposition party, the Whigs.

The nullification crisis
The South had agreed to the 1816 tariff with the assurance that it would be a temporary measure to assist postwar recovery. But the tariff remained and was even raised in 1824 and 1826. The South protested, but repre-

sentatives from the North and West controlled Congress. They needed the tariff as a protection for industry and a source of revenue.

The 1828 tariff was an "abomination" for the South. Jackson's supporters passed it to increase support from the North. The South claimed that the measure was not in the national interest but protected some states to the detriment of others. They believed the measure to be unconstitutional. South Carolina, which was in economic turmoil, led the opposition. The foremost leader in South Carolina was John C. Calhoun, Adams's vice president and about to be Jackson's vice president. In 1828, he anonymously published *Exposition and Protest*, in which he defended the "nullification" theory espoused by Jefferson and Madison: the constitution was established by thirteen sovereign states and not by the people, and therefore the states held final authority limiting the power of the national government.

Calhoun hoped to influence Jackson, but he would be bitterly disappointed; there was no rapport between the two men. Confrontations multiplied. In 1830, there was a proposal in Congress to severely restrict access to land. The West criticized the attempt, charging that it was designed to preserve Northeastern labour. Southerners attacked the measure, counting on the West's support over the tariff. A heated debate took place in the Senate between Robert Hayne of South Carolina and Daniel Webster of Massachusetts. Hayne championed states' rights and nullification, which Webster rejected in favour of the federal government's supreme authority. Calhoun was clearly behind it all and Jackson went into attack mode. During a reception, Jackson made a toast to "our union: it must be preserved." Calhoun responded that while dear, the Union was less so than liberty and could be preserved only by distributing its benefits and burdens equally. The lines had been drawn. In 1831, Jackson learned that Calhoun had criticized him for his treatment of the Seminoles in Florida. Relations deteriorated and Calhoun, sensing that his chances of influencing Jackson were nil, resigned in 1832.

The political crisis came to a head the same year. Congress again increased customs duties. South Carolina called a convention that nullified the tariff. Jackson retaliated by passing the Force Bill authorizing the federal government to collect taxes by force. Behind closed doors, however, he asked Congress to lower the tariff and Calhoun, for his part, calmed the situation by cooperating with adoption of the 1833 Tariff Act, and subsequent legislation gradually brought tariffs down to the 1816 level. Both sides saved face. Federal authority was maintained and South Carolina could claim to have made the government step back. But the other Southern states did not follow suit and it seemed that the rule of national majority had prevailed: the federal state had survived.

Other crises

Jackson stuck to his principles, but his principles were elastic, as demonstrated by several decisions he made during the crises that marked his presidency.

His politics, in fact, were personal, based on what he considered the will of the people and justified by his broad popularity. During the nullification crisis, he sided with the federal union in the name of unitary nationalism. In the Bank of the United States crisis, he opposed the nationalism of Alexander Hamilton. In the debate over relocating "nuisance" Indian tribes living east of the Mississippi, he arranged to have decisions of the Supreme Court, bastion of federal authority, overturned. In many cases, he used his veto to halt congressional initiatives that he felt violated states' rights.

The 1832 Bank crisis is worth looking at. The Bank's charter had been renewed in 1816 and did not expire until 1836. Its president, Nicholas Biddle, decided nevertheless to request a new one in 1832. He counted on beating Jackson to the punch, figuring the president would not dare oppose the Bank in an election year for fear of dividing his party. It was common knowledge that Jackson was opposed to the Bank, which had the reputation of defending the interests of big financiers and not of the people.

Congress renewed the Bank's charter, but Jackson used his veto, and the matter became the main election issue. The Bank was powerful, especially in the control it exerted over local banks. It defended stability against smaller, more speculative banks linked to farmers and developers. It represented "interests" over the people. Jackson's victory was clear-cut. His rival, Henry Clay (1777–1852), a proponent of the Bank, won only 49 votes in the Electoral College versus Jackson's 219. Convinced that his personal victory gave him a popular mandate to destroy the Bank, Jackson set about doing so even before the 1836 deadline.

The Whigs

The Bank did not go quietly. In 1833–1834, it set off a panic and a recession by calling in its commercial loans. Merchants, planters and businessmen turned against Jackson. Opposition to "King Andrew" coalesced in a new party, the Whigs (the same name used by opponents of King George III). Martin Van Buren (1782–1862), Jackson's heir apparent, won easily in 1836 against three Whig candidates from three regions, who won 124 votes compared to Van Buren's 170.

The worst recession in American history thus far struck in 1836 and would last until 1843. The disappearance of the Bank of the United States had encouraged speculation and inflation. At the same time, foreign investors, mainly British banks, had tightened credit. During the Panic of 1837, eight hundred banks failed. Businesses closed and bankruptcies were endemic. The consequences – joblessness, hunger and poverty – were dire, and Van Buren paid the price. His popular nickname was Van Ruin.

The Whigs, who had learned their lesson from defeats in 1836 and 1840, ran a single candidate, William Henry Harrison, who was also a military hero and common man in the mould of Jackson. Harrison's stunning victory (234 Electoral College votes, 60 for Van Buren) was short-lived. He died a month after his mandate began and was replaced by his vice president, John Tyler of Virginia. Tyler (1790–1862) was less a Whig than a Democrat disgruntled with Jackson's authoritarianism. Once in power, he repudiated all the elements of Henry Clay's American System that the Whigs had advocated: high tariffs, federally financed improvements in transportation and a new Bank of the United States. A rift opened between the Whig Congress and the president, now a Democrat. The quarrel would reach its climax over the issue of Texas.

Since 1821, when Mexico won independence from Spain, Americans from the South had been settling in the Mexican province of Texas. In 1830, they numbered around 7,000. In the ensuing years, over 20,000 people emigrated there while the Mexican government attempted to regain control of its territory by trying to restrict American immigration and abolishing slavery. In 1835, war broke out between Texans and Mexicans. Despite the Texans' defeat at the Alamo, the forces of Sam Houston (1793–1863) went on to win the war and Texas became independent in 1836. Admission of Texas to the Union was in the United States' highest interest, but the state was refused entry in 1837. Texas would have been the fourteenth slave state, while there were only thirteen free states. Jackson, who sympathized with the Texan cause, would only go so far as to grant diplomatic recognition.

In 1844, in a desperate bid to save his presidency, John Tyler began championing annexation. The Whigs overwhelmingly rejected the treaty and expelled Tyler from the party. Clay would be their candidate against the Democrat James K. Polk (1795–1849), a confirmed expansionist. Polk's victory in 1844 was interpreted as a mandate for expansion. Near the end of his term, Tyler got the annexation of Texas approved in Congress by a simple resolution rather than in the Senate, where he could not count on the two thirds of the votes required for a treaty. After the Oregon Treaty (1846), granting the United States exclusive control over this territory, was signed, Polk set his sights on Mexico.

The Mexican-American War, like many wars, caused discord. The president was accused of having tricked Congress, of having manoeuvred and schemed for an unjustifiable and pointless war. The war was successful, but as costs rose opposition intensified, especially among Northern, anti-slavery Whigs. It became "Mr. Polk's War." The Treaty of Guadalupe Hidalgo (1848) consolidated the American victory when California

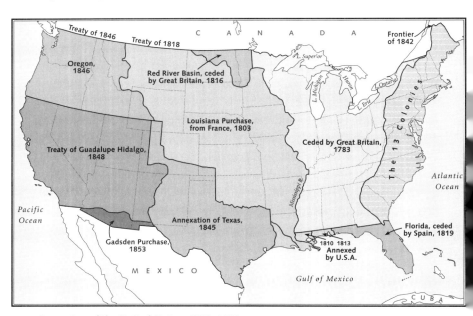

Expansion of the United States, 1783–1853

> **The Polk Doctrine**
> In the existing circumstances of the world the present is deemed a proper occasion to reiterate and reaffirm the principle avowed by Mr. Monroe and to state my cordial concurrence in its wisdom and sound policy. The reassertion of this principle, especially in reference to North America, is at this day but the promulgation of a policy which no European power should cherish the disposition to resist. Existing rights of every European nation should be respected, but it is due alike to our safety and our interests that the efficient protection of our laws should be extended over our whole territorial limits, and that it should be distinctly announced to the world as our settled policy that no future European colony or dominion shall with our consent be planted or established on any part of the North American continent.
>
> President James K Polk, in his first annual message to Congress, 1845.

and New Mexico (collectively the Mexican Cession) greatly enlarged the American territory. Between 1845 and 1848, the United States grew in size by 70 percent. It became "Manifest Destiny" that the United States should rule over the entire continent.

In 1846, the majority of Northern Whigs opposed Polk's expansionism for fear that he might reopen the question of slavery in the territories. Still, it was a Democrat who opened the Pandora's box of sectional controversy by sponsoring an amendment to a military funding bill excluding slavery from the territories acquired from Mexico. Southern Whigs and Democrats joined forces to vote against the measure and Northern Whigs and Democrats voted in favour. Sectional interest prevailed over party affiliation. The amendment was defeated in the Senate but the debate over the role of slavery had been reopened. The Wilmot Proviso, as the amendment was called, was a harbinger of the Free Soil Party's position, accepting slavery where it existed but opposing its expansion to other territories.

The 1848 elections revolved around the same problem. The Democrats chose a candidate in favour of leaving the decision to the citizens of each territory. The Whigs returned to the old formula of the military hero with vague ideas, and the Free Soilers simply wanted to focus on the issue of slavery in the territories. The strategy of Van Buren (Free Soil) drew enough votes from the Democrat (Lewis Cass) that the Whig (Zachary Taylor, 1784–1850) was elected. Sectional disputes, imputation of motives and mutual distrust dominated national life.

Taylor's election was the final Whig victory. He died in 1850 and was replaced by Millard Fillmore (1800–1874). Franklin Pierce and James Buchanan would regain control for the Democrats by winning in 1852 and 1856, but highly divisive issues dominated the political stage and leadership was lacking.

A new age: social changes

Immigration

Population growth continued apace, with 10 million in 1820, 17 million in 1840 and 23 million in 1850. Immigration exploded after 1830. In the decade from 1831 to 1840, 600,000 immigrants arrived, in the next decade more than 1.7 million. They were a part of what would be called Old Immigration from northern and western Europe, mainly Germans and Irish. The Irish were Catholic, as were half the Germans, and they were poor as a rule. They were prepared to do the hardest jobs and accept dreadful living conditions. American society, despite its opportunities, was ill-prepared to handle the massive influx of foreigners.

The Irish settled in cities because they lacked the money to homestead. They set up enclaves, supported each other and defended themselves against the fear and loathing they inspired in Protestants, who saw them as drunken brawlers. In Boston, where they were a quarter of the population in 1850, their impact on the elites was substantial. They made their mark in particular by seizing control of the Democratic party machine and providing the Catholic Church with priests and nuns. They were also well represented on police forces.

Germans arrived in even greater numbers, but they settled more often on farms farther inland. They faced the same discrimination and felt they needed to stick together. They set up community organizations and made valuable contributions to the arts and education.

Urbanization

The fundamental changes in American society in the first half of the 19th century affected mainly cities, which many Americans held in low regard. The disastrous excesses of the Industrial Revolution in England were well known. The cities were growing too quickly.

The largest cities were New York, Philadelphia, Baltimore, Boston and

Table 6
Population, urban and rural, 1820-1850

Year	Urban	Rural	Total	Percent urban/rural
1820	693,000	8,945,000	9,638,000	7/93
1830	1,127,000	11,739,000	12,866,000	9/91
1840	1,845,000	15,224,000	17,069,000	11/89
1850	3,543,000	19,648,000	23,191,000	15/85

New Orleans, the latter having replaced Charleston as the largest city in the South. The cities were growing by an average of 25 percent every ten years. Between 1820 and 1830, New York grew by 64 percent. It had over 500,000 inhabitants in 1850 and over a million in 1860. It was the largest port in the United States and its financial hub. Philadelphia was half the size of New York in 1850. Boston, the former capital of triangle trade, had moved on to trading in cotton fabric from New England textile plants, thereby continuing its traditional activities. Around 1850, New Orleans handled half the cotton produced in the United States. Cities also rose up in the interior along transportation routes. Chicago's growth was extremely fast. Whereas in 1850 it did not make the list of the ten largest cities, by 1860 it was in eighth place with 100,000 inhabitants.

Such rapid growth caused problems. Construction was frantic and speculation flourished. Cities did not have the infrastructure or financing to provide essential services, and the people crowding in tended to be poor. Sanitary conditions were appalling, with no running water, sewers or garbage collection until 1840 in many cases. Epidemics were common and even the privileged were not spared. Some had already left for the suburbs or spent summers in the country. Whatever the case, they lived in well-defined neighbourhoods with all services provided. But these affluent areas often bordered on horrific slums thronging with immigrants, blacks, criminals and derelicts. Half of all freed slaves lived in the North, most in cities such as New York, Philadelphia and Boston. Segregation was severe and widespread in schools, public transit, housing and employment. Like the Germans and Irish, the blacks set up community networks, often around churches. Between 1820 and 1850, jobs became scarcer for blacks as the Irish, in particular, moved in. Relations were tense between blacks and whites, and there were brawls and riots. Life was hard in the city and urban "culture" had more to do with competition than cooperation.

Reformism

As the problems caused by the transformation of American society worsened, an extremely varied reformist movement arose in the United States in response, taking a broader approach than the individual benefactors of the previous period. Heavily inspired by the religious awakening, this reformism was fuelled by the conviction that there was a personal responsibility to change the world for the better. People's lives could be improved by changing their environment, and reformers were convinced they knew what was good and how to achieve it.

American reformism had some unusual traits that set it apart from other reformist movements of the same period elsewhere in the world. The strong religious flavour was certainly one. So was its versatility. Everything had to be reformed; no cause was too big or too small. People could be in favour of abolishing slavery and Sunday mail delivery. The intensity of the reformism also differed by region; it was stronger in the North than in the South, where no one wanted to risk too much upheaval. Highly pragmatic and curative, it sought practical ways to remedy poverty, injustice, ignorance, vice and disease. It was an integral part of Americans' conviction that they were an example to the world and was in a long tradition of charitable works that were no match for the scope of the problems.

The sheer number of reforms could lead one to believe that the entire country was committed, but this was not the case. The 1830–1850 period was certainly a high point in American reformism, which had its ups and downs. But it was driven by a minority, albeit a very active one, that occasionally managed to form political alliances, particularly with the more reform-oriented Whigs. The major causes of reformers were temperance, abolitionism and women's rights, but education, prisons, asylums, prostitution, hospitals and orphanages were all put under the microscope and changes were proposed and implemented.

The temperance movement attracted the greatest numbers. There was a serious problem with alcohol consumption. In the 1830s, the annual per capita consumption was 26 litres (7 gallons). Given that women and children probably contributed less than men to the statistic, the problem was substantial. Some authors have even termed it an alcoholic republic. Drinking was everywhere: at work, at play, at social or political gatherings and at home. Men, primarily, would drink, get drunk, injure themselves at work and become violent with women and children. Temperance became a social movement, and young people in particular were urged to take a pledge not to drink. The American Temperance Society had 200,000 members around 1835. Their moral struggle was remarkably successful, perhaps aided by the 1837 recession. By the 1840s, alcohol consumption had diminished by about half. Some even recommended total prohibition, but it was not widely favoured.

Abolitionism was also linked to morality, and especially the moral indignation of its founder, William Lloyd Garrison (1805–1879). In 1831, Garrison began publishing *The Liberator*, which called for immediate freedom and social equality for all blacks. At first, all the figures in the emancipation struggle gravitated to Garrison, but there were nonetheless around fifty African-American abolitionist societies in the North beginning in the 1830s. People such as Frederick Douglass (1817–1895), Sojourner Truth (1797–1883) and Harriet Tubman (1815–1913) belonged to them. These former slaves worked to free their brothers and sisters, in spite of the discrimination that persisted even among the abolitionists. When Douglass, unwilling to be restricted to recounting his life as a slave, split with Garrison to pursue political action, he was called ungrateful. In 1840, the majority of abolitionists opted for partisan politics, to Garrison's chagrin, and many were involved in the formation of the Republican Party.

Women's rights
Women, deprived of the vote, made up for it by being central to the various reforms – at least the women with enough time, leisure and energy. They were usually educated women from the new middle class who had domestic help. The major causes that mobilized women were abolitionism and temperance, but also education. Through these struggles, they forged a consciousness of women's condition. They challenged women's roles and the existence of separate spheres. In 1848, the Seneca Falls Convention adopted a history-making declaration of women's rights. Lucretia Mott (1793–1880), one of the organizers, had been refused a seat at an abolitionist meeting in London in 1840 and the convention was her chance to respond.

The South and slavery

After 1793, with the cotton gin, a worker could clean (i.e., separate the grain from the chaff) fifty times as much cotton per day. By 1810, almost 27 million kilograms (60 million pounds) were being produced. In 1807 cotton exports had jumped ahead of tobacco exports, especially to England. Between 1836 and 1840, cotton exports totalled $321 million (43 percent of all exports) and between 1850 and 1860, $744 million (54 percent of all exports). Cultivation areas had spread from South Carolina and Georgia to Alabama and Mississippi, where the Indians were forced to cede their lands.

As demand for cotton increased and cultivation areas spread, there was a greater need for slaves, but public opinion outside the South was opposed to slavery. London had outlawed the practice in 1803 and Congress abolished the import of slaves in 1808. The South had to get by on natural population growth. A market developed between regions with a surplus of slaves and those in need. Between 1820 and 1860, 50 percent of the black population of the Upper South (Virginia, Arkansas, North Carolina and Tennessee) wound up on the slave market, contributing unwillingly to the expansion of the South.

Demand for cotton was linked to the Industrial Revolution, first in England then in the northern United States. New England merchants invested in new textile machines and factories. From then on, the separate callings of the North and the South were fixed and inextricably joined. Cotton farming was profitable, and planters used any available labour, including slave labour. In 1850, 55 percent of slaves were employed in cotton farming, 20 percent in other farming and 15 percent in domestic service. The South's capital was tied up in land and slaves and no one there felt the need to change that.

Slaves were not divided equally among slave owners, contrary to *Gone With the Wind*–style stereotypes about slavery. In reality, most whites did not own slaves. In 1850, a third of white landowners had one or more slaves and, of them, only half had five or more. However, 75 percent of slaves lived in groups of ten or more. Out of a population in 1850 of 6,184,477 whites, 347,525 owned slaves; 8,000 had 50 or more, 254 had 200 or more and 11 had 500 or more. The typical slave owner was a small farmer who worked the fields with a few slaves. Large planters made up

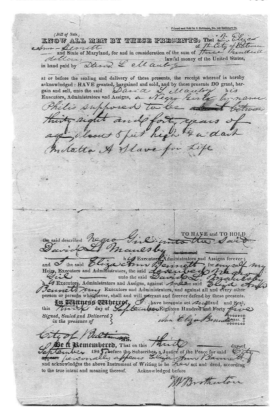

Bill of sale for a "girl by name Philis supposed to be between thirty-eight and forty years of age…" (Enoch Pratt Free Library, Baltimore)

1 percent of the South's population, small planters 23 percent and small farmers and "poor whites" 76 percent. However, all had a stake in the "peculiar institution" on which the entire social order of the South was based. The order was dominated by large planters and upheld by the conviction that the system was profitable.

The life of a slave
It is hard to generalize about slaves' living or survival conditions. Around 1850, life expectancy was 25.5 years for whites and 21.4 for blacks. Slaves were badly housed, underfed and overworked. Fevers and infections were endemic. Mortality among children of slaves was double that among white children.

The harshness of slaves' lives could depend on their sex, their age, the operation where they worked, their master and their own constitution.

For example, the worst situation for a slave might have been to work on a Louisiana rice plantation for an absentee owner under the supervision of an overseer who was quick with the whip. Work was less demanding in the big house, but the daily subordination was hard for domestics to live with. They were still slaves.

Field work was draining. Slaves aged quickly. As a rule, their diet was bland and barely adequate. Since slaves represented an investment of capital, masters tried to get the most out of them. They worked from sun-up to sundown. Cruel masters were fairly rare, but abolitionists did not have to make up horror stories of slaves branded, mutilated, beaten, whipped and killed. Any who took revenge would be starved, hanged or burned alive. The slaves resisted. Their apathy is a myth. They tried to run away or buy their freedom, they broke their tools, mutilated themselves and rebelled. Masters were well aware of the discipline and force required to keep blacks in their place.

The system's harshness meant that slaves had to stick together to survive. The essential bond was the family, with religion a close second. Marriage among blacks was not recognized, but most masters accepted it and even encouraged it to produce children as well as make men less rebellious. Marriage was a haven of comfort in a hostile world, and husband and wife worked together protecting and raising their children.

Yet families were often separated. One marriage in five broke down and one child in three was sold. The extended family became the solution. Children were taught from a young age to respect their elders, their "uncles" and "aunts"; even the other children were called brothers and sisters. Raised in this way, children separated from their parents could be quickly integrated into another community.

Religion was a powerful outlet for slaves' aspirations for freedom and justice. At first, blacks were forbidden to practise religion, but with the new religious fervour of the early 19th century, the Baptist and Methodist churches would make inroads. Masters would have preferred that the slaves practise the same religion as they did to ease social control. But Blacks created their own forms of religious expression that allowed them to survive and that are still to this day among the most solid anchors of the black community.

The industrial North

During the first half of the 19th century, the United States grew from a basically rural economy to a market economy based on early industrial capitalism.

American industry had its start in New England, where merchants reaped enormous profits. Fortunes were amassed and networks built. When obstacles to international trade arose in the early 19th century, trade turned domestic. At first, merchants invested mostly in national production. They bought raw materials and assigned the work to craftsmen and their families, and then they took the finished products and sold them. In 1800, Lynn, Massachusetts, produced 400,000 pairs of boots and shoes in hundreds of workshops using this method. The next phase involved concentrating operations in large factories using division of labour. Merchants could control costs and increase production, which was poured into the market. This is how Lynn monopolized the bargain-priced-boot market in the South and the West in no time. Similar practices were adopted in weaving, spinning and glove-making.

As early as 1790, investors had set up Slater's Mill in Providence, Rhode Island. Samuel Slater, an English immigrant, copied British machines from memory and opened the first modern American spinning mill. The great quantities of yarn produced there were then woven in cottage workshops. In 1814, all operations were combined in a factory at Waltham, near Boston. The huge mill used state-of-the-art technology and survived the return of British competition. Enormous capital, $600,000 over six years, had been invested, but profits reached 25 percent. The owners decided they could do better. Raw materials were easily accessible, the hydraulic energy to run the mills was available and everything the venture required in technology, capital and labour was present. The Boston Associates built an entire city, Lowell, around the factory. The six giant mills included housing for workers, who were recruited in the neighbouring countryside, no special skills being required. By 1836, Lowell had 17,000 inhabitants.

Of the eighty textile companies that had been incorporated in Massachusetts between 1812 and 1816, many went bankrupt with the return of British competition. But beginning in 1816, protectionist policies would eventually remedy the situation. By the 1820s, progress had resumed, driven by expanded markets, investment and the Bank of the United States and other banks. Companies diversified their operations. They moved beyond cotton into other industries and stimulated the development of cities such as Lawrence and Manchester. In 1840, the 60-kilometre (37-mile) stretch of the Blackstone River between Providence and Worcester was home to 116 spinning mills and 40 other establishments that employed 10,000 people. In the same year, there were 1,200 cotton spinning mills in operation, most of them in New England. Coal from Pennsylvania had recently become available by canal, and steam became a source of energy in addition to waterfalls and rivers.

Another major advance that would have significant repercussions for the Industrial Revolution was the development of what the British called the American System of manufacturing, based on interchangeable parts. Eli Whitney (1765–1825), the inventor of the cotton gin, was awarded a production contract for 10,000 rifles in 1798. He intended to manufacture them in a mere twenty-eight months from identical cast or turned parts. His influence spread. Standardized production opened up unimaginable possibilities. In the 1850s, using available coal to process iron, American manufacturers could build their own machinery to mass-produce sewing machines, plowing implements, nails or clocks based on the principles of the American System.

The workers

The changes brought about by industrialization affected the composition and the living conditions of the working class. The proportion of wage earners went from 12 percent of workers in 1800 to 40 percent in 1860. Most of these workers were concentrated in the North. Industrialization and division of labour meant that craftsmen lost their status and many jobs could be filled by unskilled labour. Women and children made up the bulk of the workforce in industrial spinning and weaving. Wages were low due to competition and working conditions were gruelling. The only human contact was impersonal, with managers and supervisors interested only in productivity. Hours were long, twelve to thirteen hours a day. The machines set a frantic pace. Often only children could work in cramped spaces. Even the famous Lowell Mill Girls, supposedly so well treated, were led to protest. While it was true that they were housed, given support and paid quite well at first, there was intense market pressure on management. In 1834, their wages were cut by 25 percent and 800 women went on strike. The owners were shocked and scandalized by these ungrateful, unfeminine women. More wage cuts followed in 1836–1837, and in 1840 production rates were increased.

Resistance increased, but the workers were not organized and had no strike fund or effective leadership. Worse, the law favoured management; in 1815, it had been established under common law that any strike was an illegal conspiracy. This interpretation was not overturned until 1842, when a Massachusetts judge ruled that unions and strikes were legal.

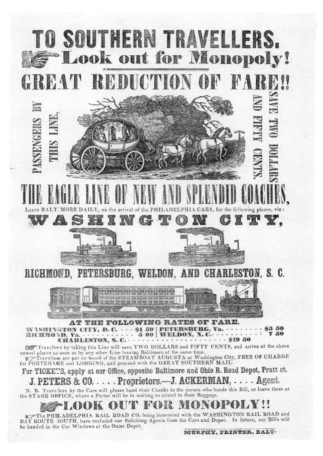

As railroads spread across the eastern states, travellers might have to take several means of transport on one journey. This announcement appeared in Baltimore in 1850. (Library of Congress)

Before the Civil War an extensive network of rail lines had spread across the eastern U.S.A., but there were few direct links between the northern and southern states. The 1857 map of the Lake Shore and Michigan Southern shows its connecting lines to the east coast. Dotted lines show planned routes westward. (Library of Congress)

Craftsmen were more organized. Carpenters, shoemakers, masons and others had a longer tradition and a more highly developed sense of their social identity and interests. Expanded voting rights increased their political awareness, and a Workingmen's Party was even founded in Philadelphia in 1828, although with a leadership comprising more reformers than workers. Other similar parties were founded in New York and Boston. Their platforms included the ten-hour working day, the abolition of debtors' prisons and universal education. In 1834, the workers' parties were absorbed by the mainstream parties. Some workers' organizations were set up in the 1830s, but they were dealt a severe blow by the Panic of 1837. The most common demand was the ten-hour day, which was achieved in several states; in 1860, it was the rule for skilled workers, but did not exist in the factories of Lowell, Lawrence or Manchester. Various trade unions were set up in the 1850s when inflation was eating away at workers' incomes, but the Panic of 1857 and the Civil War would erode workers' progress even further.

CHAPTER 6

TRIAL BY FIRE

1851–1865

Since it was founded, the United States had been internally divided. Divergent sectional interests clashed over tariffs, banks and slavery. For a time, divisions could be masked by a precarious political balancing act. In the 1850s, the balance was thrown off and two distinct societies would go on to confront each other over which values, interests and vision for the nation's future would prevail.

The crisis of the 1850s

The 1850s began with a compromise and ended with elections that touched off secession. Contentious issues had been smouldering and flaring up for decades. They centred on five major issues that divided the regions and the parties – the tariff; the Bank and currency; expansion and access to land; federal aid for transportation improvements; and slavery – the last of which increasingly polarized all the others. For years, the national Whig and Democratic parties had managed to forge strong enough alliances to trump regional interests. But by the early 1850s, large fissures had appeared in the parties and the nation.

The results of the 1848 election are a perfect illustration. James K. Polk, the Democratic architect of expansion, did not run. The voters, swept along by the military successes in Mexico, elected a military hero, Zachary Taylor, leader of the anti-expansionist Whigs. The Democratic candidate, Lewis Cass, ran for office by advocating popular sovereignty as advantageous to both the North and the South. Martin Van Buren and the Free Soil Party embodied anti-slavery sentiment, but Van Buren knew he had no chance of winning; he wanted only to publicize his cause. This was politics in 1848. The United States had gone through an incredible expansion, but one that aggravated the problem that would soon tear it apart. Fears and rivalries dominated all aspects of political life.

The national territory had tripled since 1800. The population was now 23 million, including 4 million blacks. The sixteen states of 1800 had become thirty-one by 1848. Economic development had accelerated. Agriculture had become commercialized. Factories had proliferated. Improvements in communications and transportation had nurtured an embryonic national market. The real national per capita income had doubled between 1800 and 1850. Remarkable progress had been made; ironically, it was that very progress and the march westward into the new territories that caused so much contention.

Northerners gradually came to believe that there existed a "Slave Power" that not only controlled the South but was plotting to take over the federal government and threatened freedom throughout the country. Southerners defended the constitutional rights of states and property rights that they wanted to see extended to all the territories. This was John C. Calhoun's interpretation, which became dogma in the South. Each side dug in behind political slogans about the defence of rights and freedoms as America expanded.

Not only had the North and South built different societies and different means of economic development, but each harboured animosity toward the other. To a growing number of Northerners, the South, dominated by a slave-owning planter aristocracy, was economically backward. The North, which they felt embodied dynamism and the freedom to succeed for everyone, feared being held back by the South. To Southerners, slavery was the cornerstone of their civilization, social order and economic well-being. They felt that the North profited from the South, which fuelled national economic growth, and that Northern businessmen were hypocrites who shamefully exploited their workers. The South found nothing to envy in the North because the slavery system took good care of the inferior black race. And had not all great civilizations used slaves?

The Compromise of 1850

After the victory over Mexico and the great wave of expansion, the new territory had to be organized and the question settled as to whether there would be slavery there. Requests for admission to statehood by California and Utah in 1849 brought the issue to the forefront. The boundary between Texas and New Mexico was in dispute, and there was pressure to abolish the slave trade in the national capital. Southerners demanded that the North obey the law requiring the return of runaway slaves.

In 1850, Congress set about trying to resolve all these problems. It would be the last hurrah for three senators who had had exceptional careers: Henry Clay from Kentucky, Daniel Webster from Massachusetts and John C. Calhoun from South Carolina. Calhoun would die that year and Clay and Webster two years later.

Clay first proposed an omnibus bill that called for (1) admitting California as a free state; (2) creating the territories of New Mexico and Utah, where the question of slavery would be settled by popular vote; (3) settling the boundary between Texas and New Mexico and assuming part of Texas's debt; (4) abolishing the sale of slaves in the national capital; and (5) reinforcing the fugitive slave law. Calhoun attacked the proposal and demanded that the North halt its attempts to limit slavery. Webster spoke like a unionist. He rejected the South's claims that peaceful secession was possible and encouraged the abolitionists to make compromises to keep the South in the Union. President Taylor opposed the Compromise and prepared for a confrontation with the South, but he died in the midst of deliberations. His successor, Millard Fillmore, a moderate Whig from the North, was willing to compromise with the South.

When the Senate rejected the omnibus bill, a young Democratic senator from Illinois, Stephen A. Douglas, used the tactic of separate bills so that each could vote according to his interests. The Compromise was passed and the nation breathed a sigh of relief. People were convinced the Union had been saved, but closer examination showed that divisions remained. Whigs from the North and opponents of slavery had stuck to their positions, as had the pro-slavery Democrats from the South. They represented the dominant wings of their parties. The power of the Whigs from the South and the Democrats from the North withered away as the debates raged.

Fugitive Slave Act

The Fugitive Slave Act, passed in September 1850, was a major irritant to the North. The new law significantly increased slave owners' power to reclaim their runaway slaves. They could now rely on federal authority to penalize anyone who helped or protected fugitives or even failed to cooperate.

Three Hundred Dollars REWARD.

Ranaway from the subscriber, on Saturday night last, 17th inst., my negro woman LIZZIE, about 28 years old. She is medium sized, dark complexion, good looking, with rather a down look. When spoken to replies quickly. She was well dressed and carried with her a variety of clothing. She ran off in company with her husband, Nat Amby, (belonging to John Muir, Esq.,) who is about six feet in height, with slight impediment in his speech, dark chestnut color, and a large scar on the side of his neck.

I will give the above reward if taken in this County, or one half of what she sells for if taken out of the County or State. In either case to be lodged in Cambridge Jail.

ALEXANDER H. BAYLY.
Cambridge, Oct. 19, 1857.

P. S. For the apprehension of the above named negro man NAT, and delivery in Cambridge Jail, I will give $500 reward.
JOHN MUIR.

PRINTED AT THE DEMOCRAT OFFICE, CAMBRIDGE, MD.

Reward posters for runaway slaves. (Enoch Pratt Free Library, Baltimore, Maryland, and Library of Congress)

$200 Reward.

RANAWAY from the subscriber, on the night of Thursday, the 30th of Sepember.

FIVE NEGRO SLAVES,

To-wit: one Negro man, his wife, and three children.

The man is a black negro, full height, very erect, his face a little thin. He is about forty years of age, and calls himself *Washington Reed*, and is known by the name of Washington. He is probably well dressed, possibly takes with him an ivory headed cane, and is of good address. Several of his teeth are gone.

Mary, his wife, is about thirty years of age, a bright mulatto woman, and quite stout and strong.

The oldest of the children is a boy, of the name of FIELDING, twelve years of age, a dark mulatto, with heavy eyelids. He probably wore a new cloth cap.

MATILDA, the second child, is a girl, six years of age, rather a dark mulatto, but a bright and smart looking child.

MALCOLM, the youngest, is a boy, four years old, a lighter mulatto than the last, and about equally as bright. He probably also wore a cloth cap. If examined, he will be found to have a swelling at the navel.

Washington and Mary have lived at or near St. Louis, with the subscriber, for about 15 years.

It is supposed that they are making their way to Chicago, and that a white man accompanies them, that they will travel chiefly at night, and most probably in a covered wagon.

A reward of $150 will be paid for their apprehension, so that I can get them, if taken within one hundred miles of St. Louis, and $200 if taken beyond that, and secured so that I can get them, and other reasonable additional charges, if delivered to the subscriber, or to THOMAS ALLEN, Esq., at St. Louis, Mo. The above negroes, for the last few years, have been in possession of Thomas Allen, Esq., of St. Louis.

WM. RUSSELL.

ST. LOUIS, Oct. 1, 1847.

For a long time, abolitionists had been encouraging slaves to escape, promising them help when they arrived in the North. Networks had been set up, including the famous Underground Railroad. The idea of a well-coordinated "railway" with conductors helping fugitives from station to station was very different in practice. A successful escape to the Northern states or Canada was more often the result of luck or the quick thinking of organizers. The most active smugglers were often free blacks from the North or escaped slaves. That was true of the most famous runner, Harriet Tubman. She was said to have made nineteen trips to the South and freed 300 slaves without losing a single one.

In Boston, the hub of abolitionism, the law caused extreme outrage. A mob intervened to free a fugitive. The federal government called in the troops to prevent another rescue. During the 1850s, 322 runaway slaves were returned to their masters and only 11 declared free.

It was in reaction to the Fugitive Slave Act that Harriet Beecher Stowe (1811–1896) published her novel *Uncle Tom's Cabin* in 1852. It was an instant bestseller and 300,000 copies were sold. Harriet Beecher Stowe was closely linked to American reformism. Daughter of a prominent pastor, Lyman Beecher, sister of Henry Ward Beecher, gifted orator and confirmed opponent of slavery, Harriet had never seen the South. She passionately repeated what she had heard in the North, and she touched a chord with the characters she portrayed. The novel's success helped crystallize opinion in the South as well as the Northern reaction to the law on fugitives.

The 1852 election

The Northern Whigs, furious that Fillmore had promoted popular sovereignty and vigorously enforced the law, denied him the nomination. Instead, after fifty-two ballots, they chose another general, Winfield Scott (1786–1866). Why not – it had worked in 1840 and 1848? The Democrats chose an unknown figure, at least to the wider public, in Franklin Pierce (1804–1869) of New Hampshire, who Southerners felt would be sympathetic to Southern interests.

Pierce crushed his opponent. The Democrats united behind a platform advocating strict enforcement of all provisions of the Compromise of 1850. They won votes in the South and in the North. Most Democrats who earlier had rallied to the Free Soilers returned to the party in 1852, and the urban Democratic machine was very effective among Irish and German immigrants. The Democrats enjoyed distinct advantages. Franklin Pierce would squander them all by advocating a new expansionist policy inspired by Manifest Destiny. Returning to an old formula, he supported expanding to take in Cuba first by trying to buy it from Spain. His administration then devised the Ostend Manifesto, threatening to use force to conquer the island, which would become a slaveholding territory. Pierce recognized the government of the freebooter William Walker, who had become dictator of Nicaragua in 1855 after reintroducing slavery there. Such machinations were hardly the democratic solution to national unity. Collusion between the Pierce administration and the pro-slavery expansionists lost Pierce much support in the North and reawakened old fears of the expansion of slavery.

The Kansas-Nebraska crisis

A bill aimed at politically organizing the territory to the west of Iowa and Missouri was sponsored by Stephen A. Douglas. Douglas was a strong supporter of a transcontinental railroad, which he felt would further economic development and democracy by setting up a national link. For the railhead, he favoured Chicago, in his home state of Illinois. But to open the territory, he needed the votes of Southern Democrats, who demanded that slavery be legal there. The territory was north of the line of the Missouri Compromise and, accordingly, should have been free. Douglas proposed instead following the rule of popular sovereignty. By doing so, he thought he had the support of the South and of the North, which wanted a transcontinental railroad. The second version of the Kansas-Nebraska Act was passed in May 1854 after passionate debates marked by hundreds of big public rallies decrying the act.

The act completely destroyed the Whig Party and weakened the Democrats. In the 1854 elections, the Northern Democrats lost almost two thirds of their seats. Democrats from the South controlled Congress and their party. The Republican Party would be the response to these upheavals.

Kansas bleeding

As soon as the territories were opened, pro- and anti-slavery pioneers began settling there; they were farmers from neighbouring states as well as recruits supported by anti-slavery organizations in the North or pro-slavery states such as Missouri, Georgia and South Carolina. The Kansas territorial elections of 1855 threw oil on the fire. Thousands of Missourians crossed the border to vote in the elections. After gaining office fraudulently, the pro-slavers legalized slavery. Anti-slavers were not to be outdone. In the fall they met, elected an assembly, banned slavery and requested admission to the Union as a free state. Having to choose between two territorial governments, President Pierce sided with the pro-slavers.

Open war broke out between the two groups. Seven hundred pro-slavers sacked and burned the town of Lawrence, Kansas. Five people were killed. John Brown, a wild-eyed anti-slaver, killed five people from the opposing camp as tit for tat. Murderous gangs roamed the territory. No one was ever arrested, tried or even prevented from committing violence. At least two hundred people fell victim to these deadly raids, which lasted for more than a year. The violence even reached Congress, where Senator Charles Sumner (1822–1874) from Massachusetts, a well-known anti-slaver, insulted a fellow senator from South Carolina as having taken "the harlot Slavery" as his mistress. The senator's nephew, a congressman, avenged his uncle's honour by hitting Sumner on the head with his cane. Sumner collapsed and would be absent from the Senate for two years. The North had a martyr and the South a hero who, despite a reprimand, won back his seat almost unanimously. He was even offered several canes to replace the one he had broken.

The 1856 election

As if these events were not enough to raise tensions to the boiling point, the 1856 elections took place against the backdrop of a creeping anti-immigrant crusade. The rapid growth in the number of Democratic voters because of a tripling of immigration between 1845 and 1855 disturbed many Americans. Most of the immigrants were Catholic and lived in the cities, which were regarded as dens of iniquity. Democratic Party organizers found a loyal constituency in them, helping them integrate as quickly as possible into American society. They provided jobs, helped them get the necessary documents, stepped up their naturalization and, more to the point, got them out to vote on election day.

These practices aroused scandal and concern in right-thinking Americans, especially since the immigrants, often as not Irish, competed with blacks for the most menial jobs and displayed anti-black prejudice. Countless riots attacking blacks broke out in the industrial cities of the North. It must be pointed out that the Irish in particular were also victims of the violent outbursts of their countrymen. Between 1830 and 1850, their convents, priests, nuns and neighbourhoods were attacked. Catholics were particularly mistrusted as they were not so keen on temperance. The Irish drank whisky and the Germans drank beer. Drink was associated with poverty and crime, which had to be eradicated. Immigration was seen as the cause of all problems.

The American Party, also known as the Know-Nothings, grew out of a secret society, the Order of the Star-Spangled Banner, in 1849. The name derived from the habit of party members of saying they knew nothing when questioned about the society. Similar parties, based on opposition to immigrants and the preservation of American values against the insidious newcomers, had existed before. The American Republican Party and the Native American Party were typical, but their influence remained local in the 1830s and 1840s. In the 1850s, the Know-Nothings would come to national prominence. After the split in Whig and Democratic Party ranks, the party recruited among the malcontents. Its platform called for excluding Catholics and foreigners from the civil service and a twenty-one-year waiting period for citizenship. The Know-Nothings were themselves victims of the tumult caused by the Kansas-Nebraska Act of 1854. When the party supported it in 1856, a schism occurred, and many members from the North ended up in the new Republican Party, founded in 1854.

In 1856 the Democrats ran James Buchanan (1791–1868), a compromise candidate, since neither the outgoing president, Pierce, nor Stephen A. Douglas was acceptable to Northern Democrats and would split the Southern vote. Buchanan had the virtue of not having spoken out on the Kansas-Nebraska Act. The Republicans chose John C. Fremont (1813–1890), an explorer turned senator from California. The Know-Nothings fell back on former president Fillmore. He had the support of many Southern Whigs and garnered 49 percent of the vote in ten Southern states. Buchanan, however, won all the Southern votes in the Electoral College and enough Northern states to win the election, but with only 45 percent of the popular vote. Fremont had taken eleven out of sixteen Northern states and the Republican Party established itself as a leading party. The Know-Nothings soon disappeared and anti-immigrant feeling subsided.

The Republicans, a strong anti-slavery party, had needed only two other states to take power. To Southerners, that prospect was anathema and a direct threat to their interests and their civilization.

The Dred Scott decision

In March 1857, only ten days after Buchanan's inauguration, the Supreme Court handed down a decision that threw the entire country into turmoil. In the *Dred Scott v. Sandford* case, the Court declared the Missouri Compromise unconstitutional. Scott was a slave who claimed that the time he had spent in the free state of Illinois and the territory of Wisconsin meant that he was a free man. The Constitution, according to the Court, did not recognize the right of Congress to ban slavery in the territories. Congress had no power to restrict the free movement of property across territories. Since slaves were property, this meant that slavery was legal everywhere.

Calhoun's position was now enshrined by the Supreme Court. As if to add insult to injury, the Court, in dismissing Dred Scott's case, claimed that only citizens could appeal to the Court and that blacks, whether free or enslaved, were not. The decision meant that only a constitutional amendment could ban slavery in the territories, and it required the approval of three quarters of the states to pass such an amendment. This was impossible to secure. The Democrats seemed to be entrenched in power and were emboldened by the approval they had just received. Buchanan confirmed these fears when he came down in favour of the Supreme Court's position. He was indebted to the Southern Democrats.

The decision pulled the rug out from under the Republicans, who had made excluding slavery from the territories their key issue. Even Douglas was scandalized. He had tried to ensure his party's future in the North by defending the doctrine of popular sovereignty. To many Northerners, it was clear evidence of a conspiracy by the Slave Power in Kansas.

The Democratic Party disintegrated further after the 1856 elections and the Dred Scott decision. Former Democrats and Whigs continued to join the new Republican Party. Abraham Lincoln (1809–1865) emerged in the North as a key political figure, and his experience sheds light on the period.

Abraham Lincoln and the election of 1860

Abraham Lincoln had known pioneer life. He had grown up in Kentucky, Indiana and Illinois. He came from a modest background, did not like farming and became a partner in a general store. He had little education but plenty of ambition. At twenty-three, he ran for the Illinois legislature. He was defeated but persevered, and he began studying law with a prominent attorney. In 1834, he was elected to the Illinois legislature, where he completed four terms. His law studies completed, he sat in Congress as a Whig from 1847 to 1849, and then settled down to practising law.

His interest in politics was reawakened by the Kansas-Nebraska Act. He quit the Whigs to join the Republicans and acquired an impressive reputation when he debated Stephen A Douglas in 1858 in running against Douglas for the position of senator from Illinois. He assembled a coalition capable of taking power by espousing what would become the Republican Party's articles of faith: a moral opposition to slavery, the claim that the federal government had the power to ban slavery in the territories and the conviction that slavery should eventually be eradicated nationwide because "a house divided" could not endure "half slave and half free."

Lincoln lost the senatorial election of 1858. The Illinois legislature opted again for Douglas. But he now had nationwide stature, and the Republicans chose him as their standard bearer for the presidency in 1860. He had a reputation as a moderate on the issue of slavery: although he was not an abolitionist, he felt that slavery was an evil whose spread had to be halted. He was a "trimmer" in abolitionist parlance but, to Democrats and former Whigs in favour of slavery, he was dangerous.

The Democrats were split. Northerners chose Douglas and Southerners John C. Breckenridge from Kentucky. A fourth candidate, John Bell, mustered the Whigs and the surviving Know-Nothings.

The Republicans had adopted a broader platform than the exclusion of slavery in the territories. They favoured a railroad to the Pacific, a protective tariff, free land distribution and a more liberal immigration policy. Lincoln won only 40 percent of the popular vote, but his votes were concentrated in large states, which gave him a solid majority in the Electoral College. He won not a single state in the South but nearly all the Northern states. He had clearly been voted to office by one section of the United States. In terms of the popular vote, he was a minority president whose opponents had garnered a million more votes than he had.

Southerners, recalling Lincoln's words that the Union should become "all one thing or all the other," perceived his election as a sign to secede. Moderating forces in the South lost ground, particularly after the incident at Harper's Ferry, Virginia, in 1859 when radical abolitionist John Brown led a raid on the arsenal in the hopes of beginning a slave uprising. He was caught and hanged, but panic intensified. Southerners feared slave uprisings and saw a Northern, abolitionist conspiracy at work. The radical, pro-slavery, secessionist group of Southern politicians known as the Fire-Eaters now had the upper hand.

The American Civil War

The elections were held on November 6, 1860. By November 13, the South Carolina legislature had passed a resolution calling for a special convention to study secession. On December 20, the convention passed a resolution to dissolve the Union. Events followed quickly. Within six weeks, six other states (Mississippi, Florida, Alabama, Georgia, Louisiana and Texas) had organized conventions that all ratified secession. On February 4, six of the seven secessionist states met in Montgomery, Alabama, to form a new union, the Confederate States of America.

A constitution was drafted and a provisional government formed. Jefferson Davis (1808–1889) was the president. The secessionists moved quickly. The radicals took action before supporters of the existing Union could get organized. Everything happened even before Buchanan left the White House and Lincoln took office. While Southern radicals acted swiftly, the Washington administration sat on its hands. Buchanan, in his last message to Congress in December 1860, declared secession illegal, but admitted that the federal government did not have enough authority to force a return to the Union. South Carolina saw in Buchanan's speech an implied recognition of its independence and demanded that Fort Sumter, in Charleston Harbor, be handed over. Buchanan tried to get fresh supplies to the fort on a merchant ship, but when South Carolina's forces opened fire, he retreated.

Abraham Lincoln would fill the power vacuum in Washington. In his inaugural speech of March 4, 1861, he called for a constitutional solution to bring reconciliation, but he clearly defined the limits. States could not secede since the Union predated their statehood. Slavery would be

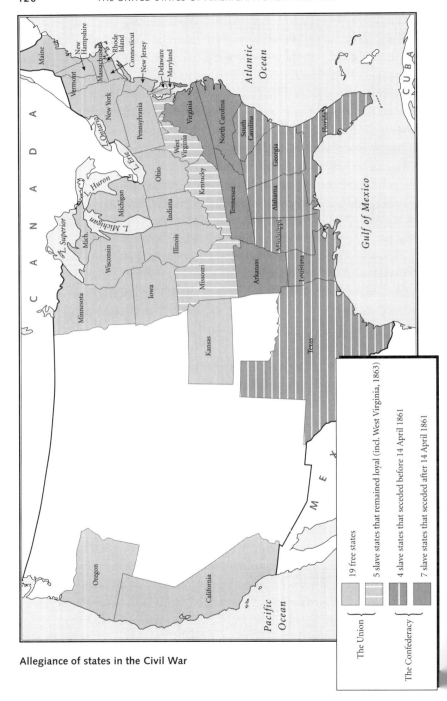

Allegiance of states in the Civil War

allowed where it already existed. Slaves could be reclaimed. There would be no slavery in the territories. The Union and its property would be protected. There would be no violence if the federal government did not have to use force.

Lincoln hoped that the Fort Sumter crisis would fizzle out on its own. But provisions were starting to run out, and he could not sacrifice a symbol of federal authority. Practically all other federal facilities had been seized. The day after he took office, Lincoln was informed that thousands of soldiers, provisions and ships would be needed at Sumter and that the commander recommended an evacuation. To avoid losing face, Lincoln decided to rescue Sumter. But he warned South Carolina that he was simply bringing fresh supplies to the garrison. If the Southerners tried to use force, they would be the aggressors. They did. Before supplies could arrive, Southerners bombarded the fort for two straight days. On April 14, 1861, the garrison surrendered.

The South had fired the first shot. The next day, Lincoln called up 75,000 militiamen into service for the federal government to put down the insurrection. The effect was lightning swift in the North, where many had been hesitant until then. People rushed to defend the Union. Jefferson Davis had already mobilized troops and there was no lack of determination in the South. Few Southerners foresaw the tragic outcome of secession; it was not certain that the North would follow through, a quick war could mean victory for the South, and they counted on foreign support.

On April 17, Virginia seceded, followed by Tennessee, Arkansas and North Carolina. But the government in Washington managed to retain the loyalty of four border states (Delaware, Kentucky, Maryland and Missouri) that would turn out to be of prime importance. And the mountainous western counties of Virginia, where slavery was less prevalent, broke away from that state and were admitted to the Union as the new state of West Virginia in 1863. The lines had been drawn.

The resources for war

From a determinist perspective, the North would inevitably win the war because of its quantitative superiority in all areas. The twenty-three Northern states had a population of 22 million. The eleven Southern states had 9 million, including 3.5 million blacks. Eighty-five per cent of industrial capacity lay in the North, along with two thirds of railroads (it was the first war in which railways played a major logisitical role). In rolling stock, horses, weapons and every other area, the North was clearly superior. Everything was produced in greater quantities.

Yet things were not so clear-cut. The South was self-sufficient in food and its cotton was sought after on international markets, so the currency required to buy goods that were lacking was readily available. The South had the advantage of a stronger military tradition and an abundance of top-flight officers. The South was waging a defensive war. It was not looking to expand and was willing to settle simply for the independence of the Confederacy. If the costs to the North were high enough for it to give up, the South would win. The South was waging total war for the survival of its civilization. To win, the North would have to overcome not only Southern armies but Southern will.

What made Northern superiority decisive was the length of the conflict. At the beginning, no one could know how the war would turn out. As fighting intensified, the disparity of resources played out in favour of the North and the Confederate states were forced to fall back on their reserves of morale. They would be drained and Southern resistance broken.

A fraternal conflict

Despite early hopes that a "fraternal" conflict would avoid the worst excesses, the Civil War was characterized by deep-seated hostilities that divided families even up to the highest levels. Lincoln's wife, Mary Todd of Kentucky, lost three brothers who fought on the Confederate side. American loyalties were divided and positions were heightened by social divides. For Southern soldiers, the conflict quickly became "a rich man's war, a poor man's fight."

In the North, workers rebelled against competition from free blacks and dreaded a massive influx of freed slaves. Lincoln had to think about the North's unity. Democrats there were divided between War Democrats and Peace Democrats, but both factions were opposed to the emancipation of slaves. The Peace Democrats, or Copperheads (the name of a venomous snake), opposed conscription and martial law and advocated armistice and a negotiated peace. Anyone suspected of disloyalty was arrested and imprisoned, 13,000 people in all. Even in the Republican Party, unity was not guaranteed. Extremists and moderates squared off. Most Republicans were more concerned about the expansion of slavery than the welfare of slaves, an issue that would still be a bone of contention after the war.

Lincoln was also forced to keep a close watch on the border states since their citizens' loyalty was questionable. In Maryland, martial law was declared, federal troops monitored the railroads, suspects were imprisoned and habeas corpus suspended. Rights violations were justified in the name of national security. The situation was worse in Missouri, where guerrilla warfare raged unchecked.

Lincoln faced numerous challenges: maintaining unity in the North, meeting the daunting needs created by the war and isolating the South diplomatically. His main advantage over his rival, Jefferson Davis, was having the machinery of an existing government, as embryonic as it may have been. Jefferson Davis had to build a Confederacy of states from the ground up, states that had traditionally guarded their independence jealously, not to mention their rights. Resources were hard to mobilize. Southern diplomats faced the major hurdle of recognition, while the North benefited from all the contacts it needed. Southerners were counting on the importance of cotton to the British and French economies, but it would never be enough to bring about diplomatic recognition. At first, planters held back shipments, hoping to force England's hand, but England found new suppliers. When exports resumed in 1862, the blockade imposed by the North was more effective and the price of cotton collapsed. King Cotton was a less powerful weapon than Southerners had believed.

Economies and finances of North and South

The war gave a significant boost to the North's economy. Rising prices caused by the army's increasing demands as well as demographic growth centred in urban areas brought increased revenue to farmers. Industrialists were not to be outdone. Soldiers needed to be clothed, shod and armed. Factories cropped up everywhere. All this development was shielded by a protective tariff, the Republicans having taken advantage of the war to put their economic platform of 1860 into effect. In 1862, the Homestead Act was passed, granting 160 acres of land to anyone twenty-one or over who would commit to living there for five years and pay a modest fee. In 1862, construction began on the transcontinental railroad.

Prosperity made financing the war easier in the North. Multiple taxes, borrowing and issues of paper money were the methods generally used, successfully, to finance the war. The treasury secretary took advantage of the war to establish a new Bank of the United States and create a national currency, in the form of demand notes known colloquially as greenbacks. The financial groundwork was being laid for a modern industrial economy. Workers, hard hit by inflation, did not make out as well.

The Confederacy had to take a different tack. The war and the blockade were devastating its economy. Central intervention was less accepted there, but was inevitable to overcome the states' frustrating slowness and objections. With a less developed economy than the North, the South had to figure out how to build and operate shipyards, armouries and foundries. The biggest problem was finding the necessary funds. Taxation was highly unpopular, and revenue from this source was almost nil. The South borrowed 35 percent of the cost of the war and, for the most part, issued paper money – so much was issued that inflation set in. In spring 1865, prices were ninety-two times higher than in 1861. In the North, inflation was limited to 80 percent.

Recruitment

In the early months of the war, both sides called on volunteers. However, the Civil War pitted Americans against Americans, and once the initial enthusiasm had faded, the war lost some of its popularity. As recruits became fewer and casualties rose, the authorities had to resort to conscription. The South led in 1862. All men between eighteen and forty-five were conscripted for three years. Substitutes could be hired and planters could be exempted by sending twenty slaves. The basic price for a substitute was $300, but the price of being replaced gradually rose to $5,000. The North ratified conscription in 1863. It applied to every man between twenty-five and forty-five. Conscripts could also send replacements or even pay $300 to be exempted. The North recruited 46,000 conscripts and 118,000 substitutes, and re-enlistment bonuses drew many volunteers. In all, half of all eligible men were conscripted in the North and 80 percent in the South.

Conscription was unevenly enforced and substitution, more accessible to the rich than the poor, caused problems. In spring 1863, there were protests throughout the North, but the worst upheaval occurred in New York between July 13 and 16. Anti-Lincoln Democrats fuelled the resentment of the urban working classes. Workers and immigrants reproached the government for conscripting the poor to free the slaves, who would

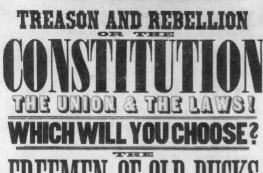

A poster published in Doylestown, Pennsylvania, 1861. (Library of Congress)

Recruiting poster for the 5th New York Cavalry. (Library of Congress)

then take their jobs. Brawls, riots, looting and lynchings left over a hundred victims. Lincoln clamped down. Troops from Gettysburg killed over a hundred rioters and put an end to the insurrection, which erupted not only over conscription but over a host of long-unresolved urban problems.

The blacks targeted by the protests helped resolve the conscription problem by signing up in droves after 1863. Two hundred thousand blacks fought in the war on the Union side.

Emancipation

Lincoln had always said that the war was fought to preserve the Union and not to abolish slavery. Although he disliked slavery, his policy had to take into account a host of factors, including the border states where slavery was legal and the unity of his own government. As the conflict dragged on, Lincoln started to feel that the North should go beyond the recruitment level so far attained. The war had to be transformed into an effort not only to beat the Confederate armies but to overturn the cornerstone of Southern society, slavery.

In August 1862, in a letter in response to an editorial in the *New York Tribune*, Lincoln prepared the public by writing: "My paramount object in this struggle is to save the Union, and is not either to save or to destroy slavery. If I could save the Union without freeing any slave I would do it, and if I could save it by freeing all the slaves I would do it; and if I could save it by freeing some and leaving others alone I would also do that."

After the victory at Antietam (September 17, 1862), Lincoln judged that the time was ripe for a first Emancipation Proclamation: unless the rebel states returned to the Union before January 1, 1863, the slaves would be free as of that date. Lincoln did not believe the South would bend to his ultimatum, which was more an attempt to strengthen the Union around a great cause: freedom for blacks.

On January 1, 1863, Lincoln issued his second Emancipation Proclamation. Slaves in the rebel states were free, but slaves in the border states as well as slaves in the parts of states already occupied by federal troops were not. His goal had been reached: advancing the cause of the war against slavery while maintaining support from conservatives. The proclamation's ambiguity made little difference to blacks, who joined the ranks of the Northern armies by the thousands.

Diplomacy

Shortly after the start of hostilities, Great Britain had declared its neutrality, recognizing the South's belligerence but not its independence. According to international conventions, Britain could now sell weapons and lend money to both sides, which it did. British merchants took advantage of the disruptions in American trade to increase their profits. While the British needed Southern cotton, they also profited from American grain. All the more reason to remain neutral.

While British public opinion, especially after the Emancipation Proclamation, sided with the abolitionist cause, the sympathies of British

"The Pending Conflict" by O.E. Woods. In one of several versions of this cartoon, the Confederate figure on the left tramples the American flag while the Union figure fights with one hand, grasping in the other the snake representing the anti-Lincoln or pacifist movement in the North. John Bull of Great Britain and Napoleon III of France observe from the sidelines. (Lithograph, Library of Congress)

leaders lay more with the South. Lincoln was particularly worried that Britain would break the increasingly effective blockade that was strangling the South. Two incidents signalled a worsening of relations between the two countries. In 1861, two Confederate commissioners were seized by an American warship while en route to England on a British vessel, the *Trent*. Britain protested, demanded an apology and prepared to defend Canada. Lincoln let negotiations drag on, then released the prisoners without an apology. Tensions eased.

The next crisis was over cruisers. The South had had six cruisers built in Britain. The ships, best known among them the *Alabama* and the *Florida*, wreaked havoc on the Northern merchant marine, sending more than 250 vessels to the bottom. Before 1863, Washington protested but did not push too hard. But after Gettysburg, as a Northern victory now seemed likely, the U.S. threatened to make the issue a cause for war. Britain made concessions to avoid provoking the Americans, but the American merchant marine had been irreparably damaged and would take decades to recover.

Military operations
In 1861, the Union's general-in-chief, Winfield Scott, proposed what he called the Anaconda Plan, meant to cut off the South by a naval blockade and control of the Mississippi waterway. Lincoln rejected the plan, preferring a more aggressive approach from the start. An attack against Confederate forces 50 kilometres (30 miles) outside Washington in Virginia and an attack on Richmond, capital of the Confederacy, could demoralize the South and end the war. Yet the First Battle of Bull Run (July 21, 1861) was a fiasco for the North. The retreat was messy, but the South was unable to follow through. The war would be neither short nor easily won. Lincoln called up 100,000 men and in November appointed General George B. McClellan to command his armies.

The second theatre of operations was in the West, where the Union was trying to control the Mississippi. Northerners were more successful there. Ulysses S. Grant by the north and David G. Farragut by the south cut off Southerners from the Mississippi. Grant won the bloody Battle of Shiloh (20,000 dead and wounded) and Farragut seized New Orleans.

On the eastern front, the year 1862 began on the same footing as 1861. Union commanding officers were trying to manoeuvre for the best position to attack the enemy's capital. McClellan marched on Richmond, but was stopped by Robert E. Lee, commander of the Army of Northern Virginia. The battles were bloody. The tactics were essentially those of the Napoleonic Wars, but the weapons had changed. Rifles and artillery had longer range and were more accurate. Infantry were mown down like hay, and cavalry charges were stopped in their tracks.

Lee next went on the offensive. The South had moved to a defensive-offensive strategy. This was a dramatic change for the Confederacy, which had gone to war simply to protect its territory. The Second Battle of Bull Run in August 1862 ended in a Southern victory. At Antietam on September 17, Lee held to a strong defensive position, pulling his 50,000 men out of a tight spot against McClellan's 80,000 men, but the result was a slaughter on both sides: a total of 4,800 dead and 18,500 wounded, 3,000 critically. Lee lost a quarter of his troops but McClellan did not pursue him. The year 1862 ended in a draw.

The war's turning point was 1863. First came Lee's victory at Chancellorsville. But on the Mississippi, the Southern forces were in trouble. The North controlled the entire Mississippi and laid siege to Vicksburg. To ease the pressure on Vicksburg, Lee proposed an offensive in Pennsylvania. There followed the great Battle of Gettysburg on July 1–3, 1863. After two days of movement on the flanks, there was a frontal assault. General George Meade, now in command of the Northern troops, lost 23,000 men and Lee, 28,000. Lee would no longer be able to invade the North, but he had not been decisively defeated.

Morale was better in the North. Emancipation had motivated the soldiers and the populace, and blacks signed up in droves. When Grant was appointed commander-in-chief, the strategy changed. Grant did not balk at losing his own soldiers. He intended to force combat and pursue, crush and demoralize the enemy by waging total war. Grant took charge of the eastern front against Lee. William T. Sherman commanded the Army of the Tennessee's offensive toward Atlanta.

The Northern steamroller continued its course, but the price was high. Lee went on the defensive; elaborate entrenchments cost him dearly. In spring 1864, Grant won victories but lost 55,000 men compared to Lee's 31,000. Finally, after the siege of Richmond got bogged down, Grant laid siege to Petersburg, where victory was also slow in coming. The siege lasted nine months and was lifted only when Lee evacuated Richmond in

April 1865. This was one week before the surrender at Appomatox.

Sherman had more success. He advanced relentlessly on Atlanta, destroying everything in his path. The siege of Atlanta began in July 1864 but seemed to get bogged down. Time pressed as elections were planned for November and Lincoln faced serious opposition. Fortunately for the Union, he was re-elected and the war could continue.

Sherman marched on Savannah, demolishing all of the South's resources and terrorizing its populace. The South was demoralized. With all the desertions, the armies dissolved. In the spring of 1865, on April 9, Lee's tattered army – the remaining 25,000 men – surrendered at Appomattox Court House, Virginia. Almost exactly four years had elapsed since the attack on Fort Sumter.

CHAPTER 7

FOUNDATIONS OF THE MODERN UNITED STATES

1865–1900

The costs of the Civil War were terribly high. In total, 620,000 human lives were lost; it was the bloodiest conflict in American history. Destruction was widespread, especially in the South, where homes were destroyed by the thousands, plantations devastated and roads, railways and factories rendered useless. The country was in chaos.

The Union had proven indestructible, but it was not the Union of the Founding Fathers. Slavery had been abolished, but through violence and, as would quickly become clear, without too much concern for the freed slaves. Thus began one of the great tragedies of American history, with the liberators gradually abandoning the former slaves to their fate and allowing segregation to take hold, another disgrace whose effects can still be felt in contemporary American society.

The North was the clear winner. All the contentious issues had been settled in its favour and, under the Republicans, a new America emerged, one of industrialization, business, speculation and, eventually, unbridled capitalism. The war had been a prime opportunity for some to get rich. Bolstered by laissez-faire policies and a belief in rugged individualism, entrepreneurs would usher in the great era of trusts and monopolies. Politicians were helpless against these captains of industry, and sectional differences made it almost impossible to pursue any consistent course of action. The Republicans, by discrediting the Southern Democrats, managed to dominate national politics while an increasingly "lily-white" Solid South was being constructed. It would be twenty years before a Democrat became president and fifty years before a Southerner did.

After the Civil War, Americans old and new – immigration had quickly resumed after being interrupted by the war, with 14 million immigrants between 1865 and 1900 – furiously set about developing the continent. Economic growth skyrocketed. The prosperity that resulted from an entire nation's work benefited only a very small segment of the population, however. The class of entrepreneurs, industrialists and financiers profited disproportionately from the energy expended by the American people.

Industrialization, urbanization, agricultural mechanization and immigration completely transformed the face of American society. Agricultural production, predominant until 1880, fell to second place in 1890, and in 1900, the value of manufactured goods was double that of agricultural commodities. Expanded markets, accelerated mechanization, mass production, access to capital, technological advances, entrepreneurial spirit and favourable government policies all contributed to American success.

The so-called Gilded Age was in fact golden for some but a time of poverty for the majority. The rapid socioeconomic changes had taken their toll on American society, and many began protesting the flagrant abuses that were a product of the triumphant new forces. Cities were growing too quickly and municipal authorities were helpless against all the problems. Changes in ownership, the rise of big business and the transformation of management exacerbated relations between capital and labour. There was massive immigration, as we have seen, and its face was changing. While Europeans remained the majority, the proportion of British and Irish declined. Between 1881 and 1890, 72 percent of immigrants still came from northern and western Europe. But between 1891 and 1900, 52 percent of immigrants came from southern and eastern Europe, and by the period 1910–1920 the proportion had risen to 70 percent. The new immigration caused worry. Immigrants now seemed harder to assimilate. Rather than Protestant, they were Catholic or Jewish. Instead of English, they spoke Italian, Polish, Russian or Yiddish. As these changes occurred at the same time as other major upheavals, people tended to blame immigrants for the prevailing anxiety.

A significant beginning was made in the years between 1870 and 1900 to remedy the abuses that marred American society. Farmers and labour unions opened the way to organized protest during the period, not to mention social thinkers and political writers such as Henry George, Edward Bellamy and Henry Demarest Lloyd. However, none of these groups or individuals could mobilize the nation's energy in a sustained enough way to bring about the many broad changes that were needed. There were victories, first at the municipal then at the state level and, aided by the prosperity that followed the Spanish-American War (1898), reformism gained support nationwide, particularly among the middle class.

There had long been opposition to trusts; the social inequalities arising from the rapid transformation of American society in the aftermath of the Civil War had been widely condemned, along with political corruption. Yet the agrarian revolt of the 1890s, which had brought to light many of these problems, failed to persuade most Americans. The middle class instead opposed agrarian demands, fearing they would cause serious social unrest. The actions of the working class during the same period did not help. Violent incidents such as the Haymarket Riot in Chicago, the clash in Homestead, Pennsylvania, and the Pullman strike alarmed members of the lower middle class, who refused to join the protesters.

Reconstruction

There had been no formal conclusion to the Civil War. Fighting had stopped, the Southern army and government had been dismantled and Jefferson Davis had been arrested and imprisoned for two years, but no other Confederate leaders were executed or otherwise penalized. There was no firm postwar policy either. How could the secessionist states be reintegrated and under what conditions? Conditions set by Congress or the president? Besides, Lincoln believed that the states had never legally left the Union; it was simply a matter of getting the governments of loyal states up and running again.

After the Emancipation Proclamation, there had been an urgent need for a ruling on the place of former slaves. In December 1863, Lincoln announced his first plan for reconstruction. He offered amnesty to Southerners (except Confederate leaders), who would take an oath of loyalty to the Union; states in which 10 percent of voters had signed such an oath and agreed to the emancipation of slaves would be allowed to set up a government. It was more an attempt by the president to destabilize the South than a postwar blueprint, and many Republicans considered the plan too generous. In 1864, Congress approved the Wade-Davis Bill proposing that 50 percent be required and the rebels excluded. Lincoln used his pocket veto to block the measure. It was clear that in Lincoln's mind nothing was definite. He kept his options open, acted with caution and occasionally dealt in ambiguity. Several members of his own party disagreed with his policy and insisted, for example, on full recognition of the rights of blacks, including the right to vote. It seems that Lincoln was ready to recognize the voting rights of blacks who had fought in the Union Army, but he apparently left no clear blueprint for the country when on April 15, 1865, he was assassinated by a Confederate sympathizer, John Wilkes Booth.

Andrew Johnson (1808–1875), a Democrat from Tennessee who had remained loyal to the Union and been chosen as Lincoln's running mate in 1864, succeeded him. The assassination completely changed the stakes. Many were now convinced that much stricter measures should be imposed on the South, and the presidency was now in the hands of a man with an unproven record.

Like Lincoln, Johnson believed that the states had maintained their constitutional status and that it was up to the president to readmit them. Johnson took office while Congress was not in session, so he unilaterally applied his plan for readmitting the states. He offered amnesty and the return of all property, excluding slaves, to all Southerners who would swear an oath of loyalty to the Union. Any officers, Confederate administrators or rich planters who were excluded could appeal directly to Johnson. Finally, he demanded that the Thirteenth Amendment abolishing slavery be ratified.

Johnson recognized the states one after another, granted thousands of pardons and appointed interim governors. By December 1865, all the seceded states had functioning governments, and the Thirteenth Amendment had been ratified. But in the meantime, the president had lost the support of radical and moderate Republicans. Developments in the South were worrisome. Former Confederates were returning to power and there was violence against blacks, who were rarely allowed the right to vote. The Southern elections sent to Congress nine ex-members of the Confederate Congress, four generals and four colonels from the Confederate army, seven former administrators of Southern state governments and even the former vice president of the Confederacy, Alexander Stephens. The more the Republicans criticized Johnson, the more he reached out to the Democrats and sought to apply his own individual policies.

The Thirteenth Amendment to the U.S. Constitution: the Abolition of Slavery. (U.S. National Archives and Records Administration)

Congress resumed sitting in December 1865 to examine the results of the Southern elections. The Southern representatives were denied seats in Congress, and a House and Senate Committee was formed to draft a new reconstruction plan. There was an investigation which revealed that democratic practices in the South were sorely lacking. Most Republicans would doubtless have been satisfied with a modicum of recognition for the rights of blacks, but this was not to be. Worse, blacks were often dispossessed of land given them by the army and Black Codes were passed in several states. The codes were an attempt to control blacks, who were treated as vagrants if they did not sign year-long work contracts. If convicted, they were consigned to employers who treated them like virtual slaves. Travel permits were required, curfews imposed and gatherings monitored.

In reaction, the Republicans set up an improved Bureau of Freedmen. Since the last years of the war, the Bureau of Freedmen had dealt with emancipated slaves. In February 1866 Congress adopted a bill granting the Bureau broad powers, but Johnson vetoed it. The bill was unconstitutional, said Johnson, because the Constitution did not provide for setting up a system to deal with the poor. Furthermore, the states most affected were not represented in Congress. An unsuccessful attempt was made to override the veto. The Democrats applauded. During a demonstration of support outside the White House, an apparently inebriated Johnson accused the Radical Republicans of being traitors along the lines of the Confederates and implied there was a conspiracy to assassinate him.

A split was only a matter of time, and it came in 1866. Congress passed a first Civil Rights Act that Johnson immediately blocked by presidential veto. This time, Congress had the two thirds of the votes necessary to override the veto. Republicans, both radical and moderate, were convinced that Congress should take charge of reconstruction, and in July they managed to charter a new Bureau of Freedmen despite another veto. They also provided constitutional guarantees to blacks by passing the Fourteenth Amendment that, while not yet guaranteeing the right to vote, recognized the citizenship of all those born in the United States or naturalized there. All would have equal protection under the law. Johnson attacked the amendment and, at his urging, ten former Confederate states rejected it. Only Tennessee approved it.

In the 1866 elections, Johnson suffered a pronounced setback. Despite his efforts, the Republicans won a two thirds majority in Congress, which they took as a mandate to impose radical reconstruction. As of March 1867, the South was treated as a conquered territory. Five separate military districts were set up, with a general in charge of each, that organized conventions to draft constitutions respecting the rights of blacks. These states would be readmitted if the constitutions were acceptable to Congress and if the new legislatures approved the Thirteenth and Fourteenth amendments. It was the beginning of Radical Reconstruction, and it would last until 1877.

In 1868, the emboldened radicals attacked President Johnson for violating an act of Congress (the Tenure of Office Act) that required Senate authorization to dismiss an administrator whose appointment had required Senate approval. Johnson had suspended the secretary of war, Edwin Stanton. The House began proceedings to impeach the president. Eleven charges were drawn up and adopted by the representatives. The Senate served as a tribunal, presided over by the chief justice of the Supreme Court. Thirty-five senators voted for conviction, one fewer than the required two thirds. Johnson remained president but had been incapacitated. He had to let Congress proceed.

The impeachment controversy paved the way for Ulysses S. Grant (1822–1885), the hero on horseback, who had almost unanimous support in the North and easily won the 1868 presidential election. The Republicans were convinced they had a popular mandate, and shortly afterward they approved the Fifteenth Amendment prohibiting states from denying the right to vote on the basis of race, colour or previous condition of servitude. But the states continued to set the conditions demanded by their voters. The remaining unreconstructed states – Virginia, Mississippi, Texas and Georgia – had to ratify the Fifteenth Amendment before being readmitted.

Scalawags and carpetbaggers
By 1870, all the former Confederate states had been readmitted into the Union and almost all were controlled by the Republican Party. It was the time of "scalawags" (whites who were "traitors" to the South by serving the North) and "carpetbaggers" (new arrivals from the North) who jumped at the chance to remake the South in the North's image. Republican voters were mainly blacks, who enjoyed a decisive influence in the reconstructed

states. However, blacks had never had supremacy in the South. There was a backlash against what was wrongly perceived as the incompetence of black-dominated radical governments. There was corruption, certainly, but it outlasted the radical governments and was also widespread in the North in the same period.

The basic reason for the growing opposition to reconstruction was the refusal of Southern whites to accept the idea that blacks could vote and hold office; they rejected the egalitarian policies adopted by the government, and in time radical reconstruction ran out of steam. The Democrats had never accepted it, and in the 1870s the Republicans retreated on the issues of social and political equality for blacks and renewed federal power. The South's corruption, inefficiency and instability were blamed on the exclusion of the former elites. By 1872, many former Confederates had regained their rights. As the Republicans became more conservative, they gradually distanced themselves from their attempts to use government power to help the lower classes. The 1873 recession diverted attention away from reconstruction, and in 1874 the Democrats regained control of Congress. The Southern Republicans were now on their own. When violence broke out again in the South, Grant did not intervene.

In the 1876 presidential election, only Florida, Georgia and South Carolina remained Republican, and the result hinged on the contested votes of these states. Republican Rutherford B. Hayes (1822–1893) was defeated in the popular vote by Samuel J. Tilden, a Democrat. But the Electoral College was deadlocked, as Tilden was one vote short, and the results were contested in four states. A deal was made: the Democrats agreed that the votes should go to Hayes and the Republicans promised to withdraw troops from the South, appoint at least one Southerner to the cabinet and fund public works in the South.

It was the end of radical reconstruction. The Republican Party virtually disappeared from the South. The radicals' policy had failed miserably. A Democratic Solid South had been created that would become increasingly "lily-white," guided by a reactionary elite that would use the same violence, courtesy of the Ku Klux Klan, and the same tried-and-true, fraudulent methods to deprive blacks of the right to vote and muzzle any opposition. The North watched apathetically, the Republicans occasionally "waving the bloody shirt" of rebellion to maintain power.

Blacks hoped that emancipation meant that they would have access to land as well as escaping the control of whites, but there was virtually no land distribution. Former slaves rejected the servitude of gang labour but many stayed with their former masters and became sharecroppers, tending a plot of land but sharing the harvest with the planter. In 1890, only 121,000 out of the 7,000,000 blacks in the South owned land. Most rural blacks remained poor, as did those who migrated to cities looking for better jobs. Almost 75 percent of blacks became sharecroppers.

The Republican vision of a new South conforming to the North's economic model did not materialize. Despite attempts at capitalist development (for example, 4,800 kilometres (3,000 miles) of railroad was built between 1868 and 1872), the South became the nation's poorest agricultural region. King Cotton, being the profitable crop, was more important than ever. The South lacked capital and financial institutions. Merchants and planters were the only ones providing credit, lending to sharecroppers in exchange for a mortgage on the next crop in what was known as the crop lien system. Interest rates were high and the price of merchandise was set by the same merchants. Farmers became trapped in debt and depended on the price of a single commodity. Production increased and prices plummeted. Between 1875 and 1894, the price of a pound of cotton fell from eleven cents to five cents. Revenue and wealth shrank after the demise of the South's diversified economy.

The recession was particularly acute in the late 1880s in the South. The Alliance, a new farmers' organization, was especially popular there. The Southern Alliance recruited mainly in Texas, Louisiana and Arkansas. By 1888, it had 250,000 members and was active on a wide variety of political fronts. Attempts were even made in 1889 to unify progressive forces by recommending that the Southern and Northern Alliances be merged with the Knights of Labor and even the Black Farmers' Alliance. The merger never happened, but the farmers' militancy led to the formation of the People's Party in 1892. The party platform represented the farmers' basic demands and, while the Populists never won control of the national government, many of the reforms they called for were implemented in later years.

The New West

In the years following the Civil War, Americans began settling the vast territory west of the Mississippi. They flocked to two large areas: the Great Plains up to the Rocky Mountains, once known as the Great American Desert, and the western plateau from the Rockies to the Sierra Nevada and the Cascade Mountains. It was the final American frontier: the mythical West.

The development of the railroad was the main impetus to opening the Great Plains, especially since the most coveted land was located along the tracks and allotted to the railway companies. Miners, cowboys and farmers quickly left their mark on the region.

The Indians

At the conclusion of the Civil War, approximately 300,000 Indians occupied the land west of the Mississippi. Some of them had been removed from the East in previous years. But the American government realized that, in spite of concentrating the Indians on reservations and signing treaties that were supposedly permanent, pressure from settlers was unstoppable. It was the same all over: Indians were concentrated on territories that were quickly invaded by prospectors and farmers as the railroad system expanded and one of the Indians' traditional sources of sustenance, the bison, was all but exterminated. In 1893, there remained a little over a thousand head of a herd that had numbered upwards of 15 million.

Indian uprisings proliferated. The Nez Perce were a typical example. Often close to whites – they had rescued the members of the Lewis and Clark expedition – the Nez Perce lived on a territory covering parts of Idaho, Oregon and Washington. In 1860, gold was discovered on their land, and they were asked to cede nine tenths of their territory for a paltry sum. The treaty was obtained illegally. The Nez Perce were asked to move. There were skirmishes in transit. The Nez Perce manoeuvred brilliantly before being cornered in the mountains of Montana. For three and a half months, they battled 2,000 soldiers in eighteen engagements and two large-scale battles. They surrendered after being promised they could return to Oregon. They ended up in Kansas, then Oklahoma.

The Indians' heroic resistance brought only a short reprieve. Victories such as the Little Big Horn in 1876, when the foolhardy George Custer was killed with all his men, did not stop the tide. In 1881 Sitting Bull, the Sioux hero, surrendered. In 1886 the Apache Geronimo was captured and exiled from his homeland. The 1890 Massacre at Wounded Knee was the final step in Indian "pacification."

Miners, cowboys and farmers

The miners arrived after the California gold rush of 1849. Rich deposits were found at Pike's Peak, Colorado, in 1859. A hundred thousand prospectors came from all over the United States. That same year, gold and silver were discovered at the Comstock Lode in Nevada. Discoveries were made in Montana, Wyoming and Idaho. Adventurers came from everywhere. Cities rose up. States were quickly formed; Nevada, for example, was admitted in 1864.

Almost everywhere the process was the same. First prospectors settled, often in a makeshift, haphazard way. They collected whatever deposits were immediately available. Then followed the companies with their expensive equipment. They mined underground. The seams were gradually depleted. Many towns became ghost towns, but the region was opening up to more long-term settlement. In the 1880s, mines were no longer an isolated frontier phenomenon but an integral part of the national industrial economy. Companies set up business in the West, where they clashed with highly militant workers' unions.

With the disappearance of the bison, the cattle industry took off. Ranchers could graze their cattle on the vast pasture lands of the plains without spending a dime. The adventure began in Texas, where at the end of the Civil War, a herd of 5 million longhorn cattle roamed free. People got the idea of herding cattle to a railhead to supply the East with meat. The first attempt succeeded in 1867. Despite the hardship – cattle died or lost weight during the trip – the venture was lucrative. People thought of fattening up the cattle before shipping them east, and cattle ranching became the norm. For two decades, cattle raising was a bonanza for the West. In the year 1880, two million cattle were slaughtered in Chicago alone. Profits were substantial: animals bought for five dollars were sold for thirty or forty dollars in Kansas City, St. Louis or Chicago.

It was the era of the legendary cowboy. He was badly paid at around thirty dollars a month, collected at the end of the long drive. He worked hard in all weather, ate badly and had few diversions. He lived in a chaotic world where violence was a constant.

Soon the plains were no longer the exclusive domain of ranchers. Farmers settled and put up fences, triggering war with the ranchers. In the end, nature took care of the problem. Between 1885 and 1887, arid summers followed by harsh winters killed 90 percent of the cattle herd. The farmers prevailed.

American farmers had long avoided the plains. The region was desert-like, with few trees, meagre rivers and streams, minimal rain and hard-packed soil. The Homestead Act of 1862 gave a certain impetus to colonization, but most farmers chose to settle on railroad lands, which had the huge advantage of being close to transportation. Only an estimated 10 percent of farmers took advantage of the Homestead Act.

The railroads fuelled development in the West and set its trajectory for growth. Railroad agents recruited pioneers east of the Mississippi and in Europe. Between 1870 and 1900, two million Europeans settled on the plains. Life was hard for Western farmers, but with improving agricultural techniques and equipment, agriculture became more productive and more fully integrated into the market economy. Farming became big business and agricultural yields increased tenfold between 1850 and 1900. But the machines of John Deere and Cyrus McCormick were expensive and farmers constantly had to go into debt. They were at the mercy of fluctuating market prices. Wheat was in high demand on international markets, but one good year did not necessarily lead to another. Climate conditions, international prices and the cost of transportation and warehousing all affected how the businesses that farms had become would fare. Between 1880 and 1900, the average farm size in the seven grain-producing states had grown from 26 to 40 hectares (64 to 100 acres).

Farmers also felt the need to organize to meet the demands of the changing economy. In the 1870s, the plains were ravaged by drought and locusts. To make matters worse, the price of grain and cotton collapsed due to international competition. The Granges, which began as secret societies in 1867, successfully united farmers in the 1870s due to economic hardship, farmers' isolation, high railroad prices and high interest rates. In 1875, 850,000 farmers belonged to Granges. They were active on many fronts: they formed cooperatives, founded banks, advocated regulatory policies for railroads and backed politicians. They achieved some success, particularly in their campaign against the railroads and the grain elevators. But renewed prosperity brought about a drop in membership. By the 1880s, the Granges had only 100,000 members.

Industrial Revolution

Jefferson had dreamed of a great rural republic populated by small, independent farmers. He had dreamed of a nation free of the liabilities of big cities, factory servitude, British mines, and the rule of privilege he had seen in France. Jefferson believed he had established this agrarian democracy and, with the Louisiana Purchase, given it room to grow. He believed that the purchase would satisfy all demand for land. Jefferson assumed he had destroyed the commercial, Hamiltonian ideal, which he felt was too close to the British one.

At first Jefferson's ideas seemed to prevail. Agriculture developed faster than industry. Even in 1860 the country was still mostly rural and agrarian. However, Hamilton won out in the end.

Less than a century after Hamilton, the United States was the most powerful industrial nation in the world. By 1900 it had discovered more coal, forged more steel, extracted and refined more petroleum, laid more railway track and built more factories than any other country. Eight principal factors made this development possible: (1) raw materials available in large quantities, (2) inventions and processing techniques, (3) communications systems, (4) domestic and external markets, (5) availability of manpower, (6) favourable government policies, (7) capital, and (8) entrepreneurial spirit.

It was a phenomenal ascent. The Civil War had further sped up the progress of the industrial system, but until 1880 agricultural production still dominated the American economy. In 1890, however, industry took the lead, and ten years later the value of manufactured goods was more than double that of agricultural products. Agriculture was worth $5 billion while industrial commodities were worth $11 billion.

In a way, the devastation of the Civil War could only slow the growth of the United States in already established sectors. It deprived the economy of too many workers not to have a negative effect, but at the same time it undeniably breathed new life into some industries. It encouraged mechanized mass production to supply the armed forces. Fortunes were amassed during the war and capital was accumulated that would finance the coming Industrial Revolution. During the crucial years of the conflict, the foundations were laid and the structures built for the American industrial revolution. The postwar United States was a republic of business.

In the 19th century, natural resources in America seemed limitless. Iron ore, essential for the steel-driven industrial revolution, was available in more than enough quantity in the Vermillion Range (more than 30 million tons was extracted in 25 years) and the Mesabi Range (more than 40 million in 10 years). Vital coal was abundant in the mines of Pennsylvania and West Virginia. Drilling for petroleum, another energy source with a promising future, began in 1859 in Titusville, Pennsylvania. Oil was also discovered in Ohio and West Virginia. Forests, quarries and mines could meet all imaginable demands.

The second phase of the Industrial Revolution, also known as the Second Industrial Revolution was characterized by several factors, the major one being new technologies that increased worker productivity and the quantity of goods produced. A production system was set up based on machines, workers and operating methods that could produce more and faster than anywhere else. Greater productivity depended not only on machines and technology but also on economies of scale, management practices, work organization and an ever-increasing demand for goods of all kinds. The population of the United States made another leap, growing from 31.5 million to 76 million inhabitants between 1860 and 1900 – all the more workers for big industry. Immigration was responsible for 14 million of these men and women.

Inventions and technical advances were quickly adopted and put to use by entrepreneurs looking for an opportunity. Before 1860, 36,000 invention patents were registered in the United States. Between 1860 and 1900, there were 440,000 in every imaginable industry. Thomas Edison invented the incandescent bulb in 1879. The new source of light would make a fortune for General Electric, which also introduced electricity to factories. The Westinghouse Electric and Manufacturing Company invented the efficient air brake for trains. In 1876 Alexander Graham Bell invented the telephone, which was the highlight of the Philadelphia Exposition, held the same year to showcase the marvels of technological progress. All these inventions were proof of the vitality of American inventiveness. Where needed, Americans also imported methods, such as the Bessemer converter for manufacturing steel. As a result, production costs were slashed. Andrew Carnegie's success in the steel industry was largely due to the speed with which he adopted the best manufacturing processes.

While Carnegie focused on processing methods, another great capitalist, John D. Rockefeller, owed his success in the oil business to his control of rail transportation. The railroad had replaced the canals as trade routes. Industrialists could obtain raw materials and distribute their production to all regions of the country. The national market gradually became interlaced with a web of railway track.

A major impetus for railway development came in 1862 when the government put the Central Pacific and the Union Pacific in charge of building a transcontinental railroad. It was completed when the two companies met at Promontory, Utah, in May 1869. Five major transcontinental networks would be built, financed by European and American capital. The railroads were the first testing ground for big business. These large national companies needed tightly controlled management, given the vast territory covered and its often sparse population. The companies made their profits from building rail lines, which was also heavily subsidized by all levels of government. The federal government gave 53 million hectares (131 million acres) of land to various companies and granted loans of $65 million. The states contributed 22 million hectares (55 million acres) of land and $228 million in loans. The railroad barons, Leland Stanford, Averell Harriman, James J. Hill, Cornelius Vanderbilt and Jay Gould, were rapacious men with often shady methods. There were many scandals and abuse was flagrant. People demanded that the extremes of the railway companies be reined in. The problem was that the government had long aided economic development through its laissez-faire policy toward regulatory interference. The captains of industry had been given free rein as well as subsidies and excessive protection from foreign competition.

Table 7
Railroad expansion in the United States, 1850–1900

Year	Miles	Kilometres
1850	9 000	14,400
1860	30 000	48,000
1873	70 000	112,000
1893	170 000	272,000
1900	192,500	308,000

Cheap Prairie land was offered by the Burlington & Missouri Rail Road Co. in 1872. The first transcontinental railroad route was opened in 1869. The Chicago and North Western Railway had reached Council Bluffs, Iowa, on the Missouri River in 1867. The Central Pacific built westwards from Omaha, just across the river, while the Union Pacific built eastwards from California, and the two met at Promontory, Utah. Other lines followed quickly, financed by an investment boom and massive land grants with which the companies attracted settlers. Later, when economic bad times hit, many lines had to merge or close down. (Library of Congress)

Trusts and monopolies

The new generation of businessmen possessed boundless ambition. The concentration of enterprises was a dominant trend in the late 19th-century business landscape. As businesses merged, they reached unprecedented proportions. Not only the mergers but downturns in the business cycle and the great recessions of 1873 and 1893 eliminated less competitive companies. Small oligopolies emerged, always on the lookout for ways to maintain their position or, better yet, improve it.

Integration was both horizontal (grouping many companies manufacturing the same product) and vertical (controlling all stages of manufacturing). The classic example of horizontal integration was Standard Oil. In 1863, John D. Rockefeller (1839–1937), who began his career as a clerk and accountant, invested his capital in a refinery in Cleveland, Ohio. He became partners with the inventor of a money-saving refining process. In 1870, he became president of the Standard Oil Company. By the mid-1870s, Rockefeller had absorbed or eliminated most of his competitors and Standard Oil was the oil giant, controlling 90 percent of the industry. Through discounts from the railroad companies and capable oversight, he controlled costs and kept his company profitable in a chaotic industry. The jolts of the 1873 recession helped him eliminate his less viable competitors. In 1882, Standard Oil set up its oil trust. In a trust, the member companies (seventy-seven in this case) submit their shares to a group of trustees (nine), who administer their combined interests. Each company receives a share of the trust's profits.

Standard Oil came to control not only refining but also pipelines, storage and distribution (vertical integration). The Standard Oil Trust served as a model for other trusts in a wide range of industries.

In 1890, Congress passed the Sherman Antitrust Act, which was far from effective as a means of fighting monopolies. The definitions of monopoly and restraint of trade were left up to the courts. The penalties were minimal. Initially, the Sherman Act was more often and more effectively applied against labour unions than against large monopolies. In 1895, in *United States v. E.C. Knight Co.*, the Supreme Court ruled that the American Sugar Refining Company did not violate the Sherman Act even though it controlled 98 percent of sugar refining. Between 1890 and 1900, the government prosecuted only eighteen cases under the Sherman Act.

Andrew Carnegie embodied the genius of vertical integration. An accountant by trade, he started out in the railroad industry. After the Civil War he expanded and, beginning in 1873, focused on the steel industry. He successfully lowered production costs and undercut his competitors by using the latest technologies and doing detailed cost analyses. He also negotiated transportation discounts. He bought out his competitors after bankrupting them through price wars. He bought iron and coal mines, railroads and ships and came to control the steel industry from mine to market. In 1900, Carnegie produced 3 million tons of steel annually, a third of national production. His annual profits were $40 million.

Many industries developed along similar lines. In textiles, tobacco, copper and food, industry barons arose and came to dominate their companies, their cities, their regions and even the national economy. The meat-packing industry, for example, saw 900 percent growth between 1870 and 1890. Industry giants Philip Armour, Gus Swift and Ferdinand Sulzberger ruled the national meat market and the city of Chicago, where their companies provided a living for 40,000 people, but often in the bleakest of conditions. Not only were farmers raising their livestock differently, people's eating habits had changed.

The Gospel of Wealth and Social Darwinism
Successful businessmen were not necessarily pleased to be called robber barons. Many believed that material success went hand in hand with social responsibility. This was the theory behind Andrew Carnegie's *The Gospel of Wealth* (1889). In it, Carnegie endorsed laissez-faire policies, hammering home his opinion that the only purpose of a government was to protect private property. Those who became rich deserved to succeed, but the rich, according to Carnegie, had an obligation to help through philanthropy.

Carnegie adhered to the prevailing social philosophy. Wealth was a sign of divine favour and the product of hard work and talent. "God gave me my money," as Rockefeller said. Similarly, poverty was a sign of laziness and lack of talent. In society, as in nature, only the strongest and best adapted and survived while the weak were eliminated. These ideas underlay the social Darwinism of Herbert Spencer and others, a theory that was sweeping the United States. It gave captains of industry justification to practise the law of the jungle by, for example, showing unwavering opposition to labour unions. The same Carnegie who wrote *The Gospel of Wealth* called in Pinkerton agents and the militia against strikers in Homestead, Pennsylvania, in 1892. The union was dismantled, and no effective workers' organization was to exist in the steel industry until the 1930s.

The cutthroat world of business required a firm hand. Any concession could endanger the company, so said the businessmen. They usually had the blessing of the public, which had absorbed the idea that success was a gift from God and the result of hard work. These were the so-called self-made men, who claimed to be from modest backgrounds. Although this was true of some, for the most part they came from wealth. Businessmen took care to maintain close relations with their churches, which gave them their blessing. A Harvard Divinity School–trained pastor, Horatio Alger (1834–1899), made a career of writing a series of popular 19th-century novels on the subject of how anyone could succeed. These inspirational rags-to-riches stories became a lucrative industry in themselves. Alger was encouraged to produce books, it was said, by the employers' association (the National Association of Manufacturers) that had supposedly distributed one of his novels in schools.

Not all the wealthy handed out their money with the altruism of a Rockefeller, Carnegie or Stanford. Many indulged in what groundbreaking economist Thorsten Veblen (1857–1929) termed conspicuous consumption in his *Theory of the Leisure Class* (1899). The excesses of the nouveaux riches were an affront: their palatial homes, their extravagant costume balls, their vacations in their Newport mansions, their jewellery, their lavish receptions and their wastefulness. It was especially galling in a society plagued by a huge disparity in wealth and income and grappling with major economic depressions.

Urbanization

Cities, integral to industrial civilization, were home to an increasing number of Americans. In 1860, only 16 cities had populations over 50,000. In 1890, 11 cities had populations over 250,000 and a third of Americans lived in cities. In 1900, 25 million people lived in cities of over 8,000 inhabitants and 30 million resided in urban areas of over 2,500 inhabitants. New York, Philadelphia and Chicago each had populations of over a million.

Industrial cities attracted people from the post–Civil War wave of immigration – so many people that in 1885, in every major city outside the South, immigrants made up the majority of the population. Chicago had as many Germans and Poles as most German and Polish cities. Boston had more Irishmen than Dublin and New York already more Italians than the vast majority of Italian cities. In 1900, three quarters of the population of Chicago was foreign-born.

The immigrants came in search of a better economic situation, and many intended to stay temporarily then return to the old country with their savings. In the 1880s almost half of Italians and Greeks returned to their country. Immigrant groups settled in cities and regions that gave them the opportunity to practise their traditional trades. The Portuguese converged on Gloucester, Massachusetts, to fish. The Italians settled in Barre, Vermont, for stonecutting or in the large East Coast cities to build railroads and subways and work in construction. Spanish cigar-makers clustered around Tampa, Florida. Others arrived with no intention of returning, including Jews fleeing persecution. Then there were the French Canadians, who settled in small towns near the New England textile mills and kept up close relations with their native country across the border for years.

Cities grew – upward and outward. Electricity provided lighting. Tramways made getting around easier. Construction fever took hold. Water mains and sewers were needed. But all this development was erratic and often led to shameless speculation and corruption. Cities were ineptly run and growing too fast. Poor-quality construction created slums where vice and crime flourished. Immigrants were an easy target for reformers to blame for the situation. The American Protective Association went further, claiming that the very existence of social and political institutions was threatened by immigrants.

In the city, the best mingled with the worst. Graceful homes and neighbourhoods, efficient office buildings of seven, ten or even twenty storeys, grandiose public buildings and architectural wonders such as the Brooklyn Bridge stood next to seedy factories and overcrowded, unsanitary workers' housing. Tenements, built by the thousands after the Civil War, were designed for maximum use of space. Usually built on 25 × 100-foot lots, they rose five floors with four dwellings per floor.

Over 1,700 people per hectare (700 per acre) were crammed into New York's Lower East Side in 1890, an extremely high density. People often succumbed to diseases stemming from air and water pollution and unsanitary conditions. In such an environment, tuberculosis, scarlet fever, smallpox, mumps and whooping cough could spread like wildfire. It is hardly surprising that the first American reforms were carried out in the city, so glaring were the problems there.

Workers resist

The Civil War had radically changed labour relations. Workers were more likely to work for large companies and take orders from a foreman hired by management.

In these new companies, workers were closely supervised and faced higher production quotas on ever-faster machines that stripped them of their expertise, since they could be operated with no training. Most industrial workers laboured ten hours a day, six days a week. Wages were low, $9 a week on average, for an unskilled worker. Employers largely neglected workers' health and safety and no state regulated working conditions.

As workers could easily be replaced, competition was fierce among workers themselves. Employers had an abundant pool of often-immigrant workers to draw from. Employment and the economy seesawed wildly, and unemployment meant serious hardship. Between 1866 and 1897 there were fourteen years of prosperity and seventeen hard ones. Even the minor depressions of 1867–1868 and 1883–1885 were not minor for those who lost their jobs. Regular work was rare. Even women and children were called upon to help make ends meet. In 1900, one fifth of the labour force was made up of women.

While times were hard, there was still hope. Most American workers lived better than workers did in Europe. Against all odds, their standard of living was improving, and despite their poverty, there was no threat of social revolution. Although they would not have admitted it, most workers had probably absorbed social Darwinism, which maintained that poverty was the result of laziness, in other words the wages of sin. Opportunities were there to be seized and, with a bit of luck, success could be achieved, and parents' hard work could eventually benefit their children. It was not fertile ground for labour organizations. Worse, there were sharp divides between skilled workers wanting to protect themselves from the immigrant masses by excluding them and industrial workers who were made up primarily of new arrivals.

Despite these obstacles, and perhaps because of them, labour organizations continued to appear. In 1866, the National Labor Union was formed to fight for the eight-hour day. Skilled and unskilled workers were invited to join the movement. Up to 300,000 members were recruited. In 1872, the organization attempted to run candidates for election. The attempt failed and the union did not survive the 1873 depression.

The Knights of Labor took up the cause. Founded as a secret society in 1869 by Philadelphia tailors, this union came out into the open in 1879 under the leadership of Terence V. Powderly. After the great railway strike of 1877, many workers joined the Knights. The organization was open to everyone, regardless of trade. Women and blacks were admitted. The union demanded an eight-hour day, the abolition of child labour, a progressive income tax and equal pay for equal work. In the 1880s, it was the largest labour organization. It counted 700,000 members in 1886 after winning a strike against the rail magnate Jay Gould and an eight-hour day for 200,000 workers.

Disaster struck soon afterward with the Haymarket massacre in Chicago on May 4, 1886. Over the objections of Powderly, who was against strikes, the Knights joined a general strike declared in Chicago. During a rally, a bomb was thrown, killing some policemen, and police in turn opened fire on the crowd; a total of eleven died. There was an immediate clampdown. Arrests and convictions followed, but most of the blame fell on the Knights. The charges were groundless, but membership declined to a hundred thousand. Employers banded together to get rid of labour organizations and announced that they would no longer negotiate. They forced workers to sign so-called yellow-dog contracts in which they promised not to join a trade union.

A rival labour organization led to the demise of the Knights of Labor. Samuel Gompers, a cigar maker from New York, insisted on the need for craftsmen to organize. He was opposed to the Knights' mass unionism and pie-in-the-sky ideals. He felt that craft organizations were the only way of effectively defending the interests of employees. He accepted the industrial status quo, opting for a business unionism in which a union was in the business of simply negotiating contracts, wages and working conditions. There was already a well-established regulatory tradition among craftsmen, with apprenticeship rules to get into a trade, and a closed shop reserved for members. In the 1870s there were at least thirty such unions.

Gompers took eight of these national craft unions and formed the American Federation of Labor (AFL) in 1886. Goals had to be concrete and short-term. The Federation had to rely on economic rather than political power. Only skilled craftsmen would be organized and the woolly-headed theories and goals of the labour reformers would be rejected.

The AFL made progress in the following years, but the major events of the turn of the century were the great strikes that marked the industrial war: the Homestead strike against the Carnegie steel mills, the Pullman strike and the miners' strikes in the West that rekindled radicalism. The violence of the conflicts, the rifts among workers, ethnic and religious divides and government intervention all proved Gompers and the AFL right. It was a choice American workers would make in ever greater numbers.

The Populist struggle

Farmers had expressed their frustration through the efforts of the Granges and the Alliance, but in the late 1880s they turned to political action. The year 1889 was a very good harvest year in the Midwest, but prices had slumped. Farmers blamed shipping companies and politicians in thrall to monopolies. In 1890, a disastrous drought struck. In June, the People's Party of Kansas was formed and ran candidates who did reasonably well, just as in the Eastern states where populist parties had been formed. In the South, farmers continued acting through the Democratic Party, a safer bet for maintaining white power.

In July 1892, a national People's Party was founded. Its presidential candidate, James B. Weaver, a Unionist ex-general, took only 22 votes out of 444 in the Electoral College, but the party elected three governors and sent several representatives to Washington.

Grover Cleveland (1837–1908), a conservative Democrat who had already served a term as president in 1885–1889, won the presidency in 1892. Almost immediately, a depression hit hard, and unemployment rose to 20 percent. Resentment polarized around the issue of the free coinage of silver. The silverites advocated an inflationary currency based on coins of widely plentiful silver. Their rival gold bugs wanted to use only gold. The old dispute between creditors and debtors was back.

In 1896, the Republicans chose William McKinley (1843–1901) as their presidential candidate. He was a proponent of a high protective tariff, and the party came out strongly in favour of the gold standard. At their convention, the Democrats were swayed by the eloquent "cross of gold" speech given by William Jennings Bryan (1860–1925). The party added free silver to its platform and chose Bryan to be its presidential candidate. The People's Party, so as not to split the silverite vote, also chose him as its candidate. The 1896 campaign marked a decisive turning point. Bryan barnstormed across the country, travelling 30,000 kilometres (19,000 miles), delivering thousands of speeches before 5 million voters on the cause of reform. McKinley led a "front porch" campaign, hardly ever leaving his home in Canton, Ohio. He was supported by the business community and promised that the tariff and a strong currency would bring back prosperity. Bryan drew 47 percent of the vote, short of McKinley's 51 percent.

It was a pronounced shift in American politics. Between 1876 and 1896, neither of the two main parties had won more than 49 percent of the popular vote. After 1896, the Republicans became the dominant political party until 1932. The People's Party had its final successes in 1896, and then quickly disappeared from the national stage.

CHAPTER 8

PROGRESSIVISM AND WAR

1898–1919

For a while after the election of William McKinley, it seemed as though life had returned to normal, and political and social tensions eased. The business sector was confident, the spectre of bimetallism had receded, commerce had recovered, factories were producing at their pre-1893 rates and prices were rising. Businesses continued merging through holding companies, which enabled a financial group to control several companies in various industries while owning only part of their shares. The recovery was bolstered when the United States went to war with Spain in 1898. Even farmers seemed cheered by improved conditions. A bushel of wheat that sold for 50 cents in 1895 rose to 80 cents in 1897, stabilized at 62 cents in 1900 then kept rising over the next twenty years.

The difficulties of the agricultural sector had diminished and the working class, despite increasing strikes, was less militant: almost half the strikes at the time were over the right to unionize. In a climate of relative well-being and social peace, the urban middle class was able to express its concerns and demand moderate reforms; it even borrowed the platform of earlier extremists.

By 1900, criticism by reformists, worker unrest and the newly conscious middle class had raised awareness in American society of the intrusiveness of big business – the tentacle-like power of financial kingpins, the abhorrent system of privilege, the existence of flagrant abuses, the corruption creeping into American life. A feeling took hold that the system should be overhauled and the abuses curbed. The dawn of the 20th century heralded ideological changes as dramatic as the economic ones. Economic activity had always been based on a philosophy of liberal individualism, but this inevitably led to abuse. The dogmas of yesteryear now seemed out of date. The idea of an individualist society gave way, at least

Table 8
Agricultural prices, 1875–1905, in dollars

Year	Butter per pound	Wheat per bushel	Oats per bushel
1875	32.5	1.01	0.367
1880	30.5	0.952	0.349
1885	26.6	0.772	0.279
1890	23.7	0.837	0.419
1895	21.2	0.505	0.193
1900	22.2	0.621	0.253
1905	24.6	0.747	0.288

Source: *Statistical History of the United States*, 293, 296, 298.

among many intellectuals and activists, to the idea of a society of collective action in the interest of all. Private property and capitalism were not cast aside, however; progressive leaders wanted to build a Jeffersonian society but within a Hamiltonian framework using Hamiltonian methods. The progressives were not revolutionaries, but they wanted to resolve the problems raised by the changes of the great industrial age and ward off potentially violent clashes within American society.

The political scene could only be a reflection of the overall social situation, and the new ideas were not the province of a single party or even of ideological wings or factions: they were held by both Republicans and Democrats, whether liberal, centrist or conservative. The progressive movement was the result of an amalgamation of ideas. While in 1901 the Republican Party, after its reformist beginnings, presented itself as the champion of high finance and the business sector, and its rival Democratic Party was the defender of the people, after that date progressivism had so overtaken both parties that their fundamental choices were almost indistinguishable. Granted, it was commonly said that the Republican Party had come to a profitable working arrangement with big business in which party leaders sought to impose ethics on it rather than eliminate it, while the Democratic Party wanted to remove the business giants. Yet once in power, the Democrats implemented Republican policy.

The United States of 1900 was a highly stratified country socially and economically. There were many extremely diverse social classes; the gaps were huge between small and large manufacturers, labour and capital, natives and immigrants, and rural and urban populations. If current trends were not reversed, it seemed as if the country was headed for a social deadlock between the privileged and the non-privileged. The struggle of the progressive movement, born of a new consciousness of these problems, fuelled by economic recovery and supported by the middle class, focused on one central theme: transforming a political economy created and dominated by big business into a fairer and more humanitarian social system that did not, for all that, reject big business or private property. The middle class rediscovered the moral obligation of service, breaking with the tradition of the smugly complacent "mugwump" (originally a Republican opposed to James G. Blaine's candidacy in 1884, and by extension a conservative who scorned the period's "dirty" politics).

Yet all the proselytizing led progressive leaders, to their disadvantage, to think of themselves as moral agents of social regeneration. Their approach hampered a movement already too easily identified with the "respectable" idealism of a middle class incapable of overcoming its contempt for immigrants and its abdication of responsibility toward the black problem. To most progressive leaders, immigrants symbolized corruption and threatened traditional American values; fear that new Americans would sully the nation's homogeneity led to racist attitudes. It was a rare progressive who could shed his racism. All in all, the progressive period was disheartening for blacks, as virtually nothing was done to counteract Southern segregationist laws.

Whatever the motivations of progressive leaders – it would be too easy to judge them selfish or fainthearted – the fact remains that the movement itself was a fascinating episode in the awakening of Americans' social conscience. The progressives carried out most of their projects between 1913 and 1916, during the first presidency of Woodrow Wilson. During these fruitful years, Wilson (1856–1924) led progressive forces from strength to strength and secured an impressive series of economic and social laws. He paved the way for a modern interventionist state that could establish the balance sought by the progressives. Wilson's task had, however, been made easier by the rise of progressivism during the presidencies of his two predecessors, Theodore Roosevelt (1858–1919) and William Howard Taft (1857–1930), to the point where, during the 1912 election, all three candidates could claim the progressive label.

In only three years, the impressive series of laws known as Wilson's New Freedom set Americans firmly on the road to reform. No one knows whether Wilson and the Democrats could have kept up the pace for long; in any case, the United States' entry into war in 1917 halted progressivism.

The 1920s marked a return to conservatism, but the subsequent Great Depression brought home to Americans the need to re-examine their society and try to improve it.

In foreign relations, the progressive era raises several questions, since a large number of progressives came out in support of American imperialism. While the United States had always been expansionist, until the end of the 19th century the phenomenon was restricted to the continent. In the late 19th century, many factors came together to propel the United States onto the international stage and set it on the road to imperialism. With its economic power, America aspired to conquer new markets and find new outlets for Americans' unbounded energy, even as its borders closed. The rise of social Darwinism convinced many Americans of their superiority over other peoples and their responsibility toward them. The social mission of the United States was easily reconciled at the time with the sermons of Protestant opinion-makers such as Josiah Strong, who maintained that Protestant values were in decline and that the United States must undertake the Anglo-Saxon mission to preserve them and spread them throughout the world. At the same time, naval officers led by Alfred Mahan argued that the United States needed to become a naval power to rise to the status to which it aspired.

Congress paid attention, expanding and modernizing the American fleet. When the crisis broke out over Cuba, which Americans wanted to liberate from its Spanish oppressors, many Americans, spurred on by a press campaign, were ready to do battle with the Spanish. The rebuilt navy played a decisive role in the "splendid little war," from which America emerged with a new imperial stature that would be championed by Theodore Roosevelt.

Its success during the Spanish-American War, confirmed by the Treaty of Paris (1898), prepared the United States for a spectacular entry into the international club of imperialist powers. In this era the United States acquired the Philippines, Guam, Puerto Rico, Hawaii, Samoa and the Cuban protectorate, while the Caribbean Sea became an "American lake" and Latin America an exclusive American domain. Under the Roosevelt Corollary (1904) to the Monroe Doctrine, America repeatedly intervened in the economic affairs of these small nations, supposedly to prevent the Europeans from doing so. When powerful American interests were at stake, as in Panama, the United States fomented unrest to justify gunboat diplomacy and allow completion of the canal, deemed indispensable from a strategic and commercial point of view.

While a large majority of Americans hailed these accomplishments, approval was not unanimous. Anti-imperialists waged a constant battle against a policy that contradicted traditional American values. In the Philippines, for example, the way an independence movement was violently crushed recalled old-fashioned colonialism, which had always been anathema to Americans. As a result, the "old imperialism" phase in the United States was short-lived, but American economic might and energy demanded that it get involved in the world to protect its stake; American interests always prevailed in foreign policy. American isolationism is revealed as a myth supporting Americans' internalized idea of their role: spreading their traditional ideals throughout a world liberated from commercial constraints (the Open Door) and presenting itself as an example, but with no direct engagement. The United States settled into its role of a supposedly neutral great power.

After Theodore Roosevelt (1901–1909), imperialist fervour declined, but Taft (1909–1913), his successor, practised "dollar diplomacy" to protect American investments in America's backyard and even beyond. Woodrow Wilson (1913–1920), while taking a moral distance from his predecessor's diplomacy, continued to support the Open Door Policy and did not hesitate to intervene massively in Haiti (1915), Cuba (1913), Santo Domingo (1916) and even Mexico (1914), whose elected government he refused to recognize.

When the First World War, which did not at first directly affect the United States, broke out in 1914, Wilson recommended that his fellow citizens remain "neutral in thought and deed." A large majority supported him and in 1916 he was re-elected with the slogan "He kept us out of war." The fateful decision to break with neutrality and enter the war was, in a way, imposed on the United States. The benefits of neutrality were many, but depended more on American ties with France and Britain than on trade with Germany, which refused to acknowledge the freedom of the seas and the rights of neutral countries and waged a vicious submarine war. In April 1917, Congress voted for war to protect the freedom of the seas, but also to help allies who had been granted huge loans and equally to preserve democracy, which they could identify with now that the Tsarist regime in Russia had collapsed.

Early stages of empire and the Spanish-American War

Nearly three centuries separated the founding of the first colony and the launch of the Spanish-American War in 1898. During those years, Americans focused their energy on developing their part of the continent. Fired by Manifest Destiny, they made their way to the Pacific, casting covetous glances toward Canada and Mexico all the while. Expansion was limited to the continent.

United States foreign policy was based on the ideas of Washington and Jefferson as well as the Monroe Doctrine (1823), reaffirmed by Polk and largely reproduced in the Polk Doctrine (1845). It focused on the need for the United States to preserve its freedom of action while avoiding permanent alliances. American exceptionalism – the idea that the United States was qualitatively different from and even superior to other nations – was invoked to outlaw any foreign interference. Such a policy must remain theoretical, however; a country's power governs its policies. In the first half of the 19th century, the United States aspired simply to develop, free from foreign interference in the hemisphere, on a continent that was opening up before it.

In 1898, the United States seemed to leap onto the international stage, achieving the status of a great power by choosing, as the Europeans had, the path of imperialism. One influential interpretation has it that the leap was an involuntary and unexpected result of American actions. Americans almost inadvertently found themselves at the head of a nascent empire. Yet the crisis of 1898 and its aftermath do not have the sudden and unexpected character often ascribed to them. The American will to power was no accident. It was fuelled by the solid support of the people and American leaders, though over heartfelt objections from certain quarters.

The United States did not suddenly become a world power in 1898. It was not isolated from the world and was well aware of the international competition for raw materials and markets. The United States was more populous than any European country except Russia and its economy was booming. Americans did not want to be outdone by the other powers, especially since they identified with the idea that it was the destiny of the Anglo-Saxon race to dominate the world and free humankind.

Spurred on by a host of pamphleteers, journalists, pastors, historians, strategists and politicians, America intended to fulfill its mission. Many were convinced that the recession of 1893 was caused by insufficient markets. Frederick Jackson Turner, the frontier historian, claimed that Americans had to find another frontier since the continent was covered. The United States looked to Latin America, particularly the Caribbean and Central America, but also toward the Pacific to secure its place in the world. The navy was expanded. From ranking twelfth in the world in 1880, it rose to sixth place in 1890 and third in 1900.

In 1867, William Henry Seward, secretary of state under Lincoln and Johnson, had approved the purchase of Alaska from Russia. In the 1880s, James G. Blaine, secretary of state under James A. Garfield and Benjamin Harrison, had pursued better relations and signed several treaties with Latin America. Since 1875, the Americans had controlled sugar production in Hawaii. In 1887, they built a base at Pearl Harbor. In 1893, the island became an American protectorate and it was annexed in 1898. Since 1878, the Americans had maintained a foothold in Samoa, which became an American protectorate in 1899. There were also failed attempts to buy the Virgin Islands and take control of Santo Domingo.

During an 1895 dispute between Venezuela and Britain over Guyana, the Americans sided with the Venezuelans and, by order of President Cleveland, Secretary of State Richard Olney sent an arrogant diplomatic note to Britain asserting that American will prevailed in the Western hemisphere. Clearly, Monroe was obsolete, and the American will to power was well in place before 1898.

Cuba, too, had long tempted the Americans. Southerners thought they had found a place to expand slavery. After the Civil War, American investment there had increased, standing at around $50 million by 1890, but strategic considerations were also important. In 1895, there was a crisis on the island when sugar sales fell. The Americans had cut Cuban sugar imports to the United States by half. Unrest spread, and the Spanish cracked down hard. Concentration camps were set up, scarcity was widespread and epidemics raged. There were almost 200,000 victims. The revolutionaries were supported by many Americans, who demanded that Cuba be freed from the Spanish yoke.

The American yellow press also played a role. Joseph Pulitzer's *World* and William Randolph Hearst's *Journal* competed for the most sensational headlines. Spanish atrocities were exposed, vilified and, when necessary, invented. Public opinion was heavily influenced by the wide-circulation newspapers, but the American government and the business community kept their calm. President Cleveland (who was in office at the beginning of the crisis) refused to back the revolutionaries and urged Spain to grant limited autonomy to the island. William McKinley, who succeeded him, was a business-oriented expansionist who was against intervention as long as Spain talked of reform. In November 1897, a *Washington Post* headline read "No War with Spain."

In early 1898, Spanish-American relations took a turn for the worse. Spanish loyalists rioted in Havana. American authorities had earlier sent the battleship *Maine* to anchor in the port of Havana on a courtesy call and to protect American citizens if necessary. On February 9, the *Journal* published a letter from the Spanish ambassador to Washington calling McKinley weak and an opportunist. Popular indignation turned to fury when on February 15 an explosion, unexplained to this day, sank the *Maine*. War fever reached a peak – the 268 victims had to be avenged. McKinley, sensing the approach of war, prepared to intervene, but he played both sides. On March 27, he asked Spain to make concessions, which they did, short of promising to grant Cuban independence. At the same time, he got $50 million in credits approved to prepare American forces, and when he reported to Congress on April 11, he asked not for a declaration of war but for authority to use force, barely mentioning the Spanish concessions.

McKinley had no doubt succumbed to popular pressure and warnings from Republicans who feared losing the next election. The war had been forced on him, but he went about it with systematic resolve. On April 19, Congress authorized the use of force but also passed the Teller amendment prohibiting the annexation of Cuba. Spain declared war on the United States on April 25. The United States opened hostilities on April 29.

To the surprise of many, the first news of the war came from the Pacific. The navy was ready. Since February, Admiral George Dewey, commander of the Pacific Fleet, had been under orders from Theodore Roosevelt, temporarily acting in the place of the secretary of the navy, to be ready to intervene in the Philippines. Many have attacked Roosevelt's initiative as an imperialist conspiracy, but that day Roosevelt was simply applying a measure that had been approved by higher authorities. Dewey destroyed the Spanish fleet off Manila on May 1, and on May 4 McKinley dispatched 5,000 soldiers to occupy the Philippines.

> **The March of the Flag**
>
> It is a glorious history our God has bestowed upon His chosen people; a history heroic with faith in our mission and our future; a history of statesmen who flung the boundaries of the Republic out into unexplored lands and savage wilderness; a history of soldiers who carried the flag across blazing deserts and through the ranks of hostile mountains, even to the gates of sunset; a history of a multiplying people who overran a continent in half a century; a history of prophets who saw the consequences of evils inherited from the past and of martyrs who died to save us from them; a history divinely logical, in the process of whose tremendous reasoning we find ourselves today....
>
> Shall the American people continue their march toward the commercial supremacy of the world? Shall free institutions broaden their blessed reign as the children of liberty wax in strength, until the empire of our principles is established over the hearts of all mankind?
>
> Have we no mission to perform, no duty to discharge to our fellow man? Has God endowed us with gifts beyond our deserts and marked us as the people of His peculiar favor, merely to rot in our own selfishness...?
>
> Albert J. Beveridge, senatorial campaign speech, first given at Indianapolis, September 16, 1898, also published as a pamphlet.

The situation was less tidy to the east. Enthusiasm was high but American forces, aside from the navy, were not ready. Regardless, they managed a landing in Cuba on June 20. The troops were ill-prepared and badly equipped, and on July 1, near Santiago, they narrowly avoided disaster. Against a position defended by 600 Spaniards, the Americans, including Roosevelt's Rough Riders, suffered losses of 1,572 men but managed to seize the hills overlooking Santiago harbour, where the Spanish fleet lay at anchor. On July 3, the Spaniards tried to get past the American blockade, but their fleet was sunk within four hours. Deprived of naval support, the Spanish soldiers in Cuba surrendered on July 17. On the 25th, Puerto Rico was occupied, and in August Manila fell to the Americans and Philippine insurgents.

It was a total victory. The United States now belonged to the club of great powers. It had leapt onto the international stage in the Caribbean, admittedly in its backyard, but also in the faraway Pacific. The Treaty of Paris of 1898 established the independence of Cuba, allowed for the purchase of the Philippines and ceded Puerto Rico and Guam. Soon afterward, Congress approved the annexation of Hawaii and Samoa.

Not everyone approved of this transformation. Opponents formed the Anti-Imperialist League. Debate over the Treaty of Paris was fierce, but the Senate ratified it by two votes. Even McKinley expressed his reservations about the acquisitions, but in the end he claimed the voice of God had instructed him to accept them. But the imperialists quickly became disenchanted. The Filipinos turned against the American soldiers. The ensuing crackdown was brutal yet drawn out, and the cost in human lives was high. Establishing freedom and democracy was not easy, and many feared for American democracy itself.

A few years after its enthusiastic beginnings, the imperial adventure was virtually over. But the United States did not turn inward. It continued to favour commercial expansion but without territorial annexations. It had also discovered that its weight gave it a big voice and that power could be profitable. The Open Door Policy in China and the American fiat in Panama imposed by Theodore Roosevelt exemplified the new approach.

The era of progressivism

The progressive era was a particularly intense period in the history of American reform movements. A strong commitment to anything hinting at the spirit of reform characterized the entire stretch of American history from 1901 to 1917. The movement got its first push at the grassroots level in the 1890s then came to national prominence with Theodore Roosevelt (who supported it throughout his presidency) and remained high on the American agenda until the Americans entered World War I in 1917.

For several years, broad swaths of society had been protesting the flagrant abuses that were a product of the triumphant new economic forces. The middle class adopted ideas considered radical in previous decades, gave them the respectability they lacked and thus permitted them to be embraced by the population as a whole. In its broadest sense, progressivism meant an attempt to improve living conditions in a society disrupted by the rush toward industrialization and its unexpected social costs. As its leading figures were middle class, the movement did not represent a challenge to economic and technological progress or capitalist society, but rather an attempt to ensure their stability by fixing their shortcomings and finding answers to the problems created by the move from a rural, agrarian society to an urban, industrial one.

The most obvious paradox had to be the inordinate wealth of the few juxtaposed with the hardship and even abject poverty of the many. Urbanization complicated the problem, bringing with it a heightened awareness of social differences on the part of less advantaged classes. Poverty was much more glaring in the city than in the country and city dwellers were much more aware of the gulf separating them. Unfair distribution of wealth went along with an unequal share of political power, also dominated by big business and the oligarchy of wealth.

To attack these problems, the progressive movement called on the cooperation of a great many individuals and associations with no real unity or shared direction except their common desire to respond to the challenges of the new social context. In every region of the country and from every class, the movement recruited members. In practice, it was much more a mindset than a clearly defined and structured movement. Indeed, there were several movements inspired by and claiming to follow the progressive ideal.

Progressives from the city did not necessarily agree with those from the country; those from the North did not see eye to eye with those from the South; and progressive industrialists did not share the views of proletarians. Kansas and Nebraska did not automatically voice the same demands as Wisconsin or Iowa. The wide variety of problems and interests at stake meant much potential for discord.

Despite the movement's pluralism, there was an underlying agreement on general principles, such as the need to quash the influence of corrupt minorities in the government; the desire to improve the political and administrative structure to favour control by the many; and the will to extend government activity into areas where it could remedy social ills.

Progressives were optimists who believed that it was possible to improve their world by mobilizing people's intelligence and energy. Their optimism expressed itself primarily in the demand for action. Leaving things to chance was not an option, and they believed in government intervention at the municipal, state and national levels. Finally, they believed it was possible to make people better by improving their environment.

For the first time in American history, Hamiltonian and Jeffersonian ideals stood side by side. By advocating government intervention to favour the general good and social justice, progressives reconciled the aspirations of Jefferson's followers with the methods advocated by Hamilton.

Progressivism arose during a period of general prosperity. Industrial production was increasing markedly, and unemployment fell by half between 1900 and 1901. By 1906 unemployment was at its lowest level in the entire 20th century, with only 0.8 percent of workers jobless. The prices of agricultural commodities, in a slump since 1873, began an upswing in 1897; they even doubled between 1900 and 1910. A feeling of confidence and well-being reappeared that had been absent since the 1880s, but other factors almost immediately raised concerns again among many Americans.

From 1898 to 1904, there was an explosion of business mergers that has not been seen since, a clear indication of the transition from industrial capitalism to financial capitalism. Out of the 318 industrial trusts listed by financial writer John Moody in 1904, only 88 existed before 1898, with capital of $1,196,000,000; the other 230 had only been set up since 1898 with capital of $6,000,000,000. It was the era when the U.S. Steel Corporation (1901), the Consolidated Tobacco Company (1902), the Standard Oil Trust (1899) and the International Mercantile Company (1902) were founded. The same phenomenon occurred in the railroad industry. In 1900, over 90 percent of the major lines were controlled by only six financial groups. In utilities, 111 combines had been formed by 1904, the vast majority since 1893.

The United States entered the 20th century with an economy plainly dominated by corporations. In 1899 they provided 66 percent of all manufactured goods; in 1909 the proportion reached 79 percent. As the 20th century dawned, business gradually became controlled by a small financial oligarchy. A dozen large banks and brokerage houses, among them J.P. Morgan and Company, Kuhn, Loeb and Company, and Kidder, Peabody and Company, controlled not only finance and the securities market but also industry and trade.

Everyone expected to profit from the new prosperity. Workers had managed until 1897 to increase their pay gradually; the economic recovery of the early century and stepped-up production led them to hope for faster improvement in their economic situation. It was not to be. While big business claimed that its monopolistic methods increased productivity, rationalized production and lowered production costs, many of its opponents in the working and middle classes doubted the benefits would be allowed to trickle down, hard hit as these people were by constantly rising prices. From 1897 to 1913, the cost of living rose by 37 percent, contradicting the claims of the big business lobby. And between 1900 and 1912, the real average annual salary was never higher than in 1890–1899. Hiring levels were higher than before, but the new urban immigration swelled the ranks of workers, providing bosses with cheap and plentiful manpower, to the detriment of workers facing rising prices.

Labour unions seized the opportunity provided by full employment to organize workers. The total number of unionized workers grew from 447,000 in 1897 to 501,000 in 1898 to 611,000 in 1900 and then climbed to 2,000,000 in 1904. Increased union membership and the rising power of labour led inevitably to confrontations between capital and labour, hence the large number of strikes (1,839 in 1900, 3,012 in 1901 and 3,642 in 1903). Unions were feared, often for the same reasons big business was, as an excessive concentration of power.

As the power of captains of industry and finance, not to mention unions, increased, the middle class of small manufacturers, merchants and professionals saw its influence decline. Prosperity itself endangered the members of a class living essentially on a fixed income and whose position relied on a certain social stasis. They felt threatened by the unions, which they associated with monopolies, by the cost of living and by the systematic corruption encouraged by big business. Trusts, whether capital trusts or labour trusts, were seen as the enemy – the source of all evil.

"That damned cowboy" – The Roosevelt era
When in 1901 President McKinley was shot dead by an anarchist, Theodore Roosevelt succeeded him. When he took office, no one except ultra-conservatives identified Roosevelt with reformism. Born into a patrician, conservative family, the new president was first and foremost a party man. Yet he was not universally admired among Republicans. He had been chosen as McKinley's running mate in 1896 to neutralize him, against the advice of party organizer and fundraiser Mark Hanna. In 1901, Hanna exclaimed, "Now look, that damned cowboy is President of the United States." He took the reins during a turbulent period of rapid change. Roosevelt immediately understood the importance of public opinion and, as a

savvy politician, knew how to reassure his party's conservative wing and satisfy popular demands. The exposure that Roosevelt gave to progressivism remains perhaps his most valuable contribution to reform. During his presidency, it became respectable and patriotic to preach certain reforms.

In his first message to Congress, Roosevelt showed great caution, taking care not to announce any revolutionary measures. He simply brought up the excesses of big business and announced his intention to consider practical measures to put a stop to them. And he was quick to take action. In February 1902, he decided to sue the Northern Securities Company, an enormous holding company that controlled almost all the railway lines in the West. While his act inspired intense dread among financiers, Roosevelt was not declaring war on all trusts. He was attacking the ones that "misbehaved themselves." Roosevelt's lawsuit caused a huge sensation among the common people. Although he was never a true trustbuster, to Roosevelt's credit he paved the way for regulating business practices by dusting off the Sherman Act (1890).

Roosevelt also played a key role in settling the coal strike of 1902: he served as a mediator in the conflict between mine owners and unions and forced a settlement, conferring a major role on the federal government in labour strikes. Before the end of his first term, he had also sketched out the first elements of a conservation policy for natural resources and secured the Elkins Act, ending certain improper practices by the railroads.

His first steps in the direction of reform earned Roosevelt widespread popularity going into the 1904 elections. He also maintained the confidence of the conservative majority in Congress, whose support he needed to implement his program and even to be re-elected. Roosevelt was chosen as the Republican candidate by acclamation. The election against Alton B. Parker was a matter of form.

As soon as he was elected, Roosevelt made the mistake of announcing that he would not run for a third term. While the president's election seemed to sanction the reform movement, Roosevelt was up against a conservative Congress that habitually stalled any progressive bills. Roosevelt managed to get only some of his recommendations adopted, and those mainly thanks to his talent for manoeuvre and compromise.

Theodore Roosevelt's second term featured increased action in the areas of railroads and conservation. In 1906, through compromise, he secured the Hepburn Act, reviving the Interstate Commerce Commission

> **The Roosevelt Corollary**
> All that this country desires is to see the neighboring countries stable, orderly, and prosperous. Any country whose people conduct themselves well can count upon our hearty friendship. If a nation shows that it knows how to act with reasonable efficiency and decency in social and political matters, if it keeps order and pays its obligations, it need fear no interference from the United States. Chronic wrongdoing, or an impotence which results in a general loosening of the ties of civilized society, may in America, as elsewhere, ultimately require intervention by some civilized nation, and in the Western Hemisphere the adherence of the United States to the Monroe Doctrine may force the United States, however reluctantly, in flagrant cases of such wrongdoing or impotence, to the exercise of an international police power…. While [our southern neighbors] obey the primary laws of civilized society they may rest assured that they will be treated by us in a spirit of cordial and helpful sympathy…. It is a mere truism to say that every nation, whether in America or anywhere else, which desires to maintain its freedom, its independence, must ultimately realize that the right of such independence can not be separated from the responsibility of making good use of it.
> President Theodore Roosevelt, in a message to Congress, 1904.

as well as raising hope of ending some of the railroad companies' most reprehensible practices. Granted, the Hepburn Act that Roosevelt got had been watered down to satisfy the conservatives, and the most progressive elements were dissatisfied. The fact remained that the act allowed the government for the first time to set the operating rules for a private company in the public interest.

After getting the Hepburn Act passed into law, Roosevelt, scandalized by the revelations of Upton Sinclair in *The Jungle* (1906), threw himself into the cause of consumer protection, launching a successful campaign in conjunction with Senator Albert J. Beveridge to regulate the quality of food and drugs. The result was the Pure Food and Drug Act and the Meat Inspection Act of 1906. The episode brought out the importance of the "muckrakers," those exposers of corruption who published scathing articles in wide-circulation magazines such as *McClure's*, *Munsey's* and *Cosmopolitan*. Ida Tarbell published her history of Standard Oil, Lincoln Steffens denounced municipal corruption and David Graham Phillips wrote about the Senate's betrayal. In his novel *The Jungle*, Upton Sinclair decried the working conditions of immigrants exploited by trusts and exposed the underbelly of the Chicago meat-packing industry, liable to turn anyone off eating its products. Roosevelt also managed to set up a genuine conservation policy for natural resources. To the chagrin of forestry and mining companies, he protected millions of acres of land that had been abandoned to private enterprise.

During the final two years of his presidency, Roosevelt, increasingly alive to public feeling, became more reformist as Congress clung fast to its conservative beliefs. His flamboyant style was off-putting to some, but the legacy he left in 1909 to William Howard Taft – whom he had personally chosen as his successor – was impressive.

While Taft announced that he would carry on Roosevelt's policies, it quickly became apparent that the old guard in Congress had been right to label him a conservative. It must be said in Taft's defence that he took office at a time when progressivism was becoming more and more demanding. The new president's lack of political instinct and his inability to gauge public opinion made him appear more conservative than he actually was. During his four years in office, he managed to alienate the conservative and progressive wings of the Republican Party and the general populace all at the same time. Yet objectively, Taft did a lot for reform. The Mann-Elkins Act was an improvement on the Hepburn Act. Taft also approved the formation of the Children's Bureau, the eight-hour day for federal government employees, the postal savings bank and the Sixteenth Amendment authorizing a federal income tax. But many progressives, even within the Republican Party, were dissatisfied. The conservatives were not at all pleased with the "persecution" of the trusts; in this regard, Taft surpassed Roosevelt, with ninety lawsuits in four years to the latter's forty-four in almost eight years.

By 1910 the Republican Party was in tatters. That year's mid-term elections were a bitter defeat. The Democratic Party had donned more progressive colours and the anti-Taft "insurgents" made up a large faction within the Republican Party. Everything indicated that Taft would be defeated in 1912.

Roosevelt could not forgive Taft for what he had done to his party or the cause of reform and decided to enter the race for the presidency. He made his first overtures within the party, but the conservatives were in such control of the machine that Taft was chosen over Roosevelt. Incensed, and sure of his popular support, Theodore Roosevelt decided to head his own political organization, the Progressive Party. In causing a schism in his party, the former president did not manage to attract all the reformists from the Republicans to his ranks, but he did destroy his old party's chances. Against these divided opponents, Woodrow Wilson, the progressive-leaning Democratic candidate, won a resounding victory. The 1912 election showed that the nation had become very clearly agreeable to change, and Wilson and his team used this popular support to pass a great many progressive initiatives into law.

The Wilson reforms

The culmination of the progressive movement was the impressive series of social and economic measures passed by the Wilson administration. In 1913, Wilson's first move was on the tariff issue. Several former presidents had divided their parties over the matter yet not a single one since the Civil War had managed to get the highly protectionist tariff reduced. Wilson succeeded where his predecessors had failed. The Underwood Tariff significantly lowered customs duties and replaced them with an income tax. In December, he set up the Federal Reserve System, which brought the American financial system broadly under national regulation.

Wilson intended to continue reforming American society through more extensive antitrust legislation. In 1914, he steered the Clayton Act through Congress and founded, under the Federal Trade Commission Act, a committee to monitor the activities of businessmen. In practice, neither measure had the teeth required and the business world quickly adapted.

That same year, Wilson announced that progressivism had achieved all its goals and that all the economic problems and abuses had been remedied. Yet he had not counted on pressure from progressives for social legislation, which had not yet been broached. For the 1916 elections, Wilson and his party clearly needed the support of progressives of all stripes or else victory could go to the Republican Party with a possibly reinstated Roosevelt. Wilson showed his flexibility by opting for bills likely to satisfy extreme reformists. This batch of measures included the Seamen's Act (1915), which aimed to increase safety for sailors and improve their working conditions; the Federal Farm Loan Act (1916), which set up a structure to ease credit for farmers; the Adamson Act (1916), which mandated an eight-hour day for interstate railway workers; and the Keating-Owen Act (1916), which prohibited interstate trade in goods manufactured by children.

The Progressive Era was a fascinating period in American history. A pluralistic and ambivalent movement born of a growing awareness of the problems of a burgeoning industrial society, progressivism tried to find ways of regulating business practices, extending democracy and ensuring greater social justice. The hoped-for results were not always achieved but, despite its shortcomings, the reforms appeared worth the effort and the outcome generally positive.

The First World War

Uneasy neutrality
Building an empire did not require annexations; that was the position taken by American administrations after the early 20th century. Theodore Roosevelt, to gain control of the Panama Canal, had fomented rebellion against Colombia, instantly recognized Panamanian independence and, through the Hay-Bunau-Varilla Treaty (1903), guaranteed the United States perpetual rights over the Panama Canal zone. A year later, Roosevelt added his Corollary to the Monroe Doctrine authorizing the United States to act in the western hemisphere to prevent European intervention. More and more the United States intervened around the globe, and the debate had shifted from whether to have an empire to how it should be run. Their control was not absolute, however, and American authorities faced a problem when war broke out in 1914.

In August 1914, the major European countries, ensnared in a complex web of alliances, went to war. Americans were greatly disturbed by the outbreak of the conflict, but they took refuge in traditional American neutrality, quickly reaffirmed by President Wilson. The United States had no direct interest in the confrontation. Its main concern was to avoid taking sides, as millions of American immigrants maintained links with their mother countries on both sides of the conflict.

Maintaining neutrality would not be easy. Both sides used propaganda to court the Americans. The British had the advantage because of cultural links and the fear inspired by the German armies. The major obstacle to remaining neutral was America's economic relations with the warring powers. The British quickly imposed a blockade against American trade with

Germany. Neutrality meant that the United States could claim the right to trade with everyone, but in practice they were forced to accept British controls. Sales to the Anglo-French allies increased from $824 million in 1914 to $3.2 billion in 1916. To break the blockade, the Germans only weapon was the submarine. In February 1915, they declared the waters around the British Isles a war zone. The United States protested against this violation of international law, which permitted merchant ships to be boarded and searched but not sunk without warning. On May 7, 1915, the *Lusitania* was sunk off the Irish coast. The British vessel was transporting war supplies, but among the 1,198 victims were 128 Americans, and there was an outcry in the United States. Wilson protested but did not break off relations with Germany. In September, the Germans softened their policy and the incidents stopped. A new crisis arose in March 1916 when the *Sussex*, a French steamship, was sunk, again with Americans on board. American protests led to German assurances that no commercial vessel would be sunk without warning. A reassuring calm seemed to settle on the issue until January 1917.

The other obstacle to American neutrality was the loans granted to the European powers. The Americans realized that for sales from the United States to continue, they had to provide credit. The American economy had been in recession since early 1913 and orders from the warring parties were helping to rally the economy. In the fall, the banks were informed that they could provide credit. American banks were authorized to float a loan of $500 million on the American market destined for France and England. Between August 1914 and April 1917, the United States lent $2.3 billion to the Entente (England/France/Russia) and $27 million to Germany. It was another strain on neutrality.

By the summer of 1916, the United States had started preparing for a possible intervention. But the 1916 election campaign was run under a pacifist banner. "He kept us out of war" was the Democratic slogan, to win over a large segment of the electorate, and Wilson won the hard-fought election.

America goes to war

In January 1917, German commanders decided that further waiting was futile since in any case the Americans had sided with the Allies. On February 1, 1917, the Germans announced unlimited submarine warfare, betting that they could win before the Americans became involved.

Diplomatic relations with Germany were cut off and in March the White House revealed the contents of a recently intercepted telegram: German minister Arthur Zimmerman had suggested to Mexico that it take up arms against the United States if the latter entered into war with Germany. In return, Mexico would be granted the territories of New Mexico, Texas and Arizona. Anti-German sentiment grew. The Mexican situation had been causing a furor for several years. Between 1914 and 1917, Wilson's attitude and policies had dragged out the civil war there. His moral diplomacy had been a total failure. His constant, futile search for the best democratic regime for Mexico foundered on the rocks of Mexican nationalism and its complexities. The Carranza government was fully recognized only in March 1917.

On April 2, 1917, Wilson stood before Congress to ask for a declaration of war against Germany in the name of the survival of democracy. Wilson's decision was partly motivated by the collapse of the Tsarist regime in Russia, since it was now possible to talk about a conflict fought in the name of democracy.

The United States went to war as an associate power, meaning that it was not in complete agreement with the Allies. Wilson wanted to participate in the war as an armed mediator to promote a new order. The Americans entered the war at the right time for the Allies. The Russian debacle had taken pressure off the eastern front, and the Germans could now concentrate their forces in the west. The submarine offensive was effective and the French and British were exhausted. The Americans were not ready, however; troops had to be recruited, trained, equipped, transported and deployed in Europe. They resorted to conscription: 2.8 million men were drafted and another 2 million volunteered. Starting in spring 1918, around 200,000 Americans arrived in Europe. Their weight would be enough to stem the Germans' final offences, and by November 1918 the war was over. The Americans had lost 52,000 men in combat and another 60,000 in the camps to Spanish flu, pneumonia and other diseases.

The effort was total. On the home front, the federal government set up agencies that effectively allocated raw materials and regulated labour. They mediated disputes between management and labour organizations, which were able to swell their ranks by loyally supporting the war effort, but radicals were hounded. The Espionage Act (1917) was used to crush

Posters from the First World War. Women played an increasing role in war production and in backing up the military, and Uncle Sam exhorted the people to buy War Bonds to help finance the war effort. (Library of Congress)

the Wobblies (Industrial Workers of the World). Companies reaped significant profits, which tripled between 1914 and 1919. Prosperity gave opportunities to the blacks who were flocking to the North as well as serving in the armed forces, yet racial tensions were greatly exacerbated by the war. In the armed forces, relations were difficult and treatment was discriminatory. Anti-black riots and lynchings were frequent in the South and the North.

The war shook up American society enormously. Women benefited from the war by entering the workforce or getting better jobs. Thousands of women also did volunteer work. Women became aware that they had to take more radical action. Taking the British suffragettes as a model, they demanded a constitutional amendment, which Wilson supported in 1917 as a war measure. In August 1920, the required states (75 percent) had ratified the Nineteenth Amendment. Neither the states nor the federal government could now deny women the right to vote.

One of the paradoxes of the United States' war experience is that a crusade to defeat German totalitarianism and promote democracy turned into a violation of civil rights and a suppression of freedom of speech at home. Radicals, critics of all stripes and Germans were persecuted. The socialist and unionist Eugene Debs was locked up for thirty-six months for a speech he had given defending the pacifist protesters. Even the Supreme Court joined the backlash.

Charting a new world order
In January 1919, President Wilson met with the leaders of the victorious powers in Paris to set the conditions of peace. Wilson had talked of peace without victory, the need to establish a fairer international order and open agreements. During the war, he had sent his advisor, Colonel Edward House, to meet with the warring parties. He had set up the Inquiry, a team of experts to advise him on the peace negotiations. There was no doubt about Wilson's good intentions and, of all the heads of state at the time, none seemed to have his authority, and American power added to his prestige.

The establishment of the League of Nations, the plan for international cooperation and peace through arbitration and Wilson's proposals for security and disarmament raised hopes all over the world and left the German government confident a solution for peace would be found that was fair and equitable for all. But the political leaders of France, Great Britain and Italy were not overly enthusiastic about Wilson's plans and were dead set on making the Germans pay.

American public opinion was not in favour of Wilson's involvement; people wanted him to settle domestic problems before fixing the evils of the entire world. The first American president to cross the Atlantic while in office, he went on a triumphant tour of Europe. Wildly cheering crowds greeted the new saviour, who took the approbation to heart. He thought he could control Georges Clémenceau (France), David Lloyd George (Britain) and Vittorio Orlando (Italy) by appealing to the people.

Right at the start, one of Wilson's ideals fell by the wayside. The defeated countries would not be participating. Wilson had rejected a hegemonic peace. What was the meaning of this meeting of the victors' club to which the defeated countries were invited only to sign the treaty?

Despite the early hitch, talks began on the basis of President Wilson's Fourteen Points. Negotiations would be long and tricky because of the personal ideas of each head of state, territorial ambitions, the difficulty of applying Wilson's broad, vague principles, France's desire for guarantees and Franco-British concerns in the Middle East. Wilson was at a disadvantage because of the complexity of the issues. His mediator's task was almost impossible when the three other leaders had their own interests to defend. How could he explain to the French, for example, that they should accept the German standpoint because a new era was beginning in which Germany would have its place. Old ways of thinking die hard. Wilson did not have the same list of priorities as his European counterparts. To Clémenceau, for example, German borders were central to the negotiations, preoccupied as the French statesman was with his country's security.

The defeated would have to pay reparations, which should only cover damage inflicted on Allied civilians and their property, but England and France went further. Germany ought to pay all war expenses, including the costs of demobilizing their combatants and pensions for their families. To justify the reparation payments, article 231 was added to the treaty. It stipulated that the Reich bore liability for all damages sustained by the Allied and associated governments and their nationals. Article 231 forced Germany to take full responsibility for the war.

Disarmament was applied only to Germany. Conscription was abolished and the army reduced to a hundred thousand men. It could not have any tanks, heavy artillery, a fleet or war planes. Wilson considered it the first step in a general disarmament, which, of course, never happened.

Wilson worked hard. But while these matters were being settled, he returned to the United States for a few weeks and it was his faithful advisor, Colonel House, who yielded on every point. When the president returned to Europe, he was quite simply flabbergasted by the outcome. He would never forgive House his "betrayal."

Wilson focused on one key project, the League of Nations. The charter's central paragraph, article 10, provided guarantees of collective security.

On May 7, representatives of the Allied powers handed over the treaty drafted in Paris to the Germans. The head of the German delegation read it and declared that it did not comply with the principles laid out in Wilson's "fourteen points" speech, but he had no choice but to sign.

Wilson returned home in July 1919 with the Treaty of Versailles in hand. He firmly believed that the treaty would quickly be approved by the Senate, and the press and public opinion seemed to be behind him. But a few senators who were needed to approve the treaty had already expressed their reservations in March. Then there were the changes proposed by opponents headed by Republican senator Henry Cabot Lodge. Some hard-liners wanted the U.S. to reject the pact. In all the commotion, Wilson rejected any compromise and instructed the Democratic senators to follow the party line.

In September 1919, battling the fatigue caused by the interminable travails in Paris, the president undertook a nationwide campaign to explain the treaty's benefits. Near the end of his trip, Wilson collapsed from a massive stroke. For two months, he was incapable of fulfilling his duties as president. He could not make the necessary compromises to get the treaty passed so the country could join the League of Nations.

Why were Wilson's foes so opposed to article 10, which could have led the United States to guarantee collective security? And why was Wilson so against any changes? Here lay the heart of the debate in American foreign policy: collective security versus the unilateralism advocated by the elder statesmen of the Republican Party. Americans preferred their traditional freedom and non-alignment to a commitment to collective security. Wilson had failed to reform foreign policy.

CHAPTER 9

THE ROARING TWENTIES TO THE NEW DEAL

1920-1939

America's massive intervention in 1917 was a deciding factor in the outcome of the First World War and consolidated the hegemony of the United States, the only country to emerge from the war stronger economically. After the inevitable restructuring difficulties after 1918, American industrial production quickly resumed and national wealth grew. That wealth, combined with political conservatism, would set the tone for the 1920s, which are traditionally associated with prosperity, prohibition and the fecklessness of a large part of the population, drunk on consumption and speculation.

Some aspects of American development during this period seemed to indicate that a new society was being built. For the first time in American history, most of the population was now urban; a new popular culture was emerging thanks to the emerging mass media and the entertainment industry; and economic expansion allowed management to reorganize production while worker salaries increased. The prosperity was an illusion, however, since wealth and income were poorly distributed. Some industries were hit hard by unemployment, and farmers went through some very lean years. As usual, blacks suffered more than whites. Race relations were tense and many episodes of intolerance tarnished the period, which came to a close with the economic collapse of 1929, an abrupt end to the decade's grand illusions.

When in March 1933 Franklin Delano Roosevelt took office, to remain there until 1945, the United States was in the depths of the Depression. Millions were unemployed, factories lay dormant, thousands of banks were closing their doors and "Hoovervilles" (shantytowns) were springing up all over. Roosevelt promised a New Deal, but his program was vague, and since he had the upper hand he did not make too many promises. The genius of F.D. Roosevelt lay in understanding that citizens' morale needed boosting more than anything, given that economics are inseparable from psychology. Americans expected vigorous action from the authorities. The New Deal, Roosevelt's highly personal initiative, would provide it.

The New Deal has traditionally been divided into two broad periods: the first, from 1933 to 1935, during which the government dealt with the most urgent matters, and the second (1935–1937), characterized more by social programs and the adoption of more Keynesian measures. This divide seems extremely arbitrary given that much of the so-called First New Deal took place during the second phase, which was also much less Keynesian than is commonly claimed. Roosevelt was rather reluctant to use deficit spending to rally the economy and hastened to rebalance the budget as quickly as possible whenever the situation improved a little. By doing so, he triggered the recession of 1937.

Central to the New Deal was Roosevelt's willingness to intervene and to experiment, and his great political savvy kept the program focused on its goals. It was thanks to him that the First Hundred Days were a success and the fifteen legislative measures that marked this phase of the New Deal, and at least partially restored confidence, were signed into law. It was also thanks to Roosevelt, who wanted to steal a march on radicals advocating miracle solutions, that the measures of the Second New Deal were passed in the run-up to the 1936 election. Roosevelt became the driving force behind the broad Democratic coalition that would throw its political weight around for decades.

In spite of popular support and early successes, opposition re-emerged once the worst was over. Hard-line Republicans, conservative Democrats and big business accused Roosevelt of leading the country down the path of socialism. The Supreme Court itself led the charge against a variety of measures. Opposition intensified from the far right and the far left, but nothing stopped the president from being triumphantly re-elected in 1936. However, after the battle over the makeup of the Supreme Court (Roosevelt had wanted to neutralize conservative judges by expanding the court), the 1937 recession and the election of a much more conservative Congress in 1938, the New Deal's impact waned. As of 1939, foreign policy problems became more pressing, and while the New Deal had an undeniable psychological, political and social impact, from an economic standpoint the results were more modest. In 1939, the United States still numbered over 9 million unemployed, the gross national product had barely reached 1929 levels and investment, which had ballooned to $9.5 billion annually between 1925 and 1929, hovered around $2 billion between 1935 and 1939.

Clearly, war-related production was what rallied the American economy from 1940 on. While the New Deal had mixed results, it holds pride of place in the American political experience. It restored confidence in capitalism and modernized the country's economic, social and political structures, and its innovations were on the whole retained by subsequent administrations. It rebuilt the presidency and redefined the role and responsibilities of the central government, which would become a major player in the American effort during the Second World War.

The Twenties

The 1920s are not immune to the mixed reviews given to euphoric periods once the illusions have faded. It is important to go beyond simplistic descriptions and see the 1920s in the continuum of American history. Demographics were a significant feature. Population growth was strong but slowing down. Birth rates were dropping due to prosperity and urbanization. The majority of Americans now lived in cities. Large companies continued to dominate economic life, leaving their imprint on the new mass culture. One major shift was in immigration. Mass immigration from Europe ended during the decade. Quotas set in 1921 and 1924 meant that the disruptive masses of foreigners would no longer be welcomed. Yet the country was as ethnically diverse as it is now.

The decade of prosperity did not exactly start that way. In 1919, Americans were more preoccupied with social unrest and the rising cost of living than the results of the Paris negotiations. The relative labour peace of 1917 and 1918 was shattered after the armistice. Wage gains were wiped out by rising prices. Government curbs on industry were lifted, anti-unionism made a comeback and workers walked off the job. The return of soldiers to the job market without proper planning threw workers' lives into turmoil. Four million workers went on strike in 1919, the highest proportion of labour (20 percent) in the history of the United States. The Boston police, textile workers and 400,000 miners went on strike. Three hundred thousand steel workers were forced to give in to strike breakers, armed guards and public opinion, which saw them as no better than Bolshevik revolutionaries, the great obsession of management and the government.

It is easy to understand the idea of a "return to normalcy" appealing to voters weary of war, unrest and inflation. This was the hollow slogan used by the Republican presidential candidate Warren G. Harding (1868–1923) in 1920. There never was a return to normalcy, but Harding won a landslide victory with 16 million votes versus 9 million for the Democrat, James M. Cox.

The economy booms

In 1920, with the war over and other countries struggling to recover, overseas sales and industrial production dropped. Unemployment reached 12 percent in 1921, and the crisis lasted until 1922. Farmers bore the brunt. There were a hundred thousand bankruptcies and 450,000 farmers lost their farms. Farmers' incomes dropped by half. Industries such as mining and textiles were hit hard. New energy sources and new technologies threw the economy into turmoil.

The recovery began in 1922 and lasted until 1929. During this flush period, gross national product rose from $75 billion to $104 billion and national income from $59.4 billion to $87.2 billion. Prices were relatively stable throughout the period, which meant that gains were real. Real individual income rose from $522 to $716 per year. Real income per worker was $1,800 in 1929, an increase of $500 over the period. These advances were due to productivity gains. In manufacturing, the workforce remained constant and working hours fell but production increased by 30 percent. Wages rose by 8 percent. Manufacturers obviously benefited from improved profit margins.

The economy appeared in good health, but overall statistics do not tell the whole story. Income was poorly distributed. The poverty threshold was $1,500 annual income in 1929 and 42 percent of families lived on less. By the end of the period, many could not afford the consumer durables produced by the factories and sold through advertising that was becoming ubiquitous. Cars, refrigerators, radios and vacuum cleaners were increasingly purchased on credit. By 1923, 80 percent of the 3.5 million cars sold in the United States were bought on credit.

The crisis of 1929 might make the advances of the earlier period seem trivial, but there was in fact genuine progress. Wages had risen but profits had ballooned by 62 percent and dividends by 65 percent. Business mergers were going full steam ahead despite legislation. During the decade, 8,000 industrial businesses went under and the holdings of the 200 largest non-financial companies rose from $43 billion to $81 billion between 1919 and 1929. Financiers and bankers were more numerous and prosperous than ever. Bank capital rose from $47 billion to $72 billion from 1919 to 1929, and 250 banks (1 percent) controlled 46 percent of all banking assets. Deposits increased from $13 billion to $28 billion. Insurance companies tripled in value.

Prosperity meant that businesses had more capital at their disposal to invest. Banks began lending money to speculators. In 1929, out of the $14 billion in loans granted by the banks, $8 billion went to stockbrokers.

Labour

Workers were somewhat less successful. After the crackdown on strikers in 1919–1920, workers were invited to share in the benefits of benevolent capitalism. These were very hard times for the union movement. While the workforce grew from 42 million to 49 million, the number of union members fell from 5 million to 4 million. Workers were encouraged to invest in companies. Insurance, medical care and leisure were increasing, but workers were still at the mercy of unemployment, long working hours and poor working conditions in the factories. Employers launched a union-busting campaign known as the American Plan. They advocated an open shop to which all workers, union or otherwise, would have access, and they set up employer-controlled company unions. All this was done with the blessing of federal authorities and the Supreme Court.

Politics

The American electorate as a whole felt that prosperity was a Republican achievement, and the party was repeatedly re-elected. Harding raised the tariff, lowered taxes, especially for the rich, and encouraged business. In 1926, a taxpayer making a million dollars paid less than a third of 1921 taxes. Harding had risen to his level of incompetence and surrounded himself with corrupt administrators and sycophants who exploited the system. The end of his presidency was marred by repeated scandals, but

Harding himself escaped censure, dying of a stroke or heart attack in 1923.

Vice president Calvin Coolidge (1872–1933) succeeded Harding, and he was such a contrast with the previous president that in 1924 he was returned to office. He was self-effacing, reticent and honest and promised to do as little as possible to affect the ongoing prosperity. Coolidge believed it was enough to avoid the "big problems." That is what he did until 1928, when he announced he would not be running again.

Herbert Hoover (1874–1964) ran for the Republicans. A millionaire engineer and former head of European relief, Hoover was a different breed from his predecessors. His presidency would crash and burn with the Depression, but in 1928 he wore the halo of Republican prosperity and was handily elected over Al Smith, a Catholic Democrat from New York City. The election illustrated the tensions and conflicts running through American society in the 1920s: tensions with immigrants and with Catholics, conflict between advocates and opponents of Prohibition, and discord between urban mass culture and traditional culture.

Repression and intolerance

The war had encouraged a rise in intolerance. The Bolshevik revolution, which many feared would engulf the world, fuelled it further. The period of anti-communism from about 1917 to 1920 – the first Red Scare – targeted union members, socialists, anarchists and foreigners. In reality, the American left was weak and fragmented. As early as 1918, the Alien Act authorized the government to deport any immigrant who was or had been a member of a revolutionary organization. In June 1919, a series of bombings in eight cities left two dead and damaged the home of the attorney general, A. Mitchell Palmer. Another bomb, set off in Wall Street in 1920, killed 38 and injured 300. Thousands of people, including non-communist American citizens, were arrested in a series of raids by federal and state security forces and close to a thousand were deported. No evidence was ever found of any grand conspiracy, but a permanent blot had been left on constitutional rights protection. Intolerance had once again been backed by the government. By the 1920s the worst excesses of the Red Scare had been calmed.

The most extreme expression of intolerance in the 1920s was the resurgence of the Ku Klux Klan. Formally re-established in 1915 by an Atlanta insurance agent who wanted to purify Southern culture, the Klan used the new advertising techniques to recruit members. By 1923 they numbered 5 million. While the Klan adopted the clothing and rituals of an earlier incarnation of the group, its activities were much more extensive. They were against blacks, certainly, but also against Catholics, Jews, immigrants and advocates of the theory of evolution – in short, anyone who the Klan felt did not conform to Puritan morality and was not American, white and Protestant. The Klan had widespread influence in the Southwest, Midwest and West, but leadership scandals led to its decline in the 1930s.

People nostalgic for a Puritan America were also prominent in the struggle against alcohol consumption and in favour of laws restricting immigration to the United States. The two movements were not new, but they culminated right at the point when America was undergoing rapid change and drew much grassroots support.

In 1925, the fundamentalists were notoriously involved in the famous Scopes Monkey Trial, which involved a teacher who had taught the theory of evolution. John T. Scopes was convicted but William Jennings Bryan, counsel for the prosecution, was called to testify as an expert on evolution. He was humiliated by Clarence Darrow, the defence counsel, who got him to admit his uncritical fundamentalist beliefs. Typical for the 1920s, the audience was nationwide since the trial was broadcast on radio.

Blacks continued migrating to the industrial cities. Nearly a million and a half relocated during the decade. The black population of cities such as New York, Detroit and Chicago doubled. Blacks lived in hard-to-escape urban ghettos and were frequently the victims of threats and violence, but they had grown more militant. Many had returned from the war changed people. In the cities, they became aware of their culture and the need for collective action. It was the time of the Harlem Renaissance, and for years the African-American intelligentsia as well as many foreigners flocked to the black neighbourhood in New York. Harlem in the 1920s was home to the famous Cotton Club, where the jazz greats performed but blacks were not allowed in as spectators. Controlled by organized crime, the cabaret presented the best jazz shows, sold prohibited alcohol and projected an image of the good life in the fast lane.

Thousands of blacks joined associations, the most influential of which in the 1920s was Marcus Garvey's Universal Negro Improvement Association and African Communities League, founded in 1914. Garvey

(1887–1940) preached pride and advocated black capitalism. He recruited hundreds of thousands of members, but his movement splintered after the failure of one of his businesses and the authorities' campaign to imprison ten of its leaders. Garvey himself was convicted of postal fraud and deported. Another association set up in 1909, the National Association for the Advancement of Colored People, progressed more slowly, numbering 90,000 members in the 1920s, but was effective in its legal actions.

Rise of mass culture

The American appetite for pleasure seemed insatiable. The automobile, radio, movies and advertising contributed significantly to the standardization of mass culture. The cultural developments that characterized the decade were rooted in the cities and the burgeoning suburbs, but rural life was not immune; the automobile brought farmers together and ended their isolation. Life, work and entertainment were all transformed by the automobile. During the decade, the number of cars on American roads rose from 8 million to 25 million. In 1929 alone, 4.8 million cars were produced. One rolled off the Ford assembly line every ten seconds, and the price was more and more affordable. Even Ford employees could sometimes afford one; its $300 price tag was equivalent to three months' wages for the best-paid workers. The automobile opened up the world and increased the possibilities for leisure.

Radio was called "an instrument of beauty and learning" by Herbert Hoover, then secretary of commerce, and Americans embraced the new medium. In 1924, 5 million homes had at least one set. In 1929, a third of all households had a radio, and 80 percent of people listened to it daily. Programming was essentially the same in the city and the country: music, sports commentary and dramas, and regular news bulletins. Networks were founded, NBC in 1926 and CBS in 1928. The first truly national hit was the Amos 'n' Andy Show (1928), created by two white men from Chicago who spoke in "black" voices. Radio created a national audience of listeners to rival the national audience of moviegoers.

During the 1920s, the already thriving movie industry got a significant boost when it moved to Hollywood so that movies could be shot all year round. Studios set up there and produced bigger movies with higher budgets. They established the star system, and the studios controlled the production, distribution and projection of movies in hundreds of studio-controlled theatres. The advent of "talkies" in 1927 caused a sensation and had an effect on consumers equally as dramatic as the introduction of radio. Between 1926 and 1930, the number of moviegoers doubled, from 50 million to 100 million a week. The most popular productions were epics such as *The Ten Commandments* (1923) by Cecil B. DeMille, tear-jerkers such as *The Beautiful Sinner* (1924) and the comedies of Buster Keaton, Charlie Chaplin and Fatty Arbuckle.

A cult of celebrity took hold, reinforced by the Hollywood publicity machine. Stars became integral to the fantasy lives of millions of fans, and studio publicity and magazines encouraged the obsession. Many people became concerned about movies' corrupting influence on morals, especially sexual ones. Movie censorship was called for, and various states set up monitoring boards. The situation heated up when Fatty Arbuckle, a major star, was charged with the rape and murder of a starlet during what was perceived as an orgy. Arbuckle was acquitted but the studios were concerned enough to impose self-censorship. They hired Will Hays, a Protestant Republican with a spotless record, to clean up the industry. It was the beginning of a system that would last until 1966. The Hays Code, developed in 1927, laid out what was and was not acceptable on screen. Right-thinking America had resisted and the industry had adapted.

Movie stars, radio personalities, sports heroes and popular musicians became the touchstones of a new, media-defined culture of celebrity. Footage exists today of Charles Lindbergh's arrival in Paris after his trans-Atlantic solo flight, Jack Dempsey's fights and Babe Ruth's home runs. Even the gangsters Al Capone and Baby Face Nelson became celebrities.

The most earnest cultural debate of the 1920s was certainly over Prohibition, which defined the period. The Eighteenth Amendment, which took effect in January 1920, and the associated Volstead Act (National Prohibition Act) of 1919 banned the manufacture, sale and transportation of alcohol.

Prohibition was doomed. Despite what progressives believed, legislating personal morality could not make people virtuous. Speakeasies cropped up by the thousands in large cities such as New York, Chicago and Detroit. Some manufactured their own alcohol while others were supplied by bootleggers linked to organized crime, already well established in

While Prohibition of alcoholic beverages had long been the law in some places, it became the law of the whole U.S.A. with the Volstead Act and the Eighteenth Amendment of 1919. The Temperance movement sprang in part from religious beliefs and in part from the social damage that excess drinking inflicted. Nationwide Prohibition was repealed in 1933 but continued locally long after. This cartoon appeared in *Stars and Stripes*, the newspaper of the American military in France, January 24, 1919. (Library of Congress)

the cities. After 1925, Prohibition was a failure in the cities, where people's urge for personal freedom was too great for enforcement to be effective. Once its failure was recognized, there was no choice but constitutional amendment, though the defeat of Al Smith, the anti-Prohibition, Catholic Democratic candidate, in the 1928 election showed just how strong was the resistance in the conflict pitting wets against drys. The Depression accelerated the process, and in December 1933 the Twenty-first Amendment was passed, repealing the Eighteenth, after the issue had again been an issue in the 1932 election campaign.

The uniformity of mass culture, especially when driven by businessmen, alienated many artists and intellectuals. Many of them had been disillusioned by the horrors of the war and America's vulgar materialism. Some emigrated to Europe, either temporarily or permanently. Writers began producing a national literature more critical of American society; Sinclair Lewis, Theodore Dreiser, John Dos Passos, F. Scott Fitzgerald, Ernest Hemingway, Eugene O'Neill and William Faulkner were among the leading figures.

The Great Depression

The prosperity of the 1920s had been sustained in the decade's final years by a speculative frenzy that took the country by storm. Not everyone played the stock market. In fact, it is estimated that four million Americans held shares and that a million and a half very actively speculated. Yet everyone talked about it. People were drawn to the stock market because of the constantly rising share prices and the easy credit. Optimism blinded people to the signs that foreshadowed the crisis.

Beginning in 1926, the large construction and automobile industries experienced slowdowns and, as of 1927, Americans were spending far less on consumer durables. The Florida real estate boom that crashed in 1926 could have been instructive and served as a warning of what happens when speculation loses all contact with reality. There had, however, been many legitimate reasons for the rise in land prices and population in Florida after 1920, among them the sunny climate, the mobility provided by the automobile and the general prosperity that accompanied American industrial development. Advertising campaigns full of bizarre, far-fetched claims began appearing. Land prices skyrocketed. Speculation was unchecked. Purchase options on swampland were bought to be sold as quickly as possible. The bubble burst when two consecutive hurricanes struck Florida. Prices collapsed. In 1928, thirty-one Florida banks failed and the following year fifty-seven went under.

The stock market frenzy began in 1928. Industrial shares rose 25 percent. How could people resist speculating when their neighbour who had bought General Motors at 99 points in 1925 had sold it at 212 points in 1928? In September 1929, shares reached their high point. Yet October 29 was the culmination of week after week of market uncertainty. On the twenty-third, the Dow Jones Index lost 21 points in an hour. On the twenty-eighth, it lost 38 points, or 13 percent of its value. The next day, Black Tuesday, 16 million shares were traded. Panic set in. Many shares could not find buyers at any price. In two weeks, $30 billion worth of value evaporated. Speculators had bought on margin (i.e., on credit); their brokers, squeezed by the banks, forced them to sell stock that was now worth far less. The stock market crisis had a domino effect.

For a while, the banks managed to stay in control. The authorities remained upbeat. No one mentioned a depression. Hoover, elected president in 1928, was reassuring. Andrew Mellon, the treasury secretary, claimed that the system would undergo a healthy correction – crises were an inevitable part of life. The *New York Times* preached patience, caution and thrift. But the stock market crisis led to a depression due to imbalances in the American economy. Wealth and income were poorly distributed. In 1929, out of 27.5 million families, 21.5 million had no savings. Thirty-six thousand wealthy families had income equal to that of 42 percent of the population and held a good third of national wealth. Many people could not buy what they needed, especially since manufacturers had cut production and laid off workers. The banks, whose assets were heavily invested in stock loans, could no longer repay worried depositors their savings. Prices collapsed and farmers, who were already in deep trouble, were hit hard.

The impact was as intense as the earlier optimism had been. The whole of American life was affected. In 1933, business volume was half 1929 levels. National income fell from $85 billion to $37 billion. Five thousand banks closed. Prices dropped by 33 percent and production by 50 percent. Unemployment became a scourge, with 6 million out of work in 1930 and 15 million in 1933. This was 25 percent of the work force. Total wages paid fell from $12 billion to $7 billion between 1929 and 1933. At a time when there was virtually no social safety net, the effect was devastating. In New York, Sidney Hillman of the Amalgamated Clothing Workers of America estimated that only 10 percent of his members had jobs. At Ford, the workforce fell from 128,000 to 37,000 in sixteen months. The plight of one-industry towns was often even bleaker. In Donora, Pennsylvania, only 277 out of 13,900 workers were employed.

At first, the stock market crisis was a distant event for the majority of Americans. Most had not invested in the stock market. Yet their lives were transformed, slowly at first then much more quickly. The psychological impact was considerable. People had been conditioned to accept responsibity for whatever happened to them. Many in the middle class who had benefited from white-collar expansion saw their dreams collapse. The jobless were plagued by shame and guilt.

The crisis was deeper than anything that had come before. Despair was widespread. Soup kitchens could not meet demand. People slept in the gutters of Oakland and foraged for food in Chicago dumps or in the garbage outside New York restaurants. Shantytowns of cardboard houses sprang up in inner cities. When a little girl who complained of hunger was told by her teacher to go home and eat, she replied that she could not because "it's my sister's turn to eat." Resources to handle the crisis were inadequate; cities, private charities and counties were overwhelmed.

President Hoover has often been accused of being a puppet of Wall Street and of doing nothing. Granted, his approach to the problem of unemployment was standard: he did not want to involve the federal government, turning instead to states, cities and private organizations. But as was traditional, he made some efforts to bail out the business community. For example, he set up the Reconstruction Finance Company that approved loans to troubled banks, industries and railroads. Yet it was too little and was perceived as inaction. Public opinion turned against him, especially after the incident of the Bonus Army. Veterans of the First World War were demanding early payment of a promised bonus. Twenty thousand of them camped out in Washington for more than a month in 1932. Their demands were not met, but many did accept compensation for their trip home. However, the remaining 2,000 were ousted under orders from General Douglas MacArthur assisted by Dwight D. Eisenhower and George Patton. The heroes of 1918 were driven away with bayonets and tear gas, their makeshift encampments burned or razed. Two veterans were fatally shot.

Hoover left office a hated and ridiculed man. He was roundly defeated by Franklin Delano Roosevelt (1882–1945), who had promised a New Deal for the American people. Exactly what was new was unclear; that it was new was enough.

The New Deal

Any Democratic candidate could probably have beaten Hoover in 1932. The election was less a victory for Roosevelt than a rejection of Hoover. During the election campaign, both parties had seemed more concerned about Prohibition than the crisis. With his political capital, Roosevelt was not overzealous. But if the past was any indication of the future, his personal history inspired confidence. His political career, begun at an early age, was interrupted when he contracted polio in 1921. The disease permanently handicapped him, depriving him of the use of his legs. He overcame the ordeal and in 1928 was elected governor of New York State.

His reputation as a reformer was well deserved, and he took measures against the Depression. With his "Brain Trust" of advisors, some of whom followed him to Washington, he adopted the position of a reformer ready to accept the contemporary reality of big business based on mass production and distribution. The Brain Trust was important, but its influence should not be overestimated since Roosevelt was essentially a pragmatist who would not ignore special interests, party bosses and other pressures.

FDR's central idea was experimentation. He was convinced that bold, aggressive action was required. His genius lay in sensing that what was needed above all was to raise American morale. When he took office on March 4, 1933, he declared that the only thing to fear was fear itself. The next day, he declared a four-day banking "holiday" to allow banks to put their affairs in order. Some banks were solvent, but others were not, setting off a panic among depositors. Congress was called to session on March 9 and the first bill introduced was the Emergency Banking Act, drafted overnight, presented to Congress at noon and passed at 9:00 p.m. Solvent banks were allowed to reopen. More unstable banks were forced to reorganize under government supervision. By mid-March, half the banks, with 90 per cent of deposits, were back in business. On March 12, Roosevelt addressed the nation on the radio in one of the "fireside chats" that became his customary way of explaining his policies. Confidence was restored and the banking crisis was over.

In his First Hundred Days, FDR managed to push fifteen other bills through Congress, all aimed at convincing people that inertia was at an end. This is what is referred to as the First New Deal, a series of emergency measures aimed at reforming an ailing system and alleviating poverty. No time was wasted. The Civilian Conservation Corps mobilized 250,000 young men to work in reforestation and conservation of natural resources for $30 a month, $25 of which had to go to dependents. Two million extra recruits were eventually hired. The Federal Emergency Relief Administration helped states deal with aid demands. The Agricultural Adjustment Act (AAA) was aimed at helping farmers by setting basic prices for the major agricultural products. Subsidies were also granted to reduce planting area and production. The Tennessee Valley Authority was set up as a public body to build dikes and hydroelectric dams, aid in the development of the six Southern states and provide them with cheap electricity. Under the National Industrial Recovery Act (NIRA), codes were established for each industrial sector. These codes were adopted by company representatives, workers and the public. The Public Works Administration allocated a budget of $3.3 billion to put people to work building roads, bridges and public buildings. In all, $4.2 billion was spent by the administration. In thousands of towns and cities across the United States today, buildings and other public works stand witness to this contribution of the New Deal.

While there was no genuine economic recovery, the climate improved. The man in charge inspired confidence, but his results were meagre. There were still 9 million unemployed in 1935. The AAA had an effect on the revenue of larger agricultural operations, but non-property-owning farmers and sharecroppers still lived in poverty. Roosevelt's initiatives were influenced by economic analysts on the one hand and planners on the other. His approach was actually quite traditional: balancing the budget as far as possible and restarting the economy by raising prices through production limits and an increase in purchasing power. His initiatives were necessarily limited by the way they were carried out. How could consulting with NIRA industrialists increase demand? How could prices be raised in a period of such high unemployment? It is also apparent that Roosevelt did not spend enough to revive the stagnant economy.

Resistance – and the Second New Deal
The situation had improved just enough by 1934 for opposition to emerge. A number of radicals and populists of all stripes criticized Roosevelt for his timidity, while conservatives felt he was destroying the American system. On the right, the American Liberty League found support among capitalist industrialists and conservative Democrats, who considered Roosevelt a socialist. That did not prevent the progressive Democrats from increasing their majority in Congress during the 1934 elections. Yet recovery seemed far off and the enthusiasm of 1933 had dwindled. The threat to Roosevelt from the left seemed more serious. The socialist novelist Upton Sinclair managed to win the Democratic nomination during the primaries for the office of California governor. He proposed a $50 per month pension for every person sixty and over. He was narrowly defeated due to a Republican disinformation campaign largely financed by the Hollywood moguls in charge of the big studios. Roosevelt sat idly by. Dr. Francis E. Townsend, a retired Long Beach physician, proposed a

plan to hand out $200 a month to all citizens over sixty. The money would have to be spent the same month. Father Coughlin, the Radio Priest heard by 40 million listeners, was an early supporter of Roosevelt but became impatient with the slow pace of reform. He was against Wall Street and international finance. In 1935 and 1936, he split with Roosevelt to form his own political organization, the short-lived Union Party. After the 1936 elections, which were disastrous for him, he withdrew for a while then returned more vociferous than ever. He denounced Communism, embraced anti-Semitism and drew closer to the fascists.

Huey Long (1893–1935) had been a Louisiana senator since 1931. Before that, he had been the state's governor, carrying out major, popular reforms. He had national ambitions. At first a supporter of the New Deal, he turned against the program in 1934. He started a movement, Share our Wealth ($5,000 in property and $2,500 income for everyone), that drew followers. A secret poll shocked the Democratic leadership in summer 1935: Long had garnered three to four million votes. A rabble-rouser who ran Louisiana like a despot, he was assassinated in 1935, preventing him from running for a third party that could have harmed Roosevelt.

The popularity of all these radicals and firebrands was evidence of a widespread dissatisfaction that Roosevelt, savvy politician that he was, could hardly have missed. The Second New Deal, his response to the dissatisfaction, was designed to undercut the malcontents. But there was more to the Second New Deal than political tactics, since the proposed measures had been on the drawing board for some time. Roosevelt picked up the pace to ensure his re-election in 1936 but he was taking the same pragmatic approach to problems, just with a little more planning. He was still after solutions.

The labour movement put pressure on Roosevelt from the left. At the 1935 convention of the American Federation of Labor (AFL), thirteen resolutions calling for a new party were presented. The previous year there had been only two. The labour movement was emerging from its 1920s dormancy. Bucking tradition, the Depression revived the labour movement. The years 1933 and 1934 were strike-ridden. Strikes were often violent and militant. John L. Lewis (1880–1969) of the United Mine Workers belonged to the AFL at first but felt that the unorganized workers of the mass-production industries (auto, steel, electricity, rubber), neglected by the AFL, represented the future. Along with Sidney Hillman of the Amalgamated Clothing Workers and David Dubinsky of the International Ladies' Garment Workers' Union, he founded the Committee for Industrial Organizations in 1935. These men were expelled from the AFL in 1936 and founded the Congress of Industrial Organizations in 1938. Unions were given a healthy boost in 1935 with the passage of the National Labor Relations Act (Wagner Act) that established workers' right to collective bargaining. The landmark Social Security Act that provided for old-age pensions and unemployment insurance was also adopted in 1935 and helped to make the union movement a major contributor to FDR's decisive 1936 victory.

The unions launched their battle against the anti-union fortress of the steel industry in 1936. In March 1937, industry giant U.S. Steel admitted defeat, and in April 280,000 steel workers were unionized. After their victory in the auto industry with the sit-down strikes of 1936 and the founding of the United Auto Workers (UAW), unionized workers enjoyed enormous early popular support. However, Little Steel (five smaller steel mills, as opposed to Big Steel, or U.S. Steel) decided on a confrontation in April 1937. Employers had hardened their position and the public was up in arms over the constant strikes. Sit-down strikes against Little Steel involved 400,000 workers. Auto-industry holdout Ford resisted the UAW, as Westinghouse, Maytag and International Harvester defied other unions. On May 30, 1937, outside the Republic Steel facilities in Chicago, the conflict turned to violence in what became known as the Memorial Day Massacre. Private guards, armed to the teeth, fired on the demonstrators. Ten were killed, including seven shot in the back, and eighty injured, thirty by gunshot. The violence escalated, and altogether eighteen workers died in summer 1937.

Roosevelt was under pressure to get involved, but he was in an impossible situation. He could no more sanction the companies and their violence than the instability caused by labour militancy. Nor could he risk losing the votes of workers, a majority of whom had voted for him in 1936. He played Solomon and criticized both. John L. Lewis would never forgive him his betrayal, but the workers continued to vote for the man they associated, rightly or wrongly, with the progress they had made. Their progress was undeniable: union membership grew from 2.6 million to 8 million between 1932 and 1940, and wages and working conditions improved. Workers also benefited from progressive laws, including the

Fair Labor Standards Act (1938) that set a minimum wage and established the forty-four-hour week.

Meanwhile, the conservative-dominated Supreme Court tackled major New Deal legislation, declaring the National Industrial Recovery Act and the Agricultural Adjustment Act unconstitutional. Elated by his historic landslide in 1936 (61 percent of the popular vote, every state but two in the Electoral College), a result of the New Deal coalition that would ensure Democratic dominance for decades (Southern Democrats, immigrants, urban political organizations, workers, farmers and blacks), Roosevelt went into action against the bastion of conservatism that was the Supreme Court. He planned to increase the number of seats from nine to fifteen by obtaining the authority to appoint an additional judge for every judge over the age of seventy who had not retired. The plan was condemned from all sides and Roosevelt alienated Congress. The confrontation was probably self-defeating, since the majority of judges had already begun modifying their decisions and Roosevelt was soon able to appoint new ones. The Social Security Act and the National Labor Relations Act were deemed constitutional. The crisis was over; the judges had got the message and FDR could appoint men to the bench, but he had lost politically.

Roosevelt himself often weakened the New Deal's effectiveness through his muddled priorities regarding his administration's different policies, his desire to be everything to everybody and his manipulative tactics. In 1936, FDR, who remained a conservative when it came to public finances, came around to the opinion of his treasury secretary and others that the private sector was now strong enough to stand on its own. Against the advice of the Keynesians, who wanted to continue priming the economic pump with federal money, he set about balancing the budget in the short term. The Roosevelt Recession followed and would be corrected in 1938 only by a massive infusion of federal money into the system.

In the 1938 elections, a more conservative Congress was elected and the New Deal went on the defensive. Its creative phase was over. As of 1939, foreign policy problems dominated the government's agenda.

The New Deal in retrospect

It has now become commonplace to claim that the New Deal was no revolution and did not really defuse the crisis. It did not do everything its admirers claimed or its enemies feared. It did not fragment big business or overturn capitalism. Instead it saved it by giving it another face: capitalism, but moderate, state-supervised capitalism. What is striking about Roosevelt and the New Deal was the willingness to explore different avenues when no one had any real idea what to do. The power and image of the presidency emerged genuinely transformed. Roosevelt's has become the standard by which all great presidencies are measured; his contribution was to establish a solid power base for the federal government, which would become a force in the lives of all Americans.

The national income was only $72.8 billion in 1939 compared to $87.6 billion in 1929. Unemployment still fluctuated around 16.5 percent of workers. Blacks were no more integrated than before and were the greatest victims of the Depression. Unionized workers had made remarkable gains, but much remained to be done. It would take another world war for the country to fully recover from the crisis and return to prosperity. The stimulus of massive war spending would bring American potential to its full flower.

CHAPTER 10

THE SECOND WORLD WAR AND THE RISE TO SUPERPOWER STATUS

Since the end of the First World War, Americans had become disillusioned, watching the escalation of international threats cautiously and from afar. Yet despite what is often claimed, the 1920 election was not a referendum rejecting the League of Nations, and while the United States was not, strictly speaking, isolationist from 1920 to 1940, the great majority of the population was undeniably against any commitment and prepared for almost any concessions to uphold the country's right to remain neutral. The country was naturally apprehensive about the illegal use of force by Axis powers in Europe and Asia but held fast to its anything-but-war policy. It basked in the illusion that it could choose if and when to get involved abroad. Its isolationism had to do with a climate of apathy toward Europe and the rest of the world that could only be dangerous. H.G. Wells had harsh words for the American eagle with the rear end of an ostrich.

Foreign policy after the First World War

During the 1920s, American leaders still had an interest in the outside world. The Republican administrations practised a conservative internationalism geared toward protecting and expanding American interests internationally. Close cooperation among bankers, businessmen and the government pushed American foreign investment from $3.8 billion to $7.5 billion between 1919 and 1929. The U.S. was active on world markets and established itself as a rising power. It was at the centre of negotiations and treaties to address imbalances in naval power among the great powers, which now included the United States. The same negotiations were aimed at curbing Japanese ambitions in the Pacific.

American initiatives to promote peace and resolve conflicts, including the question of war reparations, also stood out. The idea of outlawing war, included in the Briand-Kellogg Pact (1928) that was signed by over sixty countries, came from an American, James T. Shotwell. The Dawes (1924) and Young (1929) plans were implemented by the Americans to resolve the problem of reparations by restarting the German economy. The Germans could then pay reparations to France and England, which could repay their debts to the Americans.

In 1925, Calvin Coolidge spoke about the United States' "tranquility" at home and abroad. But all this tranquility would be disrupted in the 1930s. Japan, Germany and Italy pursued policies of aggression. In 1931, when the Japanese seized Manchuria, the United States countered by proclaiming the Stimson Doctrine under which territorial gains would not be recognized, but it did not deter Japanese aggression. In 1933, Japan withdrew from the League of Nations.

Roosevelt's foreign policy in the shadow of war

When Roosevelt took office, he had limited experience in international affairs, but his record was one of Wilsonian internationalism. Yet as a pragmatic politician, he did not try to swim against the prevailing isolationist current. During his 1932 campaign, he even renounced the idea of the United States joining the League of Nations. Everyone understood that he was appeasing isolationists such as William Randolph Hearst and his powerful press. Italy, Germany and Japan were far from his mind; it was the domestic situation that monopolized his attention. However, two moves he made signalled that he was breaking off in a new direction. In 1933, he re-established diplomatic relations with the Soviet Union. Recognizing the absurdity of not admitting that the USSR was ruled by a Communist government, he was also attempting to encourage trade and strengthen a bulkhead against Japanese expansion. In Latin America, he maintained the non-interventionist Good Neighbor policy set in motion by Hoover. He effectively nullified his cousin Theodore's Corollary to the Monroe Doctrine (1904) by agreeing in Montevideo in December 1933 that "no state has the right to intervene in the internal or external affairs of another." In 1934, the last American marines were withdrawn from

Haiti and Cuba was freed of the Platt Amendment, which had authorized American intervention in Cuban affairs. American efforts there had served to bring to power Fulgencio Batista, who ruled the island intermittently until the Castro revolution.

The mood remained isolationist throughout the 1930s, particularly after 1934, when the Nye Committee began investigating the munitions industry and the First World War. The committee's findings were grist for the mill of those who saw the 1917 intervention as a mistake caused by the "merchants of death" who had pocketed scandalous profits by dragging Americans into a war in which they had had no stake. In the climate of the Depression, it seemed obvious that the big capitalists were at fault.

Roosevelt's attempt to join the World Court was blocked in 1935. Congress bowed to a campaign orchestrated by Father Coughlin and the Hearst newspapers, and the president was forced to back down. He was also forced to accept the first Neutrality Act (1935), which aimed to protect Americans from the conflicts raging around the world from Europe to Asia to Africa. The act held that when a state of war existed between two foreign countries, an embargo should be imposed on all sales of arms to the warring parties. In October 1935, the law was tested when Mussolini's Italy attacked Ethiopia. Roosevelt refused to apply the oil embargo proposed by the League of Nations, claiming that such a measure was beyond American jurisdiction. His talk of a moral embargo was empty and meaningless.

The Ethiopian Crisis was an important step. It exemplified the incapacity of the great powers to halt aggression, and Berlin and Tokyo watched with interest. Germany began rearming in 1935 and remilitarized the Rhineland in 1936. Hitler sensed that he had nothing to worry about from the United States. When the Spanish Civil War broke out in 1936, Congress passed another Neutrality Act prohibiting the extension of loans or credits to belligerents. Meanwhile, Italy and Germany supplied Franco in what would be a proving ground for the next war.

After outlawing munitions sales and credit to belligerents, the U.S. added to the Neutrality Acts in 1937 by forcing buyers in a state of war to pay for supplies on a cash and carry basis and transport them on their own ships. The limitations of the act were immediately exposed by events in China. In July 1937, war broke out between Japan and China. Despite sympathy for China and the revulsion inspired by the Rape of Nanking, the Americans did nothing. The administration did not invoke the Neutrality

Acts, claiming that to do so would be disadvantageous to China, and furthermore there had been no formal declaration of war between the two countries. Public opinion did not waver, remaining fiercely isolationist.

In October 1937, Roosevelt tested the waters with his "quarantine" speech, in which he seemed to propose concrete actions to isolate states that spread the contagion of war. It was delivered in Chicago, the bastion of isolationist sentiment. The very next day he was forced to backtrack to journalists by admitting that he had no sanctions in mind. He had quickly understood that he had no support. In December 1937, an incident occurred that in other circumstances would have sparked a forceful American response. The *Panay*, a gunboat clearly identified as American, was attacked by Japanese warplanes on China's Yangtze River. The attack left several dead and dozens wounded and the ship was sunk. The American reaction was in stark contrast to its handling of the 1898 explosion of the *Maine*. Everyone called for moderation and accepted Japanese apologies and $2 million in compensation.

Nor did Hitler's policy of aggression provoke a strong reaction by Americans. The annexation of Austria and part of Czechoslovakia in 1938 worried Roosevelt, but he joined in the Anglo-French appeasement. A congratulatory telegram from Roosevelt to Chamberlain said, "Good man." Roosevelt was dealing with a conservative Congress, he had lost face in the Supreme Court battle, another recession was barely over and isolationist sentiment showed no signs of abating. His initiative to write a letter to Hitler and Mussolini, asking them for assurances that they would not invade thirty-one listed countries, was ridiculed by Hitler. But the isolationists applauded heartily.

The Second World War

By September 1939, the situation in Europe had again worsened, and war became a real possibility. Hitler invaded Poland shortly after signing a non-aggression pact with the USSR in August 1939. France and England were under treaty obligation to defend Poland. The Second World War had begun.

FDR's first concern was to invoke American neutrality. Voters had become more interested in international matters and their sympathy lay with the victims of the attacks, but they wanted to avoid getting involved at all costs. Roosevelt wanted to help England and France but the Neutrality Acts were still in effect. In November 1939, he managed to get the arms embargo lifted, but buyers still had to pay cash and carry the arms in their own ships.

After the so-called Phoney War from autumn 1939 to spring 1940, with no significant military operations yet launched in Europe, the Americans were greatly shocked by the French defeat in May and the emergency evacuation of the British Expeditionary Force from Dunkirk. Public opinion shifted. In September 1940, 53 percent of Americans felt that it was more important to help the British against Hitler than to stay out of the conflict. Roosevelt took the initiative to exchange destroyers for strategic British bases. The measure was supported by two thirds of the population. In the November 1940 election, Roosevelt was handily re-elected for a third term against Wendell Willkie, who won only 45 percent of the vote. (FDR was the first president to serve more than two consecutive terms, two terms having been an unwritten limit since Washington declined to serve a third.) During the campaign, Roosevelt had reassured parents that their sons would not be called up to fight on foreign soil. Yet a bill introducing man-

Many in the U.S. opposed involvement in the Second World War, though President Roosevelt did all he could to assist beleaguered Britain. The Japanese attack on the U.S. Navy base at Pearl Harbor and Germany's declaration of war against the U.S. sealed the issue. This cartoon, from the *Detroit Free Press*, May 29, 1941, shows President Roosevelt at the helm of the ship of state, before the U.S. was officially in the war. (Library of Congress)

datory registration for possible conscription of all men between the ages of twenty-one and thirty-five was narrowly passed in September 1941.

There was a battle to win over the citizenry. In December, Roosevelt announced that the United States would have to become the arsenal of democracy. Britain was running out of steam and could no longer pay cash for the supplies it needed. Under a proposed Lend-Lease program, munitions and supplies up to a value of $7 billion would be provided to any country whose defence was vital to the United States (in all, the United States would commit $50 billion to Lend-Lease aid). In March 1941, after heated debate, the bill was passed with the support of the Republicans. The isolationists sensed that the non-interventionist house was collapsing.

The United States was still formally neutral while becoming more and more involved. Secret Anglo-American meetings took place in January and February 1941 to coordinate strategy in the event the United States entered the war. When Hitler turned against the USSR in June, Lend-Lease aid was extended to Stalin. The Battle of the Atlantic was raging. Convoys transported supplies to Europe, enduring attacks from German submarines, and U.S. Navy ships escorting them had been sunk or damaged. In spite of these incidents, and the public's increasingly strong support, the Americans could not bring themselves to actually declare war. Signals were still mixed. In August 1941, Roosevelt requested that selective service, as mandatory registration was called, be extended by an extra eighteen months; the measure was passed by a single-vote majority and the ban on sending soldiers overseas was upheld.

America was in an undeclared war with Germany. Roosevelt confided to a cabinet member that he would prefer to be pushed into the conflict. War matters were decided by Congress, and a favourable vote would require persuasive arguments; the Roosevelt magic had faded.

Roosevelt found the occasion to push the country into war not in the Atlantic but in the Pacific. On December 7, 1941, the Japanese launched a surprise attack on the American base at Pearl Harbor, Hawaii. Japan was allied with Germany and Italy and its expansionist aims had been a source of concern for years. The Japanese had seized French Indochina in July 1941 and the Americans had adopted retaliatory measures that had outraged the Japanese. Negotiations with Japan were taking place in Washington when the attack occurred. The impact was devastating. The Pacific fleet was hit hard and would recover with difficulty. On December

"This is not drill." Telegram from Commander in Chief of the Pacific Fleet to all ships in the area of Hawaii, December 7, 1941. The Japanese attack on Pearl Harbor was one of the greatest military surprises in the history of warfare and a national trauma unmatched until September 11, 2001. (Library of Congress)

8, FDR obtained a war declaration from Congress by a unanimous vote minus one. The sacred alliance had been achieved. Three days later, Germany and Italy declared war on the United States. There are those who claim that Roosevelt conspired to allow the Japanese attack to occur to precipitate the United States into war. Mistakes were certainly made and intelligence misread, but there was no conspiracy to set in motion the events that would cost the United States so dearly for years to come.

America mobilizes

The nation's energies were almost completely mobilized for the war effort, and the primary architect was the central government, which controlled wages and prices, distributed raw materials, rationed consumer goods and, most notably, restarted the economy and brought prosperity through war contracts. Soon everyone was at work. In 1941, 65 million men, women and sometimes children wore a uniform or were employed in the war industry. The experience was life-changing for many and prefigured the later upheavals in American society. The president's authority was greatly expanded by the War Powers Act. He could reorganize the federal government, set up agencies, award contracts and control information.

The war cost $250 million a day. The federal budget increased tenfold. Gross national product grew from $90 billion to $212 billion. The war effort was financed by income taxes: in 1939, 4 million Americans paid income tax whereas 59 million did by the end of the conflict. The government also resorted to victory bonds of $135 billion. Prices were controlled at least partially, as were wages. Full employment had been reached. The war did what the New Deal could only partly achieve.

Production levels reached unprecedented heights. American success in the war was largely due to a relentless capacity to meet its needs better than the enemy without draining its fighting resources. Productivity gains of 25 percent in industry and of 36 percent in agriculture from 1939 to 1945 allowed lofty objectives to be met. Businessmen were called upon and were only too happy to restore their lustre after their Depression-era nosedive in public opinion. Subsidies rained down, war industries were exempted from antitrust legislation and the government awarded contracts on a cost-plus basis – production costs plus a guaranteed profit. Companies invested heavily. To the despair of many New Dealers, Roosevelt followed the advice of his war secretary, Henry Stimson, who believed that when a capitalist country went to war, businesses had to be allowed to make a profit or the enterprise would fail. The Americans produced 300,000 airplanes, 88,000 tanks, 6,500 ships and 15 million rifles, stimulating regions around the country. The West was given a major boost. Los Angeles became the second-largest industrial centre after Detroit. The South was handed most of the boot camps, and its textile industry ran at full capacity to produce the hundreds of millions of uniforms required. Nearly two thirds of all contracts were awarded to the hundred largest companies. Big business, which had dominated before the war, emerged from the international conflict even stronger. The basis of the military-industrial complex, later denounced by Dwight Eisenhower, was being laid.

The 17 million jobs created during the war, as well as union campaigns, pushed the number of unionized workers to 15 million in 1945. There was much union activism. During the recovery just before the war, strike activity had increased. As a result, the United Auto Workers had unionized Ford employees. When the war began, the government was given a non-strike pledge from most union organizations. Yet while wages rose substantially, prices and profits rose faster still. Strikes persisted, and the War Labor Board granted a 15 percent raise as a cost-of-living adjustment. It did not stop John L. Lewis from getting his 500,000 miners to walk off the job in 1943, a confrontation that forced Roosevelt to seize the mines. Lewis still won points for his miners when the owners recovered their mines. Yet most strikes were short-lived, often spontaneous and not ordered by the unions. There were several racist strikes when blacks, and especially black women, were hired for jobs usually reserved for whites.

Life in wartime

The war caused a significant population shift. Sixteen million men and women donned the uniform and "saw the world." There was a great deal of moving around within the United States. Fifteen million Americans changed residences during the war. Blacks found industrial jobs, as did women. Nearly 20 million women were working, including most married women. Black women left domestic work for factory jobs. Family values underwent a transformation. Young people enjoyed more independence. Geographic and social mobility increased. Incomes were higher but rationing made it harder to spend. Savings increased. Government slogans equated thrift with victory.

Housing was hard to find. Rents were high. The economic recovery had led many people to marry, and the war sped up the process. People had to live with rationing, long working hours and domestic worries. Couples were often separated by war and children became a heavier burden. The problem of juvenile delinquency became more acute.

Fighting was taking place on foreign soil, making the war seem a far-off reality. The government tried to raise people's awareness and unite them behind the war effort. The Office of War Information was set up to control information and promote patriotism. Hollywood helped boost the nation's morale. Over a hundred million Americans went to the movies every week, and movies like *Casablanca* (1942) were part of the propaganda. Many features depicted the Soviet Union, now an ally of the United States, in a highly favourable light. *Mission to Moscow* (1943) and *Days of Glory* (1944) belong to a genre of anti-fascist movies that celebrated the friendship between the Americans and the Soviets. Newsreel footage screened in movie theatres kept Americans informed of the war's progress. Some directors began working for the government, producing propaganda films. Hollywood stars also participated by endorsing victory bonds.

The armed forces

Thirty-one million men between the ages of eighteen and forty-four were registered for the draft. Over half the 5 million required to take a medical exam failed. The army recruited over 10 million men and women, the navy 4 million and the marines 600,000. Around 350,000 black and white women enlisted in the services. They were denied combat duty, performing traditionally female tasks. Racial discrimination was alive and well in the armed forces. The 700,000 blacks who fought for the United States were subjected to segregation and were often stuck with the most menial tasks. Many questioned fighting for a country that would treat them in such a way. Black soldiers were often attacked in the South, and race riots broke out even on military bases. The Red Cross blood bank kept black and white reserves separate. Canteens and chapels were segregated.

Blacks nonetheless made progress in the armed forces, distinguishing themselves in aviation and on the battlefield. The consciousness raised by the war was probably a major factor in the progress made by the National Association for the Advancement of Colored People (NAACP), whose membership grew from 50,000 to 450,000 between 1940 and 1946. Civil society was still riddled with opposition, and the reaction from whites escalated tragically in summer 1943, when hundreds of racial incidents broke out in forty-seven cities. The bloodiest riot took place in Detroit and left over thirty dead, including twenty-five blacks. In Los Angeles, young Mexicans suffered the wrath of sailors during the Zoot Suit Riots. The sailors objected to the way the youths dressed and their perceived lack of patriotism, even though Mexican-Americans had signed up in disproportionate numbers to serve their country.

The Roosevelt government did little to counteract discrimination, preferring to focus on the war effort. Under pressure from blacks, outright discrimination was curtailed in the war industries and the government, but the war secretary refused to turn the army into a "sociological laboratory." The army separated Japanese-American recruits into a Nisei (American-born Japanese) regiment, the most highly decorated in the Second World War.

The case of the Japanese

After Pearl Harbor, many feared a Japanese invasion of the United States and doubted the loyalty of the Issei (Japanese born in Japan) and the Nisei. People feared subversion and sabotage. The fact that there had not been any meant that there eventually would be, went the dubious logic of one report. Racism verging on paranoia reappeared. From December 8, 1941, all Issei assets were frozen. All those of Japanese origin, two thirds of whom were born in the United States, became victims of hatred toward "Japs."

In February 1942, by executive order, Roosevelt suspended the rights of enemy aliens, but only those of Japanese background were targeted.

Concentrated in the West, 110,000 Japanese were interned in a dozen camps in isolated locations as far away as Arkansas. Living conditions were rudimentary, lack of privacy was an issue, families were often separated and there was frequent tension between Issei and Nisei.

The Japanese American Citizens League, the American Civil Liberties Union and several churches were indignant over the rights violation, but to no effect. The Supreme Court ratified the decision, the worst stain on human rights protection of the entire war. Not only were the rights of Japanese-Americans violated, but many of them were dispossessed by Americans only too happy to get rid of industrious competitors and snap up their assets and property at bargain-basement prices. It was not 1948 that the government authorized partial comepnsation and not until 1989 that Congress offered an apology and appropriated more money to redress the wrong.

Women at war

With millions of men in uniform, there was a serious shortage of labour. Women would largely fill the vacuum, making up 36 percent of the workforce in 1946, compared to 24 percent at the beginning of the war. A large majority of these women were married with children. What had changed was access to industrial jobs. In the aviation industry alone, female jobs grew from 4,000 to 310,000 between 1941 and 1944. Women's contributions were appreciated; Norman Rockwell's Rosie the Riveter became a national symbol.

The change was perceived as temporary, however. Once victory had been achieved, women were expected to go back to the kitchen. Some women were not of the same opinion; they wanted to keep their jobs. Authorities began planning for layoffs of women in 1943, and when the veterans returned, there was a flood of job losses. Between 1944 and 1946, four million women were laid off. Although in most cases they had earned considerably less than men, they had acquired a degree of independence and discovered their potential. Their struggle for equal rights would resume another day.

Military operations

Militarily, the Allies adopted the American strategy: first confront the toughest enemy, Germany, even if it meant putting off the campaign against Japan. At first, the Americans were on the defensive. Hitler controlled the European continent and had advanced into the Soviet Union and North Africa. Britain resisted but suffered heavy bombing. In the Pacific, the situation was bad. General Douglas MacArthur had been driven from the Philippines, and Wake, Guam and Hong Kong had fallen. American naval power had been crippled, but luckily there had been no aircraft carriers at Pearl Harbor. At the Battle of Midway in June 1942, won by the Americans after they cracked the Japanese code, the Japanese advance was halted. The War of the Pacific would drag on, but efforts could be focused on Europe.

In the European theatre, the main problem was opening a second front. The Soviet Union was demanding a front in western Europe to relieve German pressure on the eastern or Russian front that was bleeding it white. During the winter of 1942–1943, the Soviets inflicted a costly defeat on the Germans, stopping them at Stalingrad. It was a turning point in the war. The Germans were no longer invincible, but the western front had

Posters from the Second World War. The War Bonds poster at right by artist Norman Rockwell was one of four that he painted on themes from President Roosevelt's 1941 "Four Freedoms" speech to Congress – Freedom of Speech, Freedom of Worship, Freedom from Want, and Freedom from Fear. (Library of Congress)

still not been opened. Roosevelt wanted a landing in France. Churchill objected; they would make a detour through North Africa. Between November 1942 and May 1943, the British and Americans defeated General Erwin Rommel's Afrika Corps, then moved on to Sicily and Italy, where Benito Mussolini's regime collapsed in July 1943. The Germans, however, were well-established in Italy, and the Allies did not take Rome until June 1944. Stalin was not reassured by the invasion of Italy, and during the Tehran Conference in December 1943, Churchill relented on his Mediterranean plan, but the damage had been done to relations with Stalin. Each partner had precise goals, hoping to improve its relative position on the postwar international chessboard.

The invasion of France began on June 6, 1944. In the greatest amphibious assault in history, 200,000 men and 20,000 vehicles were landed on the beaches of Normandy against fierce German resistance. In the following weeks, 500,000 additional men landed and headed inland, taking Paris on August 25, 1944.

Yet Hitler had not had his final word, and the Allied command gave him time to react by not pushing on quickly with its drive toward Berlin. The Battle of the Bulge, a counteroffensive of 250,000 men from December 1944 to January 1945, rattled the Allies, but after driving the Germans back, they continued their march into Germany. The Soviets were already on the outskirts of Berlin. Germany surrendered on May 8, 1945, Hitler having committed suicide about a week earlier. As troops invaded successive Nazi-controlled territories, they discovered the full horror of the Final Solution: concentration camps where millions of Jews, Poles, gypsies and other "undesirables" had been exterminated. American authorities had known of the existence of the camps earlier but could do little about them.

Germany had been defeated, but there was still Japan. The American strategy was to take the Pacific Islands one after another. The battles were ferocious. Nature was hostile and the Japanese rarely surrendered. The Marshall, Gilbert and Marianas islands fell. In October 1944, MacArthur began re-conquering the Philippines after the Japanese fleet had been almost totally wiped out. The invasion of Japan was within reach, but first the islands of Iwo Jima and Okinawa had to be taken to put American planes within range of Tokyo. Strategists predicted that the cost of these operations would be very high. They were right: 6,000 were killed at Iwo Jima and 7,600 at Okinawa in the first half of 1945.

Diplomatic manoeuvres

Meanwhile, the Allied leaders met at Yalta in February 1945 to try to organize the postwar world. It was the second time that Roosevelt, Churchill and Stalin had come face to face. There had been much friction during the conflict and peace looked to be hard work for this alliance of necessity united only by the will to defeat Germany. Yalta consisted of ten days of hard bargaining. Many claim that Roosevelt was in a weak position at Yalta. He needed the Soviets to open a front against Japan (the Soviet Union and Japan were not yet at war); he wanted the Soviets to be part of the future United Nations; and on the ground, the Soviets occupied eastern Europe and therefore their interests had to be taken into account. Stalin also had the advantage of meeting on his own turf.

Yalta was indisputably a major victory for Stalin. He guaranteed the USSR's entry into the war against Japan three months after the end of the war against Germany. In exchange, he was given a free hand in eastern Europe. He promised free elections in Poland but set no date or conditions. The leaders agreed to partition Germany into four zones and to exact yet-undetermined reparations. Stalin signed a treaty with nationalist China but recovered Port Arthur and part of Sakhalin.

In the poker game that was Yalta, Stalin held the best cards and played them well. The balance changed during the next conference, held at Potsdam, Germany, from July 17 to August 2, 1945. Roosevelt had died in April, shortly after beginning his fourth term, and was replaced by his vice president, Harry S. Truman (1884–1972). Although disappointed by Soviet manoeuvring in eastern Europe, Roosevelt had hoped until the end to arrive at an agreement. Truman was not as patient, especially after learning that the Manhattan Project had come to fruition. On July 16, 1945, in the New Mexican desert, an atomic bomb was detonated. Truman was emboldened by the news; he informed Churchill fully but told Stalin only that the Americans had a new weapon. The bomb in question could hasten a Japanese surrender, save numerous Allied lives and make Soviet participation in the war against Japan unnecessary.

The mood was changing even before Potsdam. On April 23, during a meeting with Vyacheslav Molotov, the Soviet foreign minister, Truman reminded him point-blank that Stalin was not fulfilling his commitments regarding Poland. He took this firm stance in spite of not being updated on the research into the atomic bomb until April 25. Many of Truman's advisors believed that Roosevelt had given too much away at Yalta and the new president fell under their influence. He would take a more forceful position at Potsdam. Still, the leaders managed to establish a policy for postwar Germany and continued to demand Japan's unconditional surrender.

War's end

A central problem for the Japanese was the fate reserved for their emperor in an unconditional surrender. American diplomats knew that the emperor was prepared to end fighting if the demand for unconditional surrender were dropped. But a bomb had been built and it only made sense to use it. The justification would be that it was used to save American lives. Roosevelt had already set up the organizational and decision-making parameters for the atomic bomb, and Truman had only to act within them. He had no reason to modify the original decision. In his memoirs, as we would expect, he takes personal credit for the decision and justifies it by the lives spared, but the decision obviously came down to more than one man's will.

On August 3, 1945, Japan announced its refusal to surrender. Three days later, the *Enola Gay* dropped Little Boy, the atomic bomb that destroyed the city of Hiroshima, leaving a staggering 80,000 dead and 30,000 wounded. Three days after that, Fat Man levelled Nagasaki, killing 40,000 Japanese and injuring 60,000. On the eighth, as promised, the Soviets entered the war against Japan. On August 14, Japan finally surrendered after being secretly assured that the emperor would be retained.

The war was over, ushering in a new era. There had been between 40 and 50 million victims, 10 million displaced people, unimaginable destruction and entire cities razed. The United States emerged in better shape than the rest; granted, 450,000 had been killed and 670,000 wounded, but all American resources were intact. In comparison, the Soviets lost 20 million people and Poland nearly 6 million. The United States came out of the conflict stronger than when it went in.

The Americans were in a hegemonic position. They alone possessed the atomic bomb, and they had the largest industrial capacity in the world, most of the oil reserves and a navy that dominated the oceans. They could no longer shirk their international responsibilities. Their vision for the world, however, would soon clash with that of the Soviets.

The postwar domestic scene

Harry Truman was stunned to succeed Roosevelt in April 1945. He was ill-prepared to take over. The Missouri senator had emerged from obscurity during the war when he headed a committee in charge of monitoring government expenditures. In 1944, when Roosevelt wanted to get rid of his overly reformist vice president, Henry A. Wallace (1888–1965), the Democratic convention chose Truman to replace him. During his few weeks as vice president, Truman had had little contact with the president and was not kept up to date on affairs. He showed exceptional strength character when he acceded to the presidency, embodying the aphorism that the job makes the man.

Domestically, the aftermath of the Second World War was cause for worry. The new president had to establish his authority, manage reconversion and demobilization of the military without creating too much unemployment, and curb inflation, all while lifting controls and relaunching the economy on a peacetime basis. Truman sketched out a twenty-one-point Fair Deal, which included the right to a worthwhile job, decent housing, protection from monopolies, adequate health care and so on.

But Truman lacked support in Congress and reconversion was tricky. The pace was faster than expected. The GIs wanted to get home and back to work. Companies needed to make the transition to peacetime productivity. Demand for consumer goods, held in check for years, returned in force before businesses could satisfy it. Prices went through the roof. The inflation rate would be 70 percent over the next four years. Meanwhile the climate was very conservative. Memories of the Depression were still fresh, and now that prosperity was back, Americans wanted to enjoy it unhampered.

Backed by stronger unions than before the war, workers demanded wage increases they felt were justified by companies' wartime profits. Labour conflicts focused on the fundamental issue of the relation between prices, profits and wages. In most cases, reconversion meant a drop in income. In the final months of 1945 there were almost 3,500 strikes, and 1946, with a total of nearly 5,000 work stoppages, set a record in American history. The number of strikers increased and stoppages were longer. The 225,000 workers at General Motors went on strike for 113 days. They were emulated by 4.6 million workers, or 14.5 percent of the workforce. Regulations were imposed but price controls collapsed at the same time, and it was clear that people had little patience with strikes that would prevent them from enjoying their peace and prosperity. Truman's support melted away like snow in the sun, plummeting from 87 percent to 32 percent between April 1945 and November 1946.

The wave of strikes in 1946 alarmed many and led to a resurgence of the more conservative Republicans with their slogan, "Had enough?" People wanted to return to "normal" life, but after the experiences of the war and the New Deal, American society was no longer the same. The government played a much larger role than before. The giant companies had remade their image, and the unions had become important partners. Labour relations had been revived and productivity was on the rise. Women's roles and family life had been transformed. Race relations, significantly affected by the mobilization of blacks into the army and the war industries, would change for good.

The mid-term elections of November 1946 installed a conservative Republican majority in Congress that was out to reassert legislative power, as is so often the case after a strong presidency. It lowered taxes, reduced spending and attacked the union movement as a too-powerful ally of the Democrats. In 1947, Congress overrode a presidential veto to pass the Taft-Hartley Act, which reconfigured labour-capital relations to favour employers. Closed shops were outlawed, strikes affecting national security could be postponed for eighty days by the president, and union officials were required to sign affidavits stating they did not belong to a Communist organization. The mood started to sour within the United States following the deterioration in relations with the Soviet Union. The first anti-subversion measures were put forward by Truman himself.

Truman desperately wanted to win the 1948 election, but his chances did not look good. His party was divided over the issue of civil rights, and the Dixiecrat splinter group was presenting a candidate, Strom Thurmond, who could cost him votes in the South. Henry A. Wallace, the former vice president and Truman's secretary of commerce, had recently been dismissed by Truman for being too moderate on the issue of relations with the USSR; Wallace formed the Progressive Party, which could potentially steal left-leaning votes. Fortunately, the Republicans had chosen the uncharismatic Thomas Dewey. Truman led the scrappy campaign of the underdog. His aggressiveness went over well. He criticized the "good-for-nothing" Congress and succeeded in rebuilding the New

Deal coalition. Despite occasionally tense relations with the unions (for example, he threatened to conscript striking rail workers into military service), he maintained the support of organized labour and increased his vote from blacks and farmers. To everyone's surprise, he won the election. He had claimed the centre – always a winning formula. Yet Truman was unable to put his program into effect, squeezed as he was by the need to counter the Soviet threat and build a foreign-policy consensus. As defence spending rose, there was correspondingly less money for domestic needs. The United States was already involved in a cold war with the USSR.

The Cold War begins

The Allies of the Second World War had had little in common aside from the will to defeat the Germans. There had been much friction during the conflict over the second front, Poland and Eastern Europe, and the surrender of Italy (from which the USSR had been excluded). But with the end of the war, problems became more frequent and acute. Belligerence became overt and rhetoric grew hostile. It quickly became apparent that the American vision of the postwar world would not be accepted by all. Even with all their power, the Americans could not impose their will universally. The atomic bomb, quickly recognized as unusable, was a disappointment as an instrument of domination.

The reorganization of the postwar world foundered on mistrust. Stalin took advantage of the war to set up a buffer zone around the USSR. His intentions were obviously suspect to the Americans, who envisioned a democratic Europe with access for American goods. American economic domination, reinforced by the atomic monopoly, was a clear threat to the independence and survival of the Communist regime. Each country wanted to keep the other at bay without resorting directly to warfare; proxy wars were the result.

In early 1946, Truman warned his secretary of state that he was through mollycoddling the Soviets; he was critical of their actions in Eastern Europe and Iran, where fighting over oil had already begun. Stalin, in a speech on February 9, 1946, spoke of the essential incompatibility between capitalism and communism. Two weeks later, Truman received a long telegram from Moscow from George Kennan, deputy head of the U.S. mission in Moscow, convincing the president that conflict was inevitable. In March

1946, Churchill delivered his "iron curtain" speech in Fulton, Missouri, with Truman's backing.

In March 1947, Truman stood before Congress to request funding to fight subversion in Greece and Turkey. Great Britain was no longer able to guarantee stability in the two countries, which had until then been

---

The Truman Doctrine

The gravity of the situation which confronts the world today necessitates my appearance before a joint session of the Congress. The foreign policy and the national security of this country are involved....

To ensure the peaceful development of nations, free from coercion, the United States has taken a leading part in establishing the United Nations. The United Nations is designed to make possible lasting freedom and independence for all its members. We shall not realize our objectives, however, unless we are willing to help free peoples to maintain their free institutions and their national integrity against aggressive movements that seek to impose upon them totalitarian regimes....

At the present moment in world history nearly every nation must choose between alternative ways of life. The choice is too often not a free one.

One way of life is based upon the will of the majority, and is distinguished by free institutions, representative government, free elections, guarantees of individual liberty, freedom of speech and religion, and freedom from political oppression.

The second way of life is based upon the will of a minority forcibly imposed upon the majority. It relies upon terror and oppression, a controlled press and radio, fixed elections, and the suppression of personal freedoms.

I believe that it must be the policy of the Unites States to support free peoples who are resisting attempted subjugation by armed minorities or by outside pressures....

The seeds of totalitarian regimes are nurtured by misery and want. They spread and grow in the evil soil of poverty and strife. They reach their full growth when the hope of a people for a better life has died. We must keep that hope alive.

The free peoples of the world look to us for support in maintaining their freedoms.

If we falter in our leadership, we may endanger the peace of the world – and we shall surely endanger the welfare of our own nation.

President Harry S. Truman, address to Congress, March 12, 1947.

considered part of its zone of influence, and British leaders suggested that the United States should replace Great Britain. To make sure the necessary $400 million would be allocated, the Communist threat had to be exaggerated. While the Soviet Union was never mentioned in the Truman Doctrine, the doctrine was intended to protect the world from that country and Communism. In the sense of being its first official document, the Doctrine initiated the Cold War, as it became known in 1947. The fight was international; the Americans would help all free countries threatened by Communist-inspired insurrections. A few months later, George Kennan publicly articulated the policy of containment of the Soviet Union in an article in *Foreign Affairs*: firmness had to be shown wherever necessary as it was the only language the Soviets understood. The next step was the April 1948 passage of the Marshall Plan, a massive $13.4 billion, five-year aid package to rebuild war-ravaged Europe and strengthen ties with America.

The Eisenhower years

Containment was the cornerstone of American foreign policy after the Second World War. The Truman Doctrine, the Marshall Plan, NATO (the Western military alliance founded in 1949) and NSC 68 (the 1950 document by the National Security Council that set American policy for the next twenty years) were all based on it. NSC 68 presented the conflict with the Soviet Union as inevitable because its amoral aims were deemed irreconcilable with American aims. Negotiating was a waste of time, it was claimed, since the Soviets could not be trusted. To deal effectively with the threat, the military budget had to be increased from $13 billion to $50 billion and the share of defence spending increased from 5 percent to 20 percent of the national budget. It was believed that the survival of the United States and the free world depended on it.

When Dwight D. Eisenhower (1890–1969) took office in 1953, containment seemed too cautious to the Republican team. Secretary of State John Foster Dulles, in particular, wanted to force the retreat of godless Communism. Soviet-dominated countries had to be liberated. The rhetoric was fierce, but the policy of liberation proved impossible in practice. Eisenhower was more realistic than his secretary of state. During the East German uprising of 1953, the Americans remained silent. In the 1956 Hungarian Revolution they stood back, ignoring all calls for help, as the

Soviets violently crushed the revolt. In the real world, it was impossible to push back the borders of Communism, and containment remained the policy in place.

Containment required that the United States respond to Soviet challenges, or what were perceived as such, all over the world. China's fall into Communist hands in 1949 caused near-hysteria in the United States. Truman and the Democrats were accused of losing China. Tension increased with the Korean War (1950–1953). Truman managed to resist General MacArthur, who wanted to extend operations to China. Eisenhower was the one who eventually ended the unpopular war. In the Vietnam War (beginning in 1959), the Americans were called upon to take over from the French, who had been driven from their former colony after their defeat at Dien Bien Phu. Washington was convinced that Ho Chi Minh took orders from Moscow. Eisenhower believed in the domino theory, according to which, if Vietnam fell, the rest of Asia would also fall. Washington accordingly backed Ho Chi Minh's rival, Ngo Dinh Diem, and his anti-Communist regime in South Vietnam. The United States was taking its first steps toward an impoverishing and destabilizing war that would soon veer out of control.

In the Middle East, with its obvious strategic importance to the U.S., the Americans also took Cold War–inspired positions. The Shah of Iran, an ally of the United States and Great Britain, was given greater power when the overly independent Prime Minister Mohammed Mossadegh was ousted in a coup fomented by the Central Intelligence Agency (CIA). Washington cultivated a friendship with Israel, but could not afford to alienate the region's oil producers. Gamal Abdel Nasser of Egypt, caught between the United States and the USSR over funding of the Aswan dam he wanted to build on the Nile, was cut off by John Foster Dulles. Nasser nationalized the Suez Canal, to the great displeasure of the French and British, who, along with the Israelis, invaded Egypt in October 1956. Eisenhower was furious. He had not been consulted about the invasion, and there was the danger of Nasser falling under Soviet influence. The U.S. forced the invaders to withdraw. In 1958, under the Eisenhower Doctrine, which held that the United States should fill any vacuum in the Middle East before the USSR did, the U.S. sent 14,000 men to Lebanon to shore up a weakened right-wing regime.

In Latin America, its traditional sphere of influence, the United States was on the lookout for any Communist inroads. A 1954 coup, once again orchestrated by the CIA, toppled Arbenz Guzman's reformist government in Guatemala. The newly installed right-wing government returned property that had been nationalized to the United Fruit Company. The Americans inspired a widespread anti-Americanism in the region by using any means to protect stability and private property. In 1958, Vice President Richard Nixon was practically stoned on his visit to Venezuela. When the following year Fidel Castro took power in Cuba, the Americans reacted predictably. Cuba would turn toward the USSR.

American policy increasingly relied on the atomic shield. Under Dulles, the approach was based on the threat of massive reprisal for any attack and a diplomacy of "brinkmanship."

McCarthyism and the Red Menace

The political climate was unsettling, and people were anxious about the constant barrage of situations they half understood: in 1949, the Soviets developed and tested an atomic bomb; that same year China fell to the Communists; and, in 1950, the Korean War broke out. Meanwhile, it was discovered that some Americans were traitors (such as the Rosenbergs and Alger Hiss). Subversion threatened. Attorney General J. Howard McGrath declared in 1949 that there were Communists "everywhere – in factories, offices, butcher shops, on street corners, in private businesses – and each carries within himself the germs of death for society." The notion was appealing. All problems had an outside source, Communism, which even threatened from within. Americans had to both contain Soviet expansionism and protect themselves from subversion. They settled into the Cold War, which justified mobilizing resources and guided social, political and intellectual life for decades.

In the United States, the shift to the right was based on a traditional anti-Communist obsession dating back to the Bolshevik revolution. The new flare-up was at first spurred on by the government's need to mobilize support for its foreign policy and by the business community's union-busting campaigns. When the political parties realized the advantage of jumping on the bandwagon, national anti-Communist crusades were launched. Between 1945 and 1952, various congressional committees held over eighty hearings into Communist subversion in the unions, education, the government, the movie industry and so on. President

The hunt for Communists was under way well before Senator Joseph R. McCarthy began making headlines.

Truman himself went as far as to approve the Loyalty Program for federal employees.

The most famous political name associated with anti-Communism was of course Joseph R. McCarthy, a Republican senator from Wisconsin. His fire-and-brimstone methods made him the most dreaded figure of that period of political and intellectual repression, but he embodied only the most extreme point of view when the witch hunt was on. In February 1950, McCarthy gave a speech in which he claimed to have in his possession a list of 205 names of Communists working within the State Department. A career was launched. McCarthy was an opportunist who played on the fears of his countrymen. What set him apart from other politicians who exploited anti-Communism was the outrageous nature of his accusations, constantly reiterated to feed public opinion. He had no list, but his simple accusation was appealing: the threat came from within. The enemy had to be flushed out. Ironically, the danger was well in the past. There had been espionage in the United States; there had been much sympathy among Americans for their Soviet ally and many had belonged to the legal American Communist Party in the 1930s. But even as the Cold War escalated and the Federal Bureau of Investigation (FBI) cracked down, the "threat" had already receded. The perception of danger, however, was heightened by the events of 1949 and exploited by the Republicans, including the rabid demagogue McCarthy. He considered the Democrats, the army and the secretary of state soft on Communist subversion. His televised attacks on the army led to his downfall.

It is ironic how remarkably few Communists there actually were compared with the many unfairly accused victims of McCarthyism. Yet once his political usefulness had been outlived (the Republicans and Eisenhower retook power in 1952) and tensions had died down somewhat after the end of the Korean War, the inconvenient senator could be dispensed with. The Senate censured him in 1954, condemned his methods and quickly stripped him of political influence. Yet it was not until the mid-sixties, when the country was plagued by other problems, that the United States finally cast off its Cold War-imposed political orthodoxy.

Time of prosperity

During the postwar years, aside from a few short recessions, the United States enjoyed uninterrupted prosperity. The affluent society was born with all its consequences for the lives of Americans and the way they perceived their society and their place within it. Between 1950 and 1970, the gross national product grew from $260 billion to nearly $1 trillion. Productivity in agriculture and manufacturing rose significantly. Jobs increased in the service industries, largely because of bigger government. In 1956, for the first time, there were more white-collar than blue-collar workers. Demand for consumer goods (fuelled by the baby boom) and Cold War military expenditures stimulated the economy. In a mood of general optimism, buoyed by tangible rewards, everyone was out to enjoy the benefits of prosperity.

Politics mirrored the emerging society of comfort, which seemed to remove all need for reformist projects such as redistributing wealth and power in the United States and, crucially, curbing big business. Economic prosperity appeared to reduce class frictions and even to homogenize American society further into a vast middle class, creating what the editors of *Fortune* called a "permanent revolution" that would provide abundance in a classless, "post-industrial" society. The 1953–1961 presidency of Dwight D. Eisenhower, a military hero and reassuring symbol, was a perfect match for the prevailing climate: middle-of-the-road political conservatism and conformity to mainstream culture, with no questioning of New Deal gains. The America of *Father Knows Best* was complacent; the reformist fervour of the 1930s and 1940s was well and truly dead.

In hindsight, it is easy to see that economic growth, rather than solving all the problems, simply masked them. There still existed social and economic disparities that would become increasingly apparent to Americans over the ensuing decades. Attention was refocused on poverty in the 1960s as a scourge of the United States, but the issue of race was what changed everything. The civil rights movement of the late 1950s and 1960s protested segregation and discrimination, ending the political inertia. The great crusade for the rights of blacks inspired other groups to demand their rights. Various ethnic groups, women frequently stuck in employment or family ghettos, students, gays and "deviants" would demand legal protection. These protest movements would become the hinge on which postwar American history would turn.

The decision of the Warren Supreme Court in *Brown v. Board of Education of Topeka* (1954) shattered many earlier certainties. Earl Warren (1891–1974) had been appointed to the Supreme Court by Eisenhower, a conservative. Yet the former Republican governor of California proved to be one of the most progressive judges in the history of the United States. In 1954, the Court struck down the *Plessy v. Ferguson* opinion, which declared that the "separate but equal" treatment at the core of segregation was legal. The Brown case dealt with education but had far-reaching effects. It set off a long wave of protest and civil disobedience that would characterize the next decade.

CHAPTER 11

HIGH HOPES... AND DOUBTS

1960-1974

In the late 1950s, few Americans suspected that the next decade would be so disruptive for their country. The vast majority joined in the general celebration of the system. People were convinced that economic growth and affluence would erase income disparity along with race and class divisions, even though it was clear that for half the population the society of abundance was more a dream than a reality.

The figures were indeed impressive. The population had reached 179 million after the highest decade-long increase in American history, thanks to the postwar baby boom. Gross domestic product grew by 37 percent from 1950 to 1960 and median family income by 30 percent. Productivity was high, unemployment was low and the price of televisions, refrigerators and washing machines was stable. The system, however, had stayed the same. Barely 2 percent of Americans controlled 80 percent of stock market shares. The pace of mergers had picked up again; the 500 largest industrial companies controlled 70 percent of production and the 50 largest, 23 percent. From 1950 to 1960, 3,404 companies were absorbed by the 500 largest ones with no objection from the Justice Department. It was felt that big business had a positive effect on society and that big government kept big business and big labour in check. People believed in popular capitalism.

The late 1950s had their share of tumult: the Soviets put Sputnik into orbit around the earth in 1957; a recession hit in 1958; demands from blacks became more insistent; there were quiz-show scandals; and Cuba was shifting to Communism. Yet when John F. Kennedy (1917–1963) was elected in 1960 and called on his fellow citizens to reach for new frontiers, there was renewed optimism. Was it really the end of complacency?

JFK: An enduring myth

Decades after dying by an assassin's bullet in Dallas, John F. Kennedy remains one of America's favourite president despite whatever revisions and re-evaluations historians have come up with. He was perceived as a valiant knight of Camelot in the '60s, then a Cold Warrior in the '70s, becoming a much more complex figure in subsequent years. His weaknesses, louche behaviour and Mafia acquaintances have all since come to light. None of this has altered his martyr status in the public mind. Historians have not been kind to him in recent years; at best, he is considered a president who had success handed to him. He could have been great, the thinking goes, had he lived longer.

Ascension

The story of John F. Kennedy begins like a fairy tale. He was born into a rich and politically powerful Irish family in Boston. His grandfather had been the city's mayor and his father, the millionaire Joseph P. Kennedy, had for a while been a confidant of Roosevelt and was named American ambassador to Britain just before the Second World War.

In frail health, Kennedy was an indifferent student at Harvard before continuing his training as a man of the world and political observer in London. When the war broke out, he served in the Pacific and emerged as a hero. Joseph Kennedy had had grand ambitions for his eldest son, Joe, who died in the war. The father transferred his ambitions to John, who was elected to the House of Representatives in 1946. In 1952, he was elected to the Senate, where he did not particularly stand out. Although a Democrat, he often voted with conservatives and avoided committing himself on controversial issues such as civil rights. His abstention during the vote on the McCarthy censure did not go unnoticed. His father happened to be a prominent supporter of the senator from Wisconsin.

Ambitious, energetic and gifted with a good head for politics, John Kennedy carefully moulded his image. In the television age, charisma, personality and style counted for much. Kennedy also knew how to cultivate the party. In 1956, he received 2,500 invitations to speak and came close to being chosen as running mate to Adlai E. Stevenson (1900–1965), the Democratic presidential candidate that year. In 1958, he was handily re-elected as senator of Massachusetts.

After two failed presidential campaigns by Stevenson, in 1960 the Democrats turned to Kennedy, who led a solid campaign during the primaries. He downplayed the Catholic factor, a liability, and won the Democratic nomination on the first ballot. He shrewdly chose Lyndon B. Johnson (1908–1973), senator from Texas and leader of the Democratic majority, as his running mate. Kennedy's youth and vitality played in his favour. He promised to give the country new momentum and talked not about deadlock but about victory over Communism.

Richard M. Nixon (1913–1994), vice president under Eisenhower and the Republican candidate in 1960, tried to play up his experience and maturity. But Eisenhower's support for him was lukewarm, and during the famous televised debates, JFK was confident and animated while Nixon appeared old and tired (he had been in the hospital). Interestingly, most who had heard the debate on the radio picked Nixon as the winner, but the opposite was true on television. The campaign did not take place entirely on television, but given the close results, the medium may well have been the deciding factor in convincing people that Kennedy was as ready for the presidency as Nixon.

He won by an extremely narrow margin with 49.7 percent of the vote, compared to 49.5 percent for Nixon. Kennedy had managed to get out the vote and build a majority based on support from Catholics, blacks (he had helped Martin Luther King get out of prison) and white Southern Democrats. While there was some doubt about the results in several states, Nixon did not contest the election. Yet Kennedy could not realistically claim to have a clear mandate.

Unlike Eisenhower, Kennedy believed that the federal government should be active, strong and visible and that the president should set the tone for the nation. He took office on these principles and surrounded himself with brilliant and energetic advisors recruited from the best universities, companies and foundations. His inaugural address, the "new frontier" speech, urged Americans to face up to their responsibilities, famously exhorting them to "ask not what your country can do for you, ask what you can do for your country." His tone was that of a Cold Warrior rather than a president concerned with the domestic situation. Accordingly, the Kennedy presidency was dominated by foreign-policy problems. The imperial reach took priority.

Like Kennedy, many analysts have pointed to Eisenhower's conservatism, inaction and hesitancy. More recent assessments take a different view. Historians consider that his "hidden hand" presidency was effective; he was invariably in control and his caution was appropriate on many occasions. Despite his anti-Communism, he did not draw the country into a crusade and he gave Americans what they wanted, economic growth. On the other hand, he neglected the problems that would overwhelm the United States in the coming years: race relations and poverty. He did little for women. Nonetheless, history has generally been kinder to him as a president than to his flamboyant successor.

Bay of Pigs

During the electoral campaign, Kennedy had criticized Nixon and the Republicans for letting America fall behind in the arms race with the USSR and standing by while Cuba fell to Communism. Both accusations were spurious and Kennedy knew it. The Eisenhower administration had approved the CIA's plan to invade the island using an anti-Castro contingent trained and supported by the CIA. It was believed that the Cubans would rise up against Castro when they heard of the invasion. Kennedy approved the plan in April 1961.

The operation was a fiasco from beginning to end. The landing was botched. The 1,400 invaders were surrounded on the beach. Castro had had time to react. The Cuban air force was not incapacitated. Kennedy refused to allow American forces to intervene directly. The people did not rise up and an attempt to assassinate Castro, supposedly timed to coincide with the invasion, failed.

Kennedy took responsibility for the botched invasion. He had carefully weighed the operation's chances for success. He had heard advice from opponents of the invasion but had come to believe it could work. An internal inquiry by the CIA revealed all the planning and organizational flaws. CIA director Allen Dulles was forced to resign. At his dismissal hearing, Kennedy admitted to him that in a parliamentary system he himself would have to resign. But no lessons were learned, and attempts continued through covert means: attacks to destabilize the Cuban economy, aid for Miami anti-Castro forces and assassination attempts against Castro with the help of organized crime.

Cuban missile crisis

After the failed invasion, Nikita Khrushchev, leader of the Soviet Union, offered all necessary help to Castro. Eighteen months later, Kennedy would discover the extent of that help. Meanwhile, Kennedy and Khrushchev met in Vienna in June 1961, and the meeting went badly. Each adopted hard-line positions, particularly on Berlin. The Soviets built the Berlin Wall in August 1961 to stop East Germans from defecting to the West and to test the Americans, who decided not to react. But confrontation was in the air.

In October 1961, Deputy Secretary of Defense Roswell Gilpatric clearly emphasized the superiority of American strategic capabilities by claiming that the United States could sustain a first strike and still devastate the USSR afterward. In spring 1962, Khrushchev learned that American missiles in Turkey, which bordered on the USSR, were operational. To protect Cuba from an American invasion (the official reason), to re-establish a certain parity and neutralize the Americans in Europe (the likely reason) and perhaps to consolidate his power, Khrushchev resolved to set up secret nuclear missile bases in Cuba. Soviet authorities no doubt hoped to present the Americans with a *fait accompli* that, albeit reluctantly, they would have to accept. Missiles had already been secretly deployed in Germany without the Americans realizing it.

It was the secrecy that dictated the intensity of the American response. In August, the CIA director warned the administration that he believed the Soviets were deploying offensive missiles in Cuba, but Kennedy had been assured that they were purely defensive. The rumour mill began churning and Kennedy was pressured into responding more strongly and authorizing flights by U-2 spy planes over Cuba. During an October 4 meeting about Operation Mongoose, Attorney General Robert Kennedy voiced American impatience with Castro (see document overleaf).

On October 14, 1962, the truth came out. Spy plane photos showed that offensive missiles capable of reaching the United States had been set up. The crisis began on October 16 when Kennedy convened a special committee of the National Security Council, EX COMM, to advise him. In the mentality of the time and of the Kennedy team, such a provocation had to be met with strong retaliation. The worst confrontation of the Cold War had begun.

The committee was torn over both the degree of the threat and the response called for. Recent evidence shows that American intelligence had

[Document image: Memorandum for Record, 4 October 1962, Minutes of Meeting of the Special Group (Augmented) on Operation MONGOOSE]

These documents show that attempts to destabilize the Castro regime had been continuing for some years before the missile crisis.

underestimated Soviet forces in Cuba; 42,000 troops were already there (twice the estimate), tactical nuclear warheads were operational and Soviet commanders on the ground were authorized to use them. The crisis certainly could have deteriorated more quickly and disastrously than the Americans had imagined.

Kennedy chose the path of public confrontation by announcing in an October 22 speech to the nation that the American navy would impose a "quarantine" (a blockade would have been an act of war) against all shipments of Soviet military supplies to Cuba. Kennedy rejected proposals for air strikes or invasion. The world held its breath waiting for the reaction from Moscow. Soviet ships changed direction or agreed to be inspected. The worst was over, but the crisis continued. Kennedy demanded that the missiles be withdrawn. Khrushchev seemed to agree, demanding guarantees from the Americans not to invade Cuba, then added in a second message that Jupiter missiles had to be withdrawn from Turkey. The crisis was resolved when it was decided not to publicly respond to the second diplomatic message while privately extending secret guarantees to Ambassador Anatoly Dobrynin that the Jupiters (which were obsolete anyway) would in fact be withdrawn. But no mention was to be made of it. Khrushchev hastened to accept the American deal.

On the one hand, Khrushchev had taken a risky gamble and provoked the United States. On the other, Kennedy may have overreacted and brought the world to the brink for no reason. Nuclear parity was probably unavoidable and Soviet missiles in Cuba could have been tolerated. Yet JFK managed the crisis well. He came out the winner and his resolve made the loser, Khrushchev, back down. At the same time, Kennedy showed restraint. He scored an undeniable public relations victory, but the fact remains that the whole episode ended in a compromise that American authorities would keep secret for decades. Fortunately, Kennedy had kept a cooler head than many of his advisors and had been lucky. It must be stressed that had there been no Bay of Pigs or Operation Mongoose (continued attempts to overthrow Castro), U.S.-Soviet relations would have been simpler, and that the Soviet drive to catch up was only reinforced by the whole crisis.

Vietnam and JFK

Kennedy's Vietnam policy was a continuation of Eisenhower's: the Vietnamese had to defend themselves. The U.S. would provide them with military advisors and aid. There was no possibility of retreat lest the dominoes fall. After the humiliation of the Bay of Pigs and the Berlin Wall, Kennedy was more determined than ever. He increased military advisors in Vietnam from 750 in 1961 to 11,300 in 1962 to 16,300 in 1963.

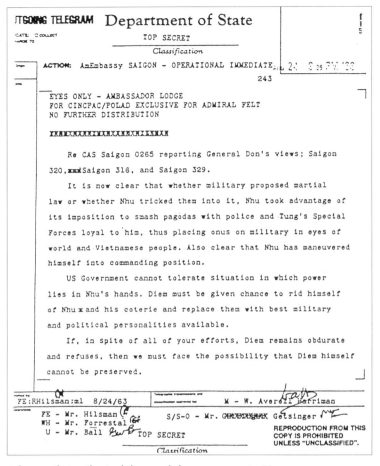

The telegram that authorized the search for a successor to Diem.

Despite American aid (in early 1961, Kennedy increased the $225 million budget earmarked for Vietnam by $42 million, writing "why so little?" in the margin), despite the special forces and the Strategic Hamlet program (fortified villages armed so that they could hold out until reinforcements could be sent), the Catholic Ngo Dinh Diem's regime appeared very fragile; he was an autocrat and had increasing numbers of enemies. Most of Kennedy's advisors were convinced they could beat the guerrillas, Communist agents backed by North Vietnam. Under Secretary of State George Ball was the exception. In November 1961, he warned Kennedy that getting involved in Vietnam would mean that five years down the road the

U.S. could have 300,000 men in the rice paddies with no way to get them out. Kennedy's response was that Ball was "crazier than hell" and that it would never happen.

Pressure was put on Diem to reform his regime. When he began persecuting Buddhists, monks immolated themselves and there was an international outcry. The American press began talking about Vietnam and Diem's excesses. Washington became convinced that he was no longer the man for the job, the one who could most effectively fight the Communists. The CIA set to work encouraging the Vietnamese military to overthrow Diem. Ambassador Henry Cabot Lodge took action after receiving a cable from Washington on August 24, 1963, that Diem was expendable. When the coup went ahead on November 1, the generals had not received the order to spare Diem and executed him, to Kennedy's surprise.

The big question about Kennedy and Vietnam is whether or not he was getting ready to withdraw Americans troops. In October 1963, while the coup against Diem was brewing, based on optimistic reports that a phased withdrawal of American troops was possible, Kennedy announced the repatriation of a thousand troops before the year's end. That decision was what sparked the controversy over his true intentions. In a September interview with prominent journalist Walter Cronkite, he also expressed doubts as to the outcome of the war. That was enough to lead admirers of Kennedy, who would be assassinated a few weeks after Diem, to conclude that he intended to withdraw American troops, and some would claim that that was precisely the reason he was assassinated. Oliver Stone's highly influential 1991 movie *JFK* argued as much. The theory is an attempt to salvage Kennedy's reputation for posterity. Nothing truly indicates that JFK was going to pull the United States out of Vietnam. The thousand men belonged to an engineering battalion due to be repatriated; in the same CBS interview, he came out against proponents of withdrawal, and in a speech he had prepared for November 22 in Dallas he mentioned again that the U.S. should not back down from the Vietnam war effort.

Civil rights

It took John F. Kennedy several years to become truly sympathetic to the cause of civil rights. Admittedly, he had to placate Southern Democrats, who could potentially block his policies in Congress. There was also the fact that popular support for black demands was not high. The politician in Kennedy did not see what he had to gain. As a result, he reneged on his promise of a bill of rights for blacks and repeatedly put off banning segregation in federally subsidized housing. Yet the unrest and demonstrations involving blacks disturbed him – they tarnished the image of the United States.

Despite lack of interest from the White House, Martin Luther King Jr. (1929–1968) and his non-violent volunteers continued to battle segregation at lunch counters and train stations in the South. King headed the Southern Christian Leadership Conference (SCLC). He had become a prominent leader of the black movement in the Montgomery Bus Boycott in Alabama in 1955. Rosa Parks had been arrested for refusing to give up her seat to a white man, a protest was organized and the company suffered financially. The Supreme Court struck the final blow when it declared Alabama's segregation laws unconstitutional. Next to be desegregated was public transit. In May 1961, the Congress of Racial Equality (CORE) and its Freedom Riders began trying to abolish segregation in interstate transportation. The Student Non-Violent Coordinating Committee (SNCC), a younger, more radical wing of the SCLC, also played an important role and tried to increase black political power by registering blacks to vote.

As support for the movement swelled, Kennedy gradually got involved. Attorney General Robert Kennedy intervened to protect the Freedom Riders in 1961. But he also allowed J. Edgar Hoover (1895–1972), director of the FBI, to wiretap King. Hoover was obsessed with Communists and suspected a King associate of being on the Communist payroll. The wiretap revealed nothing but King's extramarital affairs, but Hoover was still authorized to continue it for years afterward. JFK feared Hoover because the FBI head had knowledge of the president's many extramarital affairs. It was Hoover who notified JFK that he shared a mistress, Judith Campbell Exner, with the head of the Chicago Mafia, Sam Giancana. This was the same Giancana who had worked with the CIA to attempt to assassinate Castro. In 1962, JFK ordered federal troops to protect James Meredith, the first black student at the University of Mississippi. In spring 1963, he imposed desegregation at the University of Alabama over the objections of Governor George C. Wallace (1919–1998). In June 1963, he introduced legislation in Congress banning segregation in all public places.

The events of spring 1963 had made Kennedy think long and hard and had strengthened his commitment. King had called for a protest against "the most thoroughly segregated city in the United States," Birmingham, Alabama. There had been clashes between the non-violent protesters and police with dogs, cattle prods and high-pressure fire hoses, all of it captured by television cameras. Kennedy had come down in favour of black rights. He had moved from the margins to the centre. But there was a feeling that non-violence had reached the limits of its effectiveness.

To push the movement forward, black leaders decided to organize a March on Washington with the support of several liberal organizations. The march drew 250,000 people on August 28, 1963. The authorities, including Kennedy, were nervous. Until the last minute, they tried to temper the speakers' militancy and monitored the participants. The demonstration went well, and King's "I have a dream" speech gained him recognition as leader of the movement. However, many blacks felt that, accolades aside, non-violence was a dead end and the struggle had to be radicalized. There were lively discussions questioning non-violence, interracial mixing and apoliticism. Eighteen days after the demonstration, the horrific bombing of a Birmingham church cost the lives of four young black girls.

The Kennedy assassination

On November 22, 1963, John Kennedy was in Texas to make peace within the state's Democratic ranks in the run-up to the 1964 election. At 12:30 p.m., as he was riding through Dallas in the presidential limousine, three shots rang out over 8.4 seconds from a sixth-floor window of the Texas Book Repository. The first bullet went wide, the second hit Kennedy in the neck then Texas governor John Connally in the shoulder, wrist and leg. The third and fatal bullet hit Kennedy in the head. He was declared dead at 1:00 at the Parkland Memorial Hospital. The shooter was Lee Harvey Oswald, who worked at the Book Repository and was seen leaving the building after the shooting. He was arrested after killing a policeman who approached him. Two days later, Oswald was in turn gunned down by Jack Ruby, a petty criminal from Dallas. There was no connection between the two men.

These were essentially the conclusions of the Warren Commission (1964) and the House Select Committee on Assassinations (HSCA) (1979). The first was established by Lyndon B. Johnson, the new president, to shed light on the assassination in the immediate aftermath. The second was set up by the House of Representatives in response to doubts that had been raised. The HSCA ruled out the involvement of the Soviets, the Cubans, anti-Castro groups, the FBI, the CIA and organized crime. The committee broke new ground by raising the theory, based on acoustics, of a second gunman. In 1982, the National Academy of Sciences completely debunked the theory.

All conspiracy theorists and Oliver Stone aside, the Warren Commission's conclusions have held up remarkably well. Obviously, we can never get Oswald's full story, but the evidence indicates that he assassinated the president. There are unanswered questions about Ruby. But while it is exciting to ask questions, answers require verifiable proof. This has not materialized.

Despite the fact that the commission's conclusions have stood the test of time, hard-core conspiracy theorists have never let up, and today a majority of Americans still have doubts. It is hard to acknowledge that the most powerful man in the world, a popular president, could have his life snuffed out by a delusional nutcase. Great effects call for great causes. In conspiracy theories, the perpetrators are always big players such as Castro, Johnson or the CIA. Once he had been martyred, Kennedy was grist for the mill. Even before the Warren Report, 52 percent of Americans believed in a conspiracy. Keep in mind that 49 percent of Americans voted for him in 1960, but after his death 65 percent claimed to have done so. People remembered a happy period and a dynamic, straight-talking president, in contrast with later revelations of his weaknesses.

Kennedy's record

John F. Kennedy's life ended tragically before he could fulfill his promise. Granted, he had evolved and his work was unfinished, but we must judge him on his accomplishments and leave aside his significant health issues and personal misbehaviour, which seem not to have affected the way he governed. His legislative record is certainly slight. None of the major legislation he introduced, whether tax cuts, aid to education or health insurance, was enacted during his presidency. It was all passed under his successor, Johnson, probably helped along by Kennedy's martyrdom. In 1964, the Democrats came to power in a landslide. While JFK was limited in what he could accomplish by the conservative majority in Congress, he clearly did not show the same leadership domestically as in foreign policy. He did not make civil rights a priority. He appointed conservative judges and chose few women for federal positions of responsibility. The Supreme Court was a more influential agent for change than the presidency during this period.

Kennedy was more comfortable in the field of foreign policy, where he had more leeway. Of the Alliance for Progress, the Peace Corps and the race to the moon, only the latter two were successful. The Bay of Pigs was a failure that clearly showed to what extent Cold War ideology dominated his agenda. The same goes for the attempts to assassinate Castro. Fortunately, during the Cuban missile crisis he showed sound leadership that, after the approach to the nuclear brink, probably led to policies that eased tensions somewhat. The policy he initiated in Vietnam led to disaster, but he was neither the hero nor the villain in the sense that, once again, imperial interests took priority.

Lyndon B. Johnson

Lyndon B. Johnson took office as president in the plane bringing the body back to Washington immediately after Kennedy's assassination. Johnson would say that Kennedy had style, but he was the one who got the bills passed. And he did. He threw his skills as a negotiator and manipulator behind the legislative agenda that JFK had been unable to push through Congress. It did not hurt that the nation wanted to pay some sort of homage to the fallen president.

The Great Society

In 1964 Johnson introduced a set of domestic programs with the goal of creating a "Great Society," one without racial injustice and poverty. He secured a civil rights bill outlawing discrimination based on race, colour, sex, religion or national origin in all public places as well as in employment. He also joined the fight against poverty by securing an appropriation of a billion dollars under the Economic Opportunity Act. Lastly, the $13.5 billion tax cut requested by Kennedy was enacted. Johnson had a consensus behind him, and nothing could stand in his way.

The 1964 campaign renewed Johnson's mandate. He won in a landslide against Senator Barry Goldwater, who represented the most radically conservative wing of the Republican Party. Goldwater did not help his cause when he advocated privatizing social security and using nuclear weapons in Vietnam. Johnson won 61 percent of the popular vote and forty-six states, and the Democrats controlled both Houses. Liberals could now pass bills that the conservatives had earlier blocked.

In 1965 and 1966, Congress carried out the most significant reforms since 1935. Among the measures enacted were Medicare to protect the elderly from health-care costs, federal aid to education, a bill ensuring minorities' right to vote, Medicaid (health care for the poor), help for needy families, preschool education for needy children and the Job Corps for manpower training.

This sweeping legislation had some positive effects but failed to defeat poverty. The number of poor among the elderly was reduced from 40 percent to 16 percent between 1960 and 1974. Federal expenditures for social services doubled between 1965 and 1970 while the GNP increased by 42 percent. The general standard of living rose with productivity increases and economic growth, and the poor too benefited from the general prosperity as well as from specific programs. Yet barely a dent was made in the problem. Pockets of resistance remained; poverty among single-parent families was the same at the end of the decade as in 1963. Despite the urban slant of many programs, the crumbling cities held greater and greater concentrations of low-paying jobs, held by visible minorities whose unemployment rate was double that of whites. In 1976, 20 percent of Americans still earned less than half the median income ($15,000), considered the poverty line – exactly the same proportion as in 1963. The War on Poverty had not changed income distribution.

As reform followed reform and the government moved closer to a welfare state, demands increased and protest became widespread. The coalition could not hold because of divisions among the Democrats, torn by the demands of blacks and other minorities, while the cost of the war increased. Vietnam would be the final nail in the coffin of the Great Society.

A closer look at the victory the Democrats won in 1964 reveals the risk the party was running by supporting civil rights. The six states lost by Johnson were in the South, where he was from. A majority of whites in four Southern states voted against him. These figures dictated Republican strategy for the next few years. The fact did not escape Johnson, who told an associate that by signing the Civil Rights Act of 1964 he was handing the South to the Republicans for years to come. Another reality that did not escape Johnson was the political quicksand that was Vietnam. By 1964 he knew that the Vietnam War was leading nowhere but could not pull out. Any president who "lost" Vietnam as China had been "lost" would be crucified, he confided to a friend.

LBJ and Vietnam

Johnson continued the American engagement in Vietnam, as presidents before him had. Not being a man of half measures, he wanted to get the war over with quickly to focus on the Great Society. He wanted results but did not want to alarm the American people. As was his style, he tried to control everything, including Congress, to get the authorization needed to increase resources. In August 1964, after an almost entirely manufactured incident involving an allegedly unprovoked attack by the North Vietnamese, the Tonkin Gulf Resolution was passed, giving him authorization, which he described as being "like grandmother's nightshirt. It covers everything." He could wage war as he saw fit, as long as he did not provoke China or the USSR. Nothing would be bombed without Johnson's approval.

Public support for Johnson was high at 72 percent. In the November 1964 elections, Vietnam was rarely in the headlines, and Johnson could campaign as the candidate for peace against the dangerous warmonger Goldwater with his nuclear talk. Three months later, Johnson would implement Goldwater's policy. His victory had given him a free hand; opposition to the war was not yet overly strong. But things were still going badly in Saigon. North Vietnam was bombed to dissuade it from intervening in the South, where American bases had been attacked. Operation Rolling Thunder (sustained bombing) was launched in February 1965 and the first marines landed at Da Nang in March to protect American installations. There were 184,000 American soldiers in South Vietnam by the end of 1965, 385,000 in 1966 and 543,400 in 1968. Americans were sent to do the job that the president had once said should be done by the Vietnamese.

Washington was not dragged into the quagmire of Vietnam; it dived in headfirst. Constantly upping what the Pentagon called the "pain coefficient" would, it was believed, force Hanoi to reconsider whether the war was worth its high cost at every stage of escalation. The theory held that the more the conflict was intensified the shorter it would be, since Hanoi would agree to negotiate. Hanoi held out, prepared to pay any price to reunify Vietnam. While Ho Chi Minh was a Communist, his strength came less from his Marxism than from his nationalism.

Over three and a half years, 800 tons of bombs per day on average were dropped on North Vietnam. Between 1965 and 1973, three times as many bombs fell on Vietnam as the Allies dropped during the Second World War. The Johnson-appointed General William Westmoreland had claimed in 1967 that a threshold had been crossed and the enemy could no longer compensate for its losses. American public opinion had begun to shift, and opponents were no longer a few Quakers and pacifist intellectuals. Protests grew. Johnson blamed media disinformation, claiming that the war was going well, battles were being won, Viet Cong body counts were rising and there was a light at the end of the tunnel, but there was a credibility gap. As important a figure as Secretary of Defense Robert McNamara had begun to have doubts by late 1967. He commissioned a thorough study of the war that resulted in the Pentagon Papers, leaked to the press in 1971. And America's claims that victory was close seemed a blatant lie after the Tet Offensive of January 30, 1969.

During the Tet Offensive, the Viet Cong struck throughout South Vietnam. The American embassy in Saigon was under siege for several hours. The sheer number of targets was stunning: five large cities, sixty-four district capitals, thirty-six provincial capitals and fifty villages. The offensive failed and Hanoi's forces suffered huge losses that would take years to recover from. But American public opinion was rattled; the war was not about to end. Doves now outnumbered hawks 42 percent to 41 percent. Figures in the preceding weeks had been 56 percent for hawks and 28 percent for doves. The number of American victims was rising. The cost of the war was very high: $23 billion in 1967 with a constantly rising deficit. Inflation set in. The war struck many as immoral, yet the generals were demanding more and more soldiers. Johnson's advisors finally convinced him to change course. Victory was not in sight, and sending in more troops would not change a thing. Westmoreland's requests were turned down.

In a surprise move on March 31, 1968, Johnson announced that he had ordered a halt to the bombing of North Vietnam and requested that negotiations begin. He added that he would not run for re-election in

November. His credibility had been eroded, and during the New Hampshire primaries, he heard a warning shot when Senator Eugene McCarthy won 42 percent of votes and 20 out of 24 delegates to the Democratic convention.

Years fraught with danger
In spite of Johnson's support for civil rights – including nominating the first African-American to the Supreme Court – his presidency saw increasingly vehement demonstrations. Protesters decried not only blacks' living conditions but also the slow pace of progress. Blacks earned half what whites did. Their unemployment rate was double that of whites. The situation of young blacks was even more appalling. The cities were crumbling and blacks were becoming conscious of their situation. The black "problem" was now a problem for the urban North.

Martin Luther King Jr.'s non-violence and gradualism were challenged. The Black Muslims, an offshoot of Islam, and their eloquent spokesman, Malcolm X (1925–1965), preached pride and black separatism as well as advocating violence as a means of self-defence. Malcolm X was assassinated in 1965 by three members of the Nation of Islam, with which he had parted ways. Stokely Carmichael formed the Black Panthers with the slogan Black Power. A new generation, black and proud, began preaching armed self-defence, separatism and control of their destiny. Whites were sidelined from the civil rights movement – they were told they could never understand what it was to be black. White support declined as the black movement radicalized. In 1966, 84 percent of whites thought blacks were pushing for too much change.

The Detroit Riot in the summer of 1967 left forty-three dead, most of them black, and caused $50 million in damage while a large part of the city burned. The army had to be called in. Following the 1967 riots, President Johnson set up the Kerner Commission to determine the causes. The Kerner Report (March 1968) mentioned two societies, separate and unequal. A month later, on April 4, 1968, Martin Luther King Jr. was assassinated in Memphis by James Earl Ray. Was Ray a deranged racist or the pawn of a conspiracy? The question remains unanswered. The black ghettos exploded, with riots in 168 cities.

Meanwhile, students were flocking to anti-war demonstrations and joining the campaigns of Senator McCarthy and Robert Kennedy, who had decided to enter the Democratic nomination race. Robert Kennedy won almost all the primaries in which he ran, carried along by his crown prince image and his stand in favour of the poor, minorities and the working class. In June 1968, after winning the California primary, he was assassinated by a young Palestinian opposed to his pro-Israel policies. It seemed as though American liberalism was rudderless after the assassinations of King and Kennedy. The Democratic Party had lost the one candidate who could have rebuilt a coalition around more than opposition to the war.

Young people were particularly disaffected. It was the time of the general student revolt against the status quo. From Paris (May '68) to Tokyo to Prague to Montreal, young people were trying to change the world. At "respectable" Ivy League universities such as Columbia and Cornell students took inspiration from the Berkeley Free Speech Movement (1964), the Students for a Democratic Society and the New Left, which for years had been denouncing racism and the Vietnam War and celebrating the counterculture. An October 1967 march on the Pentagon drew 100,000 people: student activists, the New Left and the counterculture were a threat to government policies.

The Democratic party was in turmoil going into its convention in Chicago in August 1968. Vice President Hubert Humphrey (1911–1972) was almost a shoo-in for the nomination. Johnson's candidate still controlled the Democratic machine, but everyone felt the absence of Robert Kennedy, knowing the people he might have represented were outside rather than inside the convention centre. Opponents of the war gathered in Chicago, as did the Yippies (the Youth International Party of Jerry Rubin and Abbie Hoffman). Around ten thousand showed up. The police were there too, twelve thousand strong, under orders from Mayor Richard Daley, determined to crush the slightest demonstration. The Yippies, in particular, were there to cause trouble and gave Daley the excuse he needed to crack down. Violence erupted even before the convention opened and continued for four days, reaching its apex on the evening of August 28, when the Johnson–Humphrey forces adopted a pro-war position and Humphrey was nominated on the first ballot.

Demonstrators were clubbed and gassed, as was the occasional reporter, all of it caught by TV cameras. Many delegates were outraged, but Humphrey, like many Americans, found the demonstrators' behaviour more reprehensible than Daley's overreaction. In any case, it seemed it would take a miracle to reunite the fractured party. In the public's mind, it was the party of chaos.

Humphrey faced two tough adversaries: Richard M. Nixon, making his comeback with the Republicans, and George Wallace, the former Alabama governor, running for the American Independent Party. Wallace had no chance of winning but he was a wild card, as a three-way election did not guarantee a majority in the Electoral College. Right after the Democratic convention, Wallace was at 25 percent in the polls. He was a right-wing populist who preached law and order and courted the segregationist vote, and his crusade found sympathy among blue-collar Northerners who hated the demonstrators. They could not stand to see the United States humiliated. He attacked hippies, leftists, feminists and long-haired liberals.

Nixon, for his part, played up his experience. After the Democratic fiasco in Chicago, the odds were in his favour. His campaign was well financed, TV-friendly and run by professionals. He announced he had a secret plan to resolve the conflict in Vietnam. Domestically, he was close to Wallace but less extreme. He let his running mate, Spiro Agnew, combat his opponents. The Republicans followed a Southern Strategy, foreseen by Johnson and aimed at capitalizing on Southern reaction to all the recent changes.

Humphrey made a spectacular recovery by distancing himself from Johnson on the war. Many voters, not wanting to waste their vote on Wallace, returned to the Democrats, and rumour had it that negotiations with Vietnam, begun in Paris in May 1968, were advancing. On October 31, Johnson announced a halt to the bombing. South Vietnamese president Nguyen Van Thieu, possibly at the instigation of Nixon on the advice of Henry Kissinger (1923–), who was part of the American delegation, torpedoed the impending agreement. Humphrey nonetheless finished the campaign in a strong position.

The election was very close: 43.4 percent of the vote went to Nixon versus 42.7 percent to Humphrey. Wallace took 13.5 percent. The difference between the two frontrunners was a mere 500,000 votes. Nixon was a minority president with both Houses of Congress controlled by Democrats. The wounds caused by the war, youth unrest, racism and poverty had to be healed. The task seemed daunting.

The Nixon years

The American electorate had shifted to the right. Nixon and Wallace had won 57 percent of the vote. The vote was also polarized: Humphrey took only 35 percent of the white vote but 97 percent of the black vote. Nixon portrayed himself as the defender of the forgotten Americans, the silent majority who paid their taxes, did not go to demonstrations and loved America.

During the 1970s, people came to mistrust the federal government, even though it had made efforts during the New Deal and the Great Society to help millions of Americans out of hardship. Prosperity had given rise to a new middle class hostile to higher taxes and the social programs they financed. These citizens looked to liberals to criticize social upheaval and immorality, to defend traditional values and stop focusing disproportionately on minorities and the poor.

Vietnam: The exit

Nixon had promised an honourable peace. But he could not afford to "lose" Vietnam any more than Johnson could, and the war would last another four years. In May 1969, Nixon announced a phased withdrawal of American soldiers and the Vietnamization of the war with guaranteed American support for South Vietnam. Nixon wanted to negotiate from a position of strength and still hoped to deliver the fatal blow. Kissinger, now national security advisor, portrayed Nixon as the "mad bomber" as a scare tactic to frighten the Vietnamese negotiators in Paris into making concessions. As if to confirm his reputation, Nixon, without approval of Congress, ordered the invasion of Cambodia, through which the North Vietnamese were infiltrating the South.

Opposition in the United States exploded. In October and November 1969, thousands of people attended the Peace Moratorium but Nixon refused to be influenced in any way. Public anger had calmed down somewhat with the continuing withdrawals of American troops, but it flared up again with clashes in the streets and on dozens of campuses in May 1970. At Kent State and Jackson State there were casualties at the hands of the National Guard and the police. The country was in an uproar. The Senate wanted to cut off funding for the war. Bad news was everywhere: GIs were being killed, army morale was at an all-time low due to racial

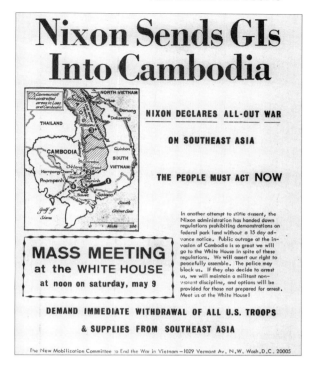

Announcement of an anti-Vietnam War rally in the *Washington Post*, May 1, 1970. Few issues more divided the country. (Library of Congress)

tensions and slackening discipline, the My Lai Massacre (the murder of over a hundred Vietnamese civilians by American soldiers) was revealed to the public, and the Pentagon Papers, which untangled the web of responsibilities and deception related to the Vietnam engagement, were published by the *New York Times*.

The atmosphere became overheated. Radicals resorted to bombing. People were afraid for their safety and Nixon was convinced that anarchy loomed. A siege mentality developed. Inflation, a chronic deficit and unemployment made things worse.

In summer 1971, Nixon made a last-ditch effort to save his presidency. He announced he would visit China, a Communist country he had been criticizing for decades. He might not get re-elected on his record: he had promised peace but extended the war; he had advocated a balanced budget but run deficits; and he had preached reconciliation but polarized the nation by linking Democrats to crime, drugs, moral decay, student radicalism, feminism, black militancy and so on. Now Nixon took on the role of architect of a new direction in foreign policy. The visit to China took place in February 1972 and the following May he was in the USSR. He succeeded in neutralizing both powers and it was rumoured that negotiations with Vietnam were progressing; Kissinger even made a premature announcement in October that the war was ending.

Wallace, a candidate for the presidency again in 1972, was the victim of an armed assault and dropped out of the race. George McGovern, the liberal Democratic candidate, could not maintain that party's coalition, and Nixon was re-elected by a landslide with 47 million votes versus 29 million for McGovern. Wallace may have been gone, but the prevailing wave of conservatism would continue for decades. Not only had the Southern Strategy worked, but Nixon had made major inroads into the urban, Catholic and ethnic vote.

On Christmas Day, 1971, Nixon ordered a final wave of bombings over North Vietnam. Negotiations resumed and an agreement was signed in January. South Vietnam was not a party to the agreement but received assurances of support. The Americans' final withdrawal in March 1973 made the conflict's outcome inevitable. In April 1975 Saigon fell and Vietnam was reunified. The war was over. The United States had sustained 58,000 dead, hundreds of thousands wounded, physically and mentally, and an astronomical cost of $150 billion. The goals of the war had not been attained. Containment had not worked. The only positive outcome was that the dominoes had not fallen either, partly due to U.S. efforts. While it was true the U.S. had not lost the war on the ground, international opinion was not wrong; the country had tasted bitter defeat.

Watergate

The Watergate scandal came of the president's obsession with secrecy and his need to control the opposition. After the Pentagon Papers were published in 1971, the White House set up a team known as the Plumbers in an office in the adjacent Executive Office Building. They were created to seal the leaks that so enraged Nixon and Kissinger. When the *New York Times* uncovered the secret bombing of Cambodia, Nixon put the FBI on the case to find the informant. Secrecy was the hallmark of the administration, and national security was invoked to hide aid given to the Shah of Iran, Ferdinand Marcos of the Philippines and Pieter Botha of South Africa. Likewise, the nature of efforts to destabilize and overthrow Salvador Allende of Chile and the aid to his successor, General Pinochet, had to remain top secret. In 1970, the Huston Plan was proposed for opening mail and for electronic surveillance of domestic radicals. Only the opposition of Hoover, who did not want anyone on his territory, killed the program.

As the 1972 campaign approached, Nixon wanted to maximize his chances. He controlled information, discredited his rivals and used dirty tricks, as he had done for his entire political career. The Plumbers' first operation was to break into Daniel Ellsberg's psychiatrist's office. Ellsberg was a researcher on the Pentagon Papers who had leaked them to Neil Sheehan of the *New York Times*. The break-in, however, uncovered nothing.

On June 17, 1972, seven men with cameras and microphones were arrested in the headquarters of the Democratic National Committee in the Watergate complex in Washington. The White House quickly distanced itself from the "third-rate burglary." The cover-up had begun. Six days after the incident, Nixon ordered H.R. Haldeman, his right-hand man in the White House, to tell the CIA and the FBI not to investigate too closely any links between the burglary and the administration. The Committee to Re-elect the President was also authorized to pay $400,000 to buy the Plumbers' silence. Judge John Sirica got the Plumbers to talk anyway, and two reporters from the *Washington Post*, Carl Bernstein and Bob Woodward, followed the trail of evidence to the White House.

In the televised proceedings of Sam Ervin's Senate committee White House Counsel John Dean admitted not only the cover-up but that the president was behind it. Even more devastating was the testimony of Nixon's deputy assistant, Alexander Butterfield, who disclosed that Oval Office conversations were recorded. Tangible evidence existed. The battle now shifted to the tapes. Nixon refused to hand them over, citing executive privilege that ensured the president could hear information and advice in confidence. Archibald Cox, who had been appointed special prosecutor, challenged Nixon's claim of executive privilege and was dismissed at Nixon's demand. On June 24, 1974, the Supreme Court voted unanimously that Nixon had to hand over the tapes to the new prosecutor, Leon Jaworski.

The tapes, even incomplete, proved that Nixon knew everything and had helped cover it up. He faced the prospect of impeachment. The House drew up the articles of impeachment to be judged by the Senate, presided over by the chief justice of the Supreme Court. The support of two thirds of senators was required for a conviction. On August 9, 1974, rather than face conviction, Richard M. Nixon became the first president in American history to step down.

Just as later there was a before and after 9/11, so there was a before and after Watergate. The scandal began a steady erosion of confidence in government. In 1964, almost 80 percent of Americans still trusted Washington to do a good job. Thirty years later, the figure stood at only 20 percent. Presidents from backgrounds as different as Jimmy Carter and Ronald Reagan would be brought to power by this mistrust.

CHAPTER 12

A TURN TO THE RIGHT

1974–2000

The Nixon administration collapsed amid total confusion in August 1974. Not only had Nixon resigned, his vice president had a few months earlier been forced to step down over charges of tax evasion and bribery. Nixon had replaced Spiro Agnew with Gerald Ford (1913–2006), the Republican House minority leader, who, once he took over as president, chose Nelson Rockefeller (1908–1979) as his vice president. Trust in institutions, especially the presidency, had been shattered. The Imperial Presidency (to use the term made popular by historian Arthur M. Scheslinger, Jr.) had its wings clipped by Congress. The War Powers Act of 1973 forced the president to consult Congress within sixty days of sending troops into combat. Congress passed other bills, including ones requiring the president to spend money appropriated, subjecting him to tighter control of campaign spending and forcing him to be more transparent.

Further alienatining many people, Ford granted Nixon a complete pardon a mere month after taking office. In doing so, he squandered his political capital and would never recover.

Economic problems were rampant. The United States was suffering the effects of the first oil crisis. Between 1973 and 1975, the price of a barrel of oil rose from $3 to $12. Inflation was galloping (a 1967 dollar was worth only 62 cents in 1975) and unemployment, at 8.5 percent in 1975 (it had reached 12 percent in 1974), soared again. Ford tried to reduce the federal budget deficit and control inflation, but he barely made a dent. In 1974, Ford projected a $60 billion deficit, and between 1970 and 1979, the dollar lost 37 percent of its value. The president was facing a Democratic opposition with tight control over Congress that regularly overrode his presidential vetoes. In 1975, the U.S. experienced the worst economic slowdown since the Great Depression. Productivity fell and the trade balance declined. Since 1971, for the first time in the 20th century, the United States had an unfavourable trade balance. Moreover, the nation's largest city, New York, was on the verge of bankruptcy.

The American economy was undergoing profound structural changes. The traditional sectors, industry and construction, stagnated while the service industries took off. The American auto industry was hit particularly hard by foreign competition. The number of American cars sold fell by eight million in 1974. There was constant soul-searching about American productivity and talk of deindustrialization; old industries were being outperformed, and the high-tech industries could not compete with other nations, the Japanese in particular. Agriculture suffered from rising fuel and fertilizer prices. Farmers went into debt and many declared bankruptcy.

In foreign policy, Ford had trouble exerting leadership. He kept Henry Kissinger as his secretary of state and pursued détente with the Soviet bloc, but Americans cared little about peripheral conflicts when the domestic situation was dire and American institutions themselves were under fire. Kissinger and Ford were forced to back down over confronting the USSR and Cuba in the Angolan civil war when Congress decided to cut off funding. Ford signed SALT I (Strategic Arms Limitation Treaty) and accepted the status quo in Europe under the Helsinki Treaty. These episodes illustrated the Soviet rise and the relative decline of the United States, yet the U.S. economy had never been in real danger of collapse. This may be easy to say in hindsight; what is certain is that the American climate of opinion at the time reflected genuine anxiety.

The Carter years

Although hampered by a deep lack of trust, Ford ran for re-election in 1976. The Republican Party narrowly granted him the nomination, fearing that his rival, Ronald Reagan (1911–2004), would push the party too far to the right and hand the election to the Democrats. Jimmy Carter (1924–), former governor of Georgia, won the Democratic nomination, billing himself as a Washington outsider, open and honest. He wanted to distance himself as far as possible from the corruption and cover-up of Watergate. "I will never lie to you," he promised the American people.

Carter led a shrewd campaign. He presented himself as a simple man, a born-again Christian and a conservative who would control government spending. But at the same time, he pledged to defend the poor, the elderly, working people and farmers. His choice of the liberal Walter Mondale (1928–) as his running mate backed up his claim. The election attracted little interest (53 percent of voters turned out) and Carter won 50 percent of the popular vote versus 48 percent for Ford. Carter was supported by 90 percent of black voters, ensuring his victory in seven Southern states.

Carter's problem was that he ran as a Washington outsider and turned out to be incapable of handling the complexities of Beltway politics. His relations with Congress were difficult, and he refused to engage in the usual horse-trading with legislators. His closest advisor, Hamilton Jordan (like many in Carter's inner circle, from Georgia and unfamiliar with Washington ways), waited weeks before meeting with Tip O'Neill, Speaker of the House and the most powerful Democrat in Congress.

Carter also alienated many liberals with his conservative policies. In many ways, Carter prefigured Reagan. Carter did not believe that the country's problems could be solved through a redistribution of wealth and power, a Democratic staple since the New Deal. He favoured deregulating airlines, railways and trucking. He removed price controls on oil and natural gas. His priority was fighting inflation by reducing federal spending, even if it meant more unemployment. The problem was that inflation persisted. It was at 10 percent in 1978 and 12.4 percent in 1980. Interest rates skyrocketed (to 20 percent in 1980), with the usual consequences.

Carter had banked on a change of image and political climate. In his inaugural procession to the White House, he made his way on foot dressed in a business suit. To demonstrate energy conservation during his inaugural address, he turned the thermostat down and donned his old cardigan. He carried his own luggage in airports and stayed overnight with American citizens. His symbolic gestures, unfortunately, were overshadowed by failed policies. Admittedly, Carter was not helped by events outside his control, among them the 1979 oil crisis and the Iranian revolution, but the political consequences for him were still disastrous; near the end of his term, he was less popular than Nixon had been after the Watergate scandal.

The nation was fractured politically and divided socially and economically. Income and wealth remained poorly distributed. There were still 26 million Americans living below the poverty line. They were overwhelmingly black, Latino and Indian. A shocking 27 percent of black families were poor versus 7 percent of white families. Unemployment stood at 50 percent for young blacks. The number of black families headed by single mothers increased dramatically.

Some progress was made. A black middle class took shape thanks in part to affirmative action, but whites cried reverse discrimination. In 1978, the Supreme Court partially agreed with Allan Bakke, a white student denied admission to the University of California under quotas that favoured minorities. The decision stipulated that affirmative action could exist, but only in cases where a history of discriminatory treatment could be proved. Bakke was admitted to the school. There were the beginnings of a resurgence of racism, and the Ku Klux Klan gained ground. Anti-busing demonstrations erupted in several cities, protesting policies that encouraged integration by assigning and transporting children to selected schools. Blacks, however, were no longer willing to accept injustice. The Indians, the poorest of the poor, were also making demands, but the era of great causes was waning. The struggle moved into the communities, where the playing field was smaller but militancy was high.

Americans turned inward, focusing on their health, well-being and environment. In response to environmental special interest groups, Congress passed legislation to protect endangered species, curb pollution, limit or ban pesticide use and so on. At the same time, a growing number of Americans were embracing conservative values, sceptical that the government could solve every problem. They wanted to limit the welfare state. Proposition 13 was passed by referendum in California in 1978 as a tax revolt: property taxes were reduced, as was the government's leeway for social and education spending. The conservatives were supported by many blue-collar Americans alarmed about the direction the country was taking, but mainly by the religious right, which mobilized around opposing abortion and defending traditional family values. In 1979, the Moral Majority was founded by Virginia television evangelist Jerry Falwell and others as a political lobby demanding stricter laws against pornography and homosexuality and supporting smaller government. At the same time, they demanded an increase in defence spending. In a few months, the movement drew millions of members and millions of dollars. Conservative think tanks and right-wing magazines joined the network of support for politicians increasingly sympathetic to the New Right cause.

One of the favourite targets of the New Right was the feminist movement. Since the '60s, many women and feminist organizations had made strides in ensuring political, economic and legal equality. The doors of medicine and law faculties were opened to female students. The number of women in the job market was constantly rising, but women's wages remained lower than men's. The Equal Rights Amendment (ERA) was passed by Congress in 1972 and presented to state legislatures to be ratified; it was intended to enshrine the principle of equal pay for equal work. New Right opposition focused on the amendment as well as the legalization of abortion (*Roe v. Wade*, 1973). Feminism was blamed for family breakdown and the rising divorce rate. The pro-life movement demanded a constitutional amendment defining life as beginning at conception. The pro-life/pro-choice battle over women's right to abortions would continue for decades. The ERA was stalled and in 1982 its proponents were forced to admit defeat and withdraw it.

Carter and foreign policy

Jimmy Carter had limited experience in foreign policy. He had cut his teeth at the Trilateral Commission (an organization bringing together opinion leaders from Europe, North America and Japan for discussions that could potentially influence national policies), but had done little more. Carter harboured illusions that he could completely overhaul foreign policy, making human rights its centrepiece. The process was arduous. Carter quickly had to reassure several dictators who were U.S. allies that national security requirements would take precedence over human rights. In Iran, South Korea, the Philippines and South Africa, American policies remained fundamentally unchanged. Argentina, Uruguay, Chile and Ethiopia saw their practices re-evaluated on the basis of their human rights record. China escaped condemnation but not the USSR, which rejected American criticisms. In Nicaragua and Iran, the new American focus on human rights encouraged liberation movements, leading to a paradoxical outcome for the United States. The dictator Anastasio Somoza was driven out of Nicaragua only to be replaced by the Marxist-leaning Sandinistas. In Iran, the Shah was overthrown in favour of an Islamic republic that seized the American embassy and fifty-seven hostages.

Carter managed a few major successes. The return of the Panama Canal to the Panamanians by 2000 was approved, after a fierce battle in the Senate, by a one-vote majority in 1978. The Camp David Accord was a master stroke when Carter convinced Israel and Egypt to bury the hatchet in March 1979. The accord fell short in not addressing the thorny issues of Jewish settlements and the future of the Palestinians, but it helped defuse tensions in the Middle East for a while.

Beginning in 1979, just as the economic situation was worsening domestically, a host of problems arose on the world stage. Carter at first tried to establish relations with the Sandinistas in Nicaragua, but Congress denied him the necessary funding. The Sandinistas quickly allied themselves with the Cubans and the Soviets. When unrest spread to neighbouring El Salvador, the United States chose to back the far right despite its extremism. Anti-Communism and American interests in the region trumped human rights.

Iran was an even worse debacle. After the hostages were seized in November 1979, the crisis went on for 444 days. TV screens showed daily images of the hostages, and Carter's inability to secure their release by negotiation or force (an attempted airborne commando raid ended in disaster in the Iranian desert) exasperated Americans and made them question the president's leadership just as he was preparing for the upcoming election. Secretary of State Cyrus Vance, who had always preferred the diplomatic route and restraint on every issue, resigned. This left the way clear for Zbigniew Brzezinski, the national security advisor and fervent Cold Warrior who considered any loss on the international stage a Soviet victory.

The December 1979 invasion of Afghanistan by Soviet troops prompted Carter to react forcefully, putting an end to détente. The Soviets had succumbed to the same arrogance of power as the Americans in Vietnam, though they had the added excuse that the danger was on their borders. Carter imposed an embargo on American grain destined for the USSR (to the great chagrin of American farmers), organized a boycott of the Moscow Olympic Games scheduled for summer 1980, put forward the Carter Doctrine (which proclaimed the Persian Gulf to be of vital interest to America) and eventually resumed the arms race and shelved SALT II.

For some time now, the Americans had seized every chance to gain a march on the Soviets. Moscow was concerned by America's recognition of the Beijing regime. The Camp David Accord, signed without Soviet consultation, was an affront. U.S. demands that the USSR withdraw the combat brigade that had been in Cuba since the 1960s, in full view of the Americans, was a shock. The Soviets' refusal almost guaranteed that the draft agreement for SALT II would be derailed. Perhaps American problems and Soviet arms parity had gone to the Soviets' heads, leading them to underestimate the American response, but the international situation in the late 1970s bore a startling resemblance to some of the worst days of the Cold War.

The Reagan era

This climate of tension and conservatism was the backdrop to the 1980 elections. The population, 226 million, had increased by 11.5 percent over the previous decade. Population growth was slowing; the birth rate was down and the population was aging. There were as many people over thirty as under. Life expectancy had risen to seventy-four for whites and sixty-eight for blacks. Men and women got married two years later than in 1970. Fifty-one percent of women had a paid job; they represented 46 percent of the work force. The population was 75 percent urban and was migrating from the east toward the south and the west. From 1970 to 1980, the northeast grew by 0.2 percent while the south gained 20 percent and the west 23.9 percent. Retirees, whose numbers had grown by 50 percent over the decade, were concentrated in the Sunbelt.

Politically, the census confirmed the country's shift to the right. In 1980, conservative politicians were flying high, and the highest flyer had to be Ronald Reagan. Reagan was a former Hollywood star and television host turned two-time governor of California. For years, he had been a Roosevelt admirer and a Democrat. He had been the president of the Screen Actors Guild, had led the anti-Communist struggle in the film industry and then, after his second marriage to Nancy Davis and the decline of his movie career, became the spokesman for General Electric. He remodelled himself as a conservative Republican and gave hundreds of speeches all over the country extolling the virtues of the American political system. In 1964, he delivered his career-making speech when he introduced Barry Goldwater at the Republican convention.

During his years as governor in Sacramento he was certainly a conservative who took a heavy hand with protesting students and welfare recipients, but he was also a pragmatist who reformed welfare and approved one of the most liberal abortion laws in the country. In 1976, he had been beaten to the Republican nomination by Ford, but in 1980 he was unstoppable. He chose the moderate George H.W. Bush (1924–), whom he had defeated for the nomination, as his running mate.

Jimmy Carter, despite his unpopularity, ran for re-election. He avoided the primaries, claiming to be entirely preoccupied by the hostage crisis. Ted Kennedy tried hard to sell his own candidacy, but the Democratic convention chose Carter. The campaign was completely dominated by the energetic Reagan, while Carter tried to appear above the fray. Reagan constantly asked Americans whether they were better off than four years before. He rallied conservatives of various stripes by opposing the ERA and, contrary to his earlier stance, abortion. He promised to put the Soviets in their place. As one worker from Cleveland put it, "When he negotiates with the Russians, he'll do it with a gun on the table." He also promised a balanced budget, with tax cuts, reduced spending and an increase in the defence budget. He embraced the theories of the supply-siders, economists who favoured stimulating the economy through supply rather than demand. One of their theories held that entrepreneurs and investors who benefited from tax cuts would make a higher profit and create more jobs; prosperity would spread through a trickle-down process. Before being won over by Reagan, George H.W. Bush had described the whole idea as "voodoo economics."

Reagan won the election with 10 percent more of the popular vote than Carter and 489 votes in the Electoral College compared to only 49 for Carter. Only 53 percent of the voters had voted. Reagan was elected by just over a quarter of Americans. While the electorate had certainly embraced Reagan's values, they were also expressing their dissatisfaction with Carter. The key element of the victory was almost certainly the electoral realignment. The traditional Republican base that wanted balanced budgets, smaller government, strong national defence and respect for law and order grew to include many Southerners concerned about blacks' gains, along with Sunbelt voters and followers of the new morality and Christian fundamentalism. Ironically, of the two candidates Reagan was the less religious. But in 1980, voters were won over by the Republican program of prayer in schools, a ban on abortion, a mandatory death sentence for selected crimes, the rejection of the ERA and an end to busing.

End of the Democratic coalition

The era of the Democratic coalition created by the New Deal and continued by Kennedy and Johnson was well and truly over. At the same time as the United States' relative position on the world stage shifted, the ideology of a majority of Americans was changing. These changes led to the Republican rebirth and domination. Between 1968 and 2000, the Republicans won six out of nine presidential elections and even managed on occasion to take control of one or both Houses.

On the very day Ronald Reagan was inaugurated as president, the Iranians released the hostages in a gesture that was also a snub to Carter, who was deliberately stripped of credit for their liberation. Reagan emissaries might have had something to do with this "coincidence."

Reagan and his team were masters of political symbolism: the substance of issues and causes was less important than rhetoric and appearances. The Great Communicator was an expert in presidential image-making. His inaugural ceremony harked back to the pomp and circumstance of the Kennedy years. His speeches referred to the American dream and his upbeat optimism inspired hope in Americans in general, and particularly among conservative supporters, that America was taking a new direction.

Like F.D. Roosevelt and Lyndon B. Johnson, Ronald Reagan was relatively busy in the first few months of his first term. He pushed through Congress his major tax cut program (25 percent on income tax over three years), slashed many social programs and significantly increased military spending. The new president benefited from his ability to make decisions at a time when Americans thought their leaders incapable of doing so. For example, he got tough with the air traffic controllers during their 1981 strike, declaring the situation an emergency and firing more than 11,000 controllers who defied his order to return to work. Reagan was also lucky. The economic recovery was attributed to "Reaganomics" when it had nothing to do with them; the trickle-down theory, inspired by Alexander Hamilton and Andrew Mellon, had failed, leading instead to the rise of a new, speculation-driven "casino" society. Even the attempt on his life by John Hinckley Jr. in 1981 was lucky in its way: it brought on an even greater wave of sympathy for him. The Los Angeles Olympics of summer 1984, wrapped in the American flag, were represented as proof that the United States, and by extension its presidency, had experienced a renewal: Americans were standing tall again.

In terms of foreign policy, a hard-line approach to relations with the USSR dominated Reagan's first term. The "evil empire," as he described the Soviet Union, had to be defeated, and "Star Wars" (the Strategic Defense Initiative) would be the answer to security. After the fiasco in Beirut (241 marines were killed in October 1983 and American troops were withdrawn), the U.S. invaded Grenada and attacked Muammar Gaddafi's Libya, increasing the president's first-term popularity and distracting attention from his failed Middle East policy. In Central America, there was a return to the tradition of propping up repressive right-wing regimes – in El Salvador, for example.

Reagan was re-elected to office in 1984. It was an unequivocal victory for his personal popularity. He won 59 percent of the vote against the team of Walter Mondale (1928–) and Geraldine Ferraro (1935–), the first female running mate in a presidential election. Only Minnesota and the District of Columbia voted for Democratic candidates. However, the Democrats did keep control of the House and gained two Senate seats.

Assessing the Reagan presidency

On the positive side, Ronald Reagan put the presidency back on track and showed leadership to segments of the American population concerned and unhappy about their changing society. To these millions of Americans demanding a return to a more reassuring climate, Reagan spoke of a new beginning and inspired what many called, despite the apparent contradiction in terms, a conservative revolution.

The downside of Reagan's presidency was his limited success in meeting the expectations he had raised, primarily economic ones. After talking at length about a balanced budget, Ronald Reagan got Americans accustomed to $200 billion deficits. The huge budget deficit, deepened by tax cuts inspired by the supply-siders, shrank the government's manoeuvring room for years to come. In eight years the national debt, half of which was foreign-held, tripled. Ronald Reagan was responsible for as much of it as his thirty-nine predecessors combined. Along with a formidable trade deficit, the debt signalled a decline in American economic power and world leadership. In an attempt to maintain leadership, Ronald Reagan and his secretary of defense, Caspar Weinberger, adopted a policy of accelerated rearmament. They earmarked $1.7 trillion for defence over five years. As well as contributing to the deficit, this policy made the Pentagon ripe for corruption and at least partly led President Mikhail Gorbachev of the Soviet Union, also being squeezed domestically, to review his foreign policy and broach the subject of disarmament with the American president. It is hard not to see the irony in the unintended consequences and the credit Reagan was given for them.

Disappointing his more committed supporters, Reagan also failed to deliver on dismantling the welfare state. Certainly his deficit limited its growth for years to come, but the gains of the New Deal and the Great Society remained largely intact; to the disappointment of reactionaries, he had not turned out to be the man who would shape a conservative future.

Conservative circles are unlikely to rate Ronald Reagan highly. Conservative icon Barry Goldwater gave Harry Truman top marks, ranked F.D. Roosevelt second, consigned Nixon to the bottom rank and was critical of Reagan, who he felt was badly advised and had no excuse for the Iran-Contra mess that came to a head in 1987. If he had not known about it, he had failed to do his job; if he had known about it, he had lied, according to Goldwater. That episode indelibly marred the Reagan presidency. It began when journalists uncovered a deal by the administration to sell arms to Iran in exchange for hostages. The Reagan administration had in 1980 openly denounced Iran, which was at war with Iraq. Profits generated by the sales were funnelled to the Nicaraguan Contras in clear violation of a congressional amendment (the Boland Amendment, 1984) banning aid to the Contras. The White House was aware of the deal but Reagan's subordinates protected him. Admiral John Poindexter, the national security advisor, would say that he did not want the president to know, and his underling Lieutenant Colonel Oliver North would say that he had not told the president but had assumed the president knew. Reagan would claim not to remember.

While the "Irangate" scandal dominated Reagan's second term, it was not the only low point. Despite the 1984 landslide re-election and the successful negotiations with the Soviet Union, it seemed as though the administration was running out of steam and losing its nerve, especially in 1986–1987. The *Challenger* space shuttle disaster, while not Reagan's responsibility, had a dampening effect. The presidential team, clearly more divided than before, was damaged by a whiff of conflict of interest and several jumped ship. Around the same time as the rise of the Democrats in the November 1986 mid-term elections, news of the arms-for-hostages negotiations broke in the newspapers. The Tower Commission Report in 1987 left serious doubt as to whether Ronald Reagan was capable of controlling a White House plagued by lax organization. The president seemed less and less on top of the issues, he was distracted, he had aged and his contacts with the press were becoming less frequent. He rarely went beyond brief answers to questions shouted by journalists as helicopter blades whirred, making any real exchange impossible. Presidential competence and credibility were questioned. Scandals on Wall Street and among fundamentalist preachers made things worse. When in late 1987 shares on Wall Street suffered a historic collapse, one wag declared, "None of this would have happened if Ronald Reagan were still president." Despite all this, Reagan had enough residual popularity to pass on the presidency to George H.W. Bush.

Only when the sound and fury around the exercise of power have settled down, among both supporters and adversaries of Reagan, can a fairer assessment made of his presidency. While the responsibility was not solely his, peace and prosperity were maintained under his administration – despite or perhaps because of his bellicose rhetoric. Ronald Reagan was indisputably a popular president, as his success at the polls indicates, both on a personal level and in terms of approval for his policies. He partly restored the tarnished image and credibility of the presidency. Americans needed reassuring after the Nixon/Ford/Carter debacle and he certainly restored their confidence. In 1976, recent presidential history might have led people to believe that the office was gruelling and inhuman and no one could politically survive a term. The simple fact that Ronald Reagan finished two terms, which had not been done since Eisenhower, was a positive contribution. It is another matter to judge how well he served his terms and whether he was more concerned about image than content; whether his ignorance of the issues and his flippancy, masked by an unshakeable optimism born of ideological certainty, were the keys to his success and survival.

In the aura of a presidential office that is glorified, imperial and almost deified, fallible humans will inevitably appear inadequate. Ronald Reagan certainly had episodes (the failure of the Bork nomination to the Supreme Court, his pro-Contra policy) that brought home the limits of presidential power. Like other presidents, he also suffered from the wearing effect of being in power and the gaps between promises, expectations and accomplishments. But he also proved that a popular man with limited abilities, but tuned into heartland America and its enduring values and symbols, can wield presidential power, or a semblance of it, in a credible way and hold on to it despite serious gaffes. Irangate is ample proof of how well-liked he was: such a series of misdeeds, mistakes and blunders still could not bring him down – although a major factor was perhaps that Americans felt the presidency could not recover from another blow to its prestige. Reagan seemed somehow impervious to scandal; one Democratic congresswoman called him the "Teflon president."

Yet time could well reveal the full extent of weaknesses in the presidency, especially at the economic level. The United States has been a debtor nation since 1985. Long-term debt threatens the economy in general and complicates any government initiative. The debt tripled under Reagan to $2.8 trillion. Interest on the debt rose to $216 billion annually in 1988. The trade deficit stood at $171 billion in 1987. Poor distribution of wealth and income continued to be a monumental flaw in the American system. Budget deadlines were constantly extended with no added resources to meet them. While historians' first assessment has been fairly kind, the revision that is certain to follow, based on the economic fallout and Irangate, could be scathing.

Next in line: George H.W. Bush

Reagan's second term, as mentioned, was less successful than his first. The gap between rich and poor had widened. People were scandalized by excessive wealth and revolted by conspicuous consumption. The new wealth was sometimes obtained fraudulently. Wall Street seemed to be run by sharks playing with junk bonds to take over companies to form larger and larger conglomerates. During this time, middle-class incomes remained largely stagnant. The success of the yuppies (young urban professionals) was much in the news, but they represented only 5 percent of their age group. Too many of the jobs created were low-paying service-industry jobs. Many families needed two salaries to survive. Federal taxes may have been cut but local and state taxes and social security deductions increased. Poverty still plagued 13 percent of the American population, affecting blacks (30 percent) and Hispanics (26 percent) disproportionately.

Children under eighteen made up 40 percent of the poor and lived for the most part in single-parent households.

When George H.W. Bush took office in 1988, an era had ended. The euphoria had been dispelled by the stock market crash of October 1987. Scandals were rocking the nation. Accumulated deficits were taking their toll. Reagan had always refused to acknowledge that simply cutting social spending could not make up the gap between lower tax revenue and increased military spending. Yet foreign policy based on the spending increase had brought results. By resorting to Star Wars, the U.S. had made the Soviet regime, bogged down in Afghanistan, reel under the costs of the arms race. The new cold war that Reagan had been fomenting for years settled into a détente in the final year and a half of the Reagan administration. Uncertainty overcame the United States as people realized that the country could not continue down the road of deficits and "imperial overextension" in a world that was no longer bipolar.

1988 election

The Democrats were in disarray in 1988. Gary Hart (1936–), a Colorado senator, took the lead at first but was forced to drop out over a sexual indiscretion. Michael Dukakis (1935–), governor of Massachusetts, won the nomination. For his running mate, Dukakis had passed over Jesse Jackson, the black leader who had led an effective campaign on his Rainbow Coalition platform, in favour of Lloyd Bentsen, a senator from Texas.

The Bush–Quayle machine (Dan Quayle was an Indiana senator with dubious qualifications) crushed the opposition using negative ads, simplistic slogans and unfounded accusations. Bush spoke of a "kinder, gentler America." His catchphrase was "Read my lips: no new taxes." The Democrats were portrayed as spendthrift liberals (dirty words on the right) who were soft on crime and unpatriotic.

Bush won with 54 percent of the popular vote and 426 Electoral College votes. The Democrats completely controlled Congress, however. The new president was not considered a true conservative and many Republicans found him suspect. Bush came from an East Coast patrician background. His father, Prescott Bush, had been a banker and senator. George H.W. studied at Yale after serving in the air force during the war. He made his money in oil in Texas, then was drawn to public service and politics. He made his mark more as a public servant than as a politician, serving as ambassador to the UN, U.S. envoy to China and director of the CIA. He had had little influence on and little in common with Ronald Reagan, but managed to portray himself as his heir. It was the first time since 1836 that a sitting vice president had been elected to succeed the president.

Troubled beginnings
Reagan's public-finance legacy, with its tax cuts and constantly rising expenditures, could not continue indefinitely, and Bush was the one who paid the price. First the savings and loan crisis erupted. These mortgage lending associations had been deregulated in 1982, allowing them to diversify into commercial investments. In the late 1980s, lenders ran into trouble due to risky investments and bad management. The government had to guarantee losses to the tune of $200 billion. A recession followed in 1990 and unemployment rose to 7 percent in 1991 then to 8 percent in 1992. After an eight-year upturn, recovery was stalled by the federal debt and the fact that lower levels of government could not run deficits and had to find new sources of revenue, which put a strain on personal finances. Bush himself was forced to go back on his promise not to impose new taxes and would never be forgiven by many Republicans.

End of the Cold War
Since the mid-eighties, Mikhail Gorbachev had been trying to withdraw from the arms race because the Soviet Union was on the verge of bankruptcy. He loosened Russia's stranglehold on Eastern Europe. The Soviets withdrew from Afghanistan in 1988 and the symbol that was the Berlin Wall was demolished in 1989. The changes came fast. A year later, the two Germanys were reunited, Communists were driven from power in a series of satellite countries and even the USSR was shaken. In April 1991, the Warsaw Pact, the Eastern counterpart of NATO, was dismantled. In summer of the same year, there was an attempted coup against Gorbachev by former Communist Party higher-ups. The coup failed but the break-up was inevitable. Russia under the leadership of Boris Yeltsin managed to reassemble a community of independent states, but Georgia, Azerbaijan and Estonia, for example, had left the Soviet orbit.

The disintegration of the Soviet empire, long desired but unexpectedly fast and wide-scale, caught the Americans off guard as they found themselves the only dominant military power. They hoped to reap the dividends of peace, but problems would strike what had become the world's sole policeman. The "new world order" put demands on a country that needed a chance to catch its breath. The challenges were new: ethnic and civil wars, the war on drugs and the struggle against the proliferation of nuclear, chemical, biological and ballistic weapons. The invasion of Panama and the arrest of its dictator, Manuel Noriega (a former CIA collaborator), in December 1989 and January 1990 was an example of the new tactics. Overcoming fears that potentially embarrassing secrets could come to light, the United States went in to stop a notorious trafficker and oust a dictator: the big-stick policy but with irreproachable motives.

Gulf War I

The new international order tempted many to test American will. One of these was the fiercely ambitious Saddam Hussein. Hussein had benefited from American support during the Iran-Iraq war, but in August 1990 he stepped out of line and invaded neighbouring Kuwait to seize its oil reserves. Washington naturally perceived the invasion as a threat to stability in the region and to Saudi Arabia, its vital ally. With Kuwait's oil at stake, this infringement of international law and American interests could not go unanswered. There had to be a show of American power.

George H.W. Bush headed a broad international coalition to fight Hussein and shrewdly secured UN support and Soviet neutrality. Troops began to be massed in the region, and it took months to transport enough forces for the overwhelming military operation envisioned by the high command. Once the war had been deemed operationally feasible and worthwhile, Bush prepared the American public: Saddam Hussein was a criminal tyrant whose regime was a threat to world peace. The problem with this noble rhetoric was that it masked a much different reality. Saddam Hussein was indeed a bloodthirsty tyrant, but the U.S. had been satisfied with him for years as a stabilizing influence on a united Iraq who minimized friction between Sunnis, Shiites and Kurds. The Americans' position seemed to imply that they would now do anything to get rid of him.

Once preparations were finished, a UN ultimatum was delivered to Saddam Hussein in late November 1990 demanding a withdrawal from Kuwait by January 15, 1991. When Hussein did not comply, Congress on January 16 authorized President Bush to launch the international force into action. An air campaign in late January began Operation Desert Storm and destroyed Iraqi defences. The American media gave the war blanket coverage, and the first bombings took place in time for the TV news. Information was controlled. The war was sanitized. Boasts were made of smart bombs that struck with "surgical" precision, stealth bombers and Patriot missiles that intercepted Iraqi Scud missiles. The accuracy of these claims would be questioned after the war. The ground offensive began on February 24. In a hundred hours, General Norman Schwarzkopf's forces overwhelmed the greatly overestimated enemy. Kuwait had been liberated and the road to Baghdad lay open.

Bush and American policy-makers preferred a stable region with Saddam Hussein remaining in power to a destabilized region and a country breaking apart under ethnic and religious pressures, a breakup that could lead to increased influence by Shiite-dominated Iran. That decision was a boon to Saddam Hussein as his Iraqi opponents, who believed the U.S. genuinely intended to oust him, stuck out their necks, only to be decapitated by the dictator while the Americans stood by. George Bush Sr. chose not to take Baghdad or be an occupying power in a harsh and hostile land rife with internal conflict, with results that could have been costly and possibly futile. The lesson was lost on George Bush Jr. after September 2001.

The Iraqi people paid the highest price during the next ten years of economic sanctions and constant attacks aimed at curbing the "Iraqi threat." Meanwhile, a strengthened Saddam maintained his façade as a dangerous power and eliminated his opponents, and the region remained stable.

The American people were pleased that the victory came with minimal American bloodshed but were frustrated not to see a rogue state brought down. The United States had proved its status as the sole international military power but had solicited financial support from its allies, which assumed 80 percent of the cost of operations. An environmental disaster resulted from the war when the retreating Iraqis set fire to Kuwaiti oil wells, and the Iraqi people were left to their fate. This cast doubt on what the new world order actually meant.

Clinton takes the reins

Most pundits felt that after the Gulf War, Bush with his 90 percent approval rating would be handily re-elected in 1992. Yet the country's slump continued. Unemployment was high and there was stiff competition from Japan and Europe. The economy would come back to haunt George H.W. Bush. "It's the economy, stupid" went the slogan of Bill Clinton (1948–), the new star of the Democratic Party. Clinton, former governor of Arkansas, great admirer of John F. Kennedy, opponent of the Vietnam War and a skilled communicator, called himself a New Democrat. He was new in many ways: he belonged to the baby boom generation, admitted smoking marijuana (albeit not inhaling), acknowledged that welfare recipients should show responsibility, billed himself as tough on crime and advocated private investment as a means of job creation. His position in favour of the family and children was inspired by his wife, Hillary Rodham Clinton, a prominent lawyer who had long been involved with these issues. Reforming health care was also a central plank in his platform.

Bush's party was divided. His economic policies were a disappointment, and he proved unable to ride the wave of the Gulf War triumph to election victory. Pat Buchanan, an ultraconservative isolationist, attacked him during the primaries, accusing him of having advanced no national interest with the Gulf War. Bush defeated Buchanan in the primaries, but at the convention in August Buchanan declared that a religious and cultural war was under way in the United States for no less than the soul of the country. Buchanan's remark recalled one particular recent incident in the culture wars: the 1991 battle between Clarence Thomas and Anita Hill. Clarence Thomas, a black conservative who was colour-blind on legal and constitutional matters, was nominated for a seat on the Supreme Court. During his confirmation hearings, Anita Hill, a black lawyer, accused Thomas of sexual harassment while she had been his assistant during the Reagan years. Thomas claimed to be a victim, criticized the methods of the all-white Senate committee and, naturally, denied everything. Anita Hill and her feminist supporters criticized her treatment at the hands of the all-male committee. Thomas was confirmed to the Supreme Court, but by a thin margin. Passions were running high, and each side accused the other of cultural politicking and playing the race or gender card.

The debate that had raged for years around the phenomenon of "political correctness" had spread out from college campuses into the world of politics and then into the media. The right saw the Clintons, with their platform of radical feminism, abortion on demand and gay rights, as their sworn enemy. Even Bush himself was not conservative enough for his party's right wing. The Republicans had freed up the political centre for Clinton, and he seized the opportunity.

A wild-card third candidate made an appearance in 1992, eventually damaging Bush more than Clinton. Texas millionaire Ross Perot channelled voter mistrust and anger toward the two traditional parties. Making the national debt his crusade, he spent millions of dollars on a media-heavy campaign and managed to rake in 20 million votes. Clinton won 45 million votes versus 39 million for Bush. In the Electoral College, Clinton won 370 votes, Bush 168 and Perot none. It was a clear rejection of Bush, and the Democrats still controlled both Houses.

Bill Clinton's policies were varied and often put him at odds with his own party. He was first and foremost a pragmatist who was against invasive government; he made efforts to control the deficit, and his Supreme Court appointments were fairly moderate. Despite his campaign promise, he arrived at a compromise with the Pentagon over gays in the army by proposing a "Don't ask, don't tell" policy. He expanded police forces and supported a ban on most assault rifles. He benefited from the economic recovery as annual growth reached 4 percent. Yet Clinton suffered a huge defeat over a central issue in his platform: health care. He handed the file to his wife, Hillary, who produced a report in late 1993. The reform died in Congress because the plan was complicated and impossible to sell to interest groups; the Chamber of Commerce, the National Association of Manufacturers, the pharmaceutical companies and doctors all opposed it.

In foreign policy, Clinton seemed just as tentative as Bush when it came to adapting his policies to new conditions. Iraq policy had not changed, but Clinton tried to avoid too much American muscle-flexing in the style of Reagan or Bush. His first intervention, in Somalia, turned to disaster and troops were withdrawn in 1994. The setback explains his waffling over Bosnia and even Haiti. In the war-ravaged Balkans, Clinton backed the UN against the Serbs and entered negotiations for the Dayton Accords in 1995. As a result, the United States had a presence in the region, if only to save face, whereas its slow response earlier reflected its lack of interest in the disintegration of Yugoslavia. The Kosovo crisis of 1997–1999 was reminiscent of the Iraq crisis; while his crimes were overlooked in the 1995 Dayton Accords, Serb leader Slobodan Milosevic, like Saddam Hussein, was later portrayed as a bloodthirsty tyrant.

Economically, Clinton spearheaded free trade and globalization, which were the sources of the recovery. He strongly defended NAFTA (North American Free Trade Agreement), which added Mexico to the free-trade agreement signed with Canada in 1988. He prevailed over the objections of American labour by garnering support from Republicans open to free trade. Soon afterward, he also continued efforts begun by Bush to create an American hemispheric market, the Free Trade Area of the Americas (FTAA). He remained open to China and backed the creation of the World Trade Organization (WTO) to conclude trade agreements and resolve disputes.

The 1994 mid-term elections displayed Clinton's vulnerability and signalled the wave of conservatism sweeping the country. Clinton had been plagued by problems. Members of a far-right cult, the Branch Davidians, had barricaded themselves in Waco, Texas, and when their compound was stormed by government agents, seventy-eight cult members, including children, had died. The Clinton administration was accused of murdering them. A similar incident had occurred in Ruby Ridge, Idaho, when two members of a patriot militia had been killed in a confrontation with the FBI. On a personal level, Clinton and his wife had invested in a failed real estate venture in Arkansas, and when rumours of the so-called Whitewater scandal began circulating, the Republicans naturally jumped on them. Even more unsettling, an employee of the state of Arkansas, Paula Jones, claimed that Clinton had sexually harassed her when he was the state governor. Awkwardly for him, the Supreme Court eventually decided that the case could be heard before Clinton left office.

The mid-term elections in November 1994 brought a Republican landslide. The president was left with an anti-government, anti-tax Congress that promoted the Conservative Revolution and the New Order. Success went to the heads of House Speaker Newt Gingrich and his cohort. As a result of their extreme opposition to government and their determination to impose their morals and undermine social programs, the Republicans quickly sank in the polls, and Clinton capitalized on the rumblings of discontent by promising a balanced budget and deep cuts in the federal bureaucracy. When the federal government was shut down in late 1995 due to a budget standoff, the Republicans were blamed, not Clinton. In January 1996, Clinton announced that the era of big government was over. The new Democrat was looking like the Republicans he had collaborated with on welfare reform.

Clinton's chances for re-election in 1996 improved considerably as he exerted his leadership and presented himself as a president for all Americans, a centrist who defended common values. Right-wing arrogance and weak Republican leadership made his task easier. When General Colin Powell, the architect of the Gulf War, showed no interest in the presidency, the Republicans were left with Senator Robert Dole (1923–), an old political hand who seemed out of touch with the times and with his own party and its newfound conservatism. Having lived there for thirty-five years, he was also the epitome of the Washington insider so reviled in 1994.

Clinton won an election in which voter turnout was less than 50 percent. The lack of interest can be put down to cynicism, poor mobilization by both parties, lack of information, and apathy towards politics. The country seemed to be run by an acceptable leader and voters seemed satisfied with Democrat-Republican power sharing, the Republicans having retained control of Congress.

Despite his 1996 victory, a booming economy and legislative accomplishments, Bill Clinton's second term was calamitous. There had never been a shortage of scandals surrounding Clinton, and the many Clinton-haters were lying in wait. During his 1992 campaign, Gennifer Flowers had caused a media sensation by claiming to have had an affair with him. The suicide of Vincent Foster (he had left a note condemning the Washington sport of ruining careers), Hillary's former law partner and White House counsel, had triggered rumours of a so-called conspiracy involving the presidential couple. Then the full force of the long-simmering Whitewater scandal broke, in which Foster had been involved. Troopergate was unleashed by an article that claimed there had been an attempt to silence Arkansas state troopers who knew about Clinton's sexual indiscretions. By January 1994, a special prosecutor had been appointed to look into the allegations.

The media frenzy began in early 1998, fuelled by the special prosecutor, who had expanded his investigation of Whitewater to include sex in the

White House. Despite all the alleged revelations, Clinton's popularity held up. It seemed that as long as the rumours were not backed up by proof that a crime had been committed, Americans were willing to overlook his personal morality in favour of his capable leadership.

In August 1998, Clinton himself admitted in testimony before a grand jury that he had had an "inappropriate" affair with Monica Lewinsky, a White House intern who had been manipulated by a supposed friend who was working closely with the office of Special Prosecutor Kenneth Starr. As all the sordid details of the affair came out, Clinton continued to maintain that he had committed no crime and to protest the invasion of his private life.

The battle to impeach Clinton ended up before Congress in February 1999, but in the meantime other events had rearranged the political landscape. The November 3, 1998, mid-term elections were shattering. The Republicans lost seats in the House and the Democrats held on to the Senate. Impeaching the president would be more difficult. Newt Gingrich resigned as Speaker of the House, and it later came out that he had also had an affair. His unfortunate replacement, Robert Livingston, was forced to step down for the same reason.

On November 19, 1998, Kenneth Starr testified before the House Judiciary Committee. After a four-year investigation costing $40 million, he could find nothing to corroborate the allegations he was formally investigating. That had not stopped him from releasing a 445-page report with 3,000 pages of supporting documents in September outlining eleven possible motives for impeachment as well as Clinton's sexual habits. Shortly afterward, a contrite Bill Clinton apologized for his wrongful behaviour. The public was largely sympathetic to him.

The Republicans refused to back down, even though they almost certainly did not have the votes to win a conviction. On December 19, Bill Clinton was charged with perjury and obstruction of justice. His trial before the Senate was presided over by the chief justice of the Supreme Court. On February 11, 1999, he was acquitted on both counts when several Republican senators broke ranks and voted with the Democrats. The vote fell far short of the required two-thirds majority; the senators had refused to inflict possibly irreparable damage on the presidency based on allegations of personal immorality or a sex scandal. The constitutional *coup d'état* had failed. The Comeback Kid could finish out his term.

2000 election: George W. Bush

The presidential election that unfolded in fall 2000, while uninspiring in itself, ended in dramatic suspense on election night, November 7.

During the primaries, Al Gore Jr. had been the frontrunner for the Democratic nomination. While there had been an attempt by former senator Bill Bradley to reinvigorate the party with more liberal positions, Gore, as Clinton's heir, seemed more likely to rally voters. The Republicans, for their part, were demoralized and divided after Dole's defeat and the failure of the impeachment. The conservative wing still carried weight in the party, but Republicans needed a new, more moderate-seeming candidate who embodied renewal. They came up with George W. Bush, governor of Texas and son of former president George H.W. Bush. He quickly became the darling of the party with his "compassionate conservatism" (although his policies back in Texas had been for the most part extremely conservative). He was closely connected to oil interests and a product of Republican tradition. The other star of the party was Arizona senator John McCain, a Vietnam War hero who was, however, an outspoken and often nettling critic of the party.

Gore and Bush accepted the nominations at their national conventions. Gore teamed up with Joe Lieberman, a senator from Connecticut. Dick Cheney, who had been secretary of defense for Bush Sr., was chosen to lend authority to the younger Bush's candidacy, which was less than impressive to Americans. Bush's résumé was in fact slim, his malapropisms famous, his knowledge of issues sorely lacking and his foreign-policy experience non-existent. Once again, a wild-card third candidate appeared. Ralph Nader, a lawyer and crusader for consumer rights and the environment, ran as a candidate for the Green Party. Nader attacked the Democrats from the left by accusing them of being too centrist and forsaking liberal principles. As the campaign progressed, the Democrats urged Nader to withdraw to avoid stealing votes from them in a tight race.

The campaign was lacklustre. Bush started out with a slight lead in the polls. His accomplishment was avoiding serious mistakes and admitting his limited qualifications while promising to seek advice, in foreign policy, for example. That was the tactic used in the second televised debate. Gore rose in the polls after the third debate, on topics including health care. He adopted more liberal positions, and the two candidates were almost neck and neck going into November 7.

On that day, Gore received a majority (by 400,000) of the popular vote, but the Electoral College tally would determine the winner. Over the entire evening, predictions by the major American networks flipped back and forth. It finally became apparent that Florida's twenty-three Electoral College votes would be the deciding factor. The situation degenerated into an unimaginable travesty. Gore was first declared the winner in Florida by CNN, and the other networks followed suit. Two hours later, they all announced that the result was too close to call. Not until 2:00 a.m. was Bush declared the winner, but it still was not quite true. Gore conceded to Bush then recanted, much to Bush's annoyance. The final count depended on results from Florida, where the election was close (a 1,700-vote lead for Bush) and there had been charges of irregularities. The Democrats demanded a recount. The state was awarded to Bush, but Gore legally contested the results. The case wound up before the Supreme Court, which ruled in a narrow five-to-four decision that the recount should have been done within forty-eight hours, handing the victory to Bush. The Supreme Court, whose influence had been an election issue for both parties, had indirectly elected George W. Bush as the forty-third president of the United States. The difference proved to be 930 votes in Florida. A series of recounts sponsored by various news organizations confirmed that Bush had indeed won the state.

EPILOGUE

After George W. Bush's election we enter the territory of recent history, where a historian must tread carefully given that not all aspects are known and the broad strokes that writing history requires can easily be shown to be imprecise or open to correction as new facts come to light and are analyzed. Certain Bush administration policies toward terrorism and Iraq will need to be re-evaluated.

Let us briefly recall that the early months of George W. Bush's presidency were not particularly noteworthy. Predictable decisions were made by a president who, behind his conciliatory words, hid a dogged inflexibility. What was perhaps more surprising was Bush's ability to bounce back; he behaved as though he had been given massive voter approval. He revelled in playing the president for all Americans, possibly to make people forget the razor-thin victory of an "accidental" president and the fact that most Americans had voted for Gore. More worrisome still, 51 percent of people who voted for Bush had reservations about their vote.

The terrorist attacks against the World Trade Center in New York City on September 11, 2001, completely re-launched Bush's presidency, which had seemed to be drifting. His popularity in summer 2001 had stood at 50 percent, a recession had hit, unemployment had risen by a million people in one year, the budget surplus left by Clinton was disappearing and the Dow Jones was dropping. Bush had seemed in over his head. After the immediate shock of the terrorist attack, he pulled himself together and became commander-in-chief of a nation under siege.

Bush's presidency was reinvigorated, as Reagan's had been after the attempt on his life in 1981. Bush would increasingly become Reagan's spiritual son. He had never hidden his fascination with the Reagan era, and his references to traditional values were inspired by it. His ideas and language were often the same. His worldview was similarly black and white. "If you're not with us, you're against us," Bush declared. The world was divided into good and evil, and the evildoers, as in a western movie, would be caught dead or alive. Ninety percent of Americans were now behind him. After September 11, Bush focused on weapons of mass destruction and the war on terror, to the exclusion of most other factors in foreign policy.

September 11 had a devastating effect. Americans were shaken by a new vulnerability. The terrorist threat would demand single-minded American resolve. When, where and how to become involved in world affairs was no longer up to them. In his politician's mind, George Bush also understood quickly that the outside threat was convenient to him and that by maintaining it, he might be able to coast until the next election. In all likelihood he was less calculating than this, but it was obvious that a besieged president under attack along with all of America would be difficult to challenge.

George W. Bush was in no way prepared to steer foreign policy. During the election campaign, he had criticized Bill Clinton for being too activist and had come out against a nation-building role for the United States. He assembled an international coalition under his leadership to crush Taliban-led Afghanistan, where Al Qaeda and Osama bin Laden, the mastermind of the attack, had been given shelter. The victory was quick and decisive. George W. Bush deserves full credit, not that the imbalance of forces left any doubt as to the probable outcome. Unfortunately, bin Laden was not captured and the attack on home soil was not fully avenged.

Problems arose when the United States proceeded as though the war against the Taliban were just a first step. The war was won in November 2001. By January 2002, President Bush, in his State of the Union address, was raising the spectre of an "axis of evil" – Iran, Iraq and North Korea – that was building weapons of mass destruction and supported terrorism. These countries were a threat to world peace and the American government would take action against them. There was an international outcry against the possibility of an expanded war on terror.

Opposition, especially in Europe, was widespread. It was brushed aside with a sneering remark about "old Europe" by Donald Rumsfeld, the secretary of defense. In September 2002, after countless efforts to sway the American public, the National Security Council announced a new doctrine that justified pre-emptive strikes against anyone threatening the security of the United States.

The 2002 mid-term elections were just around the corner. Since September 11, the Democrats had been unable to find any politically advantageous position. They were paralyzed with fear of being accused of lacking patriotism or playing into enemy hands in a nation at war against terrorism. Yet reasons for voter discontent were everywhere: the economic slump, corporate scandals, the stock market, eroding pension funds, unemployment and vanishing jobs. These conditions would normally lead to a trouncing of the presidential party in the mid-term elections. But debate centred on Iraq, and George W. Bush had contrived to negotiate with the UN on the question of Iraq, mollifying the fears of centrist voters.

The Republicans' 2002 victory brought them a comfortable majority in both Houses and gave added legitimacy to Bush when it came to the war in Iraq. The U.S. could continue negotiating with the UN or act unilaterally if necessary. This was a major turning point. It meant that if the UN failed to approve American plans, the unilateralists could declare it ineffectual.

There was a misconception that Secretary of State Colin Powell's multilateralists had prevailed when Security Council Resolution 1441 was passed unanimously on November 8, 2002. Bush had already been won over by the firebrands. Cheney, Rumsfeld, Richard Perle, Paul Wolfowitz and Elliot Abrams had chosen to provoke, manufacture and maintain a crisis designed to wipe out a hated regime. The necessity of a pre-emptive war was doubtful, and yet Saddam Hussein would not allow UN weapons inspectors to prove it.

The American invasion of Iraq was lightning-swift. Intense bombing began on March 19, 2003, the first strikes in a war that is now almost universally agreed to have been unnecessary and unjustified. Baghdad fell on April 9. Strongman Saddam Hussein was overthrown, went into hiding and was eventually captured by the American army in December 2003 and executed by the new Iraqi government.

On May 1, 2003, Bush made a splash for the troops and the cameras by jetting onto the aircraft carrier USS *Lincoln* wearing a flight suit and against a backdrop that featured a banner proclaiming "Mission Accomplished." But there were some major flaws in the Pentagon's plans. Baghdad descended into chaos. The city was torn by bombs, destruction and pillaging. Efforts to set up democratic institutions amid sectarian tension ran into difficulties. American intelligence had fallen short, the strategy of

Donald Rumsfeld's Pentagon was ill-suited to a long occupation and the "administrators" had been slow to install their Iraqi replacements.

Backed by approval ratings still approaching 60 percent in late 2003, George Bush continued to repeat his stay-the-course mantra, but more problems soon appeared. The weapons of mass destruction were nowhere to be found. The administration's arguments were collapsing and the goals of the occupation remained elusive. American soldiers expecting to be greeted as liberators became targets instead as Iraqi Sunnis and Shiites clashed.

Iraq was the backdrop to the 2004 presidential elections. John Kerry, senator from Massachusetts, was the Democratic candidate with John Edwards, senator from North Carolina, as his running mate. The Democrats diligently criticized the Bush administration and held up their leader's Vietnam record while offering no real alternative course of action. The uncharismatic Kerry was no match for the Republicans' "positive" campaigning; the war on terror and the support for moral values won out over economic issues. In many states, Republican strategy could be distilled down to "God, gays and guns" (for, against, for). Bush was also aided by a booming economy.

George W. Bush won with 51 percent of votes (116 million Americans had voted out of the 212 million eligible to vote) and a 3.5-million-vote majority. While the president who had billed himself as a unifier in 2000 certainly had a stronger mandate, his country was increasingly divided, its reputation tarnished internationally. As Bush's second term began in 2005, after four years of the war on terror, there was more terrorism than ever. Iraq aside, Tunisia, Bali, Madrid and London had been hit. As casualties and costs mounted, the increasingly isolated U.S. became entrenched in a war that made daily headlines in the Arab world. Iraqi insurgents, with every car bomb and assassination, systematically destroyed the possibility of any cooperation with the occupier.

Public opinion turned gradually against the war. By the end of 2005, barely a third of Americans approved of the way George W. Bush was handling the war, and 40 percent even felt that the effort was wasted. Democrats demanded an exit strategy that would "bring the boys home."

There were false hopes. For example, the December 2005 Iraqi elections unfolded surprisingly well, but the situation rapidly deteriorated. The Bush administration hoped to save the day once again, but 2006 was a disaster. Despite all assurances that it had a winning strategy in Iraq, the administration was clearly changing it constantly to adjust to events and forces outside its control. The 2006 mid-term elections became a referendum on George W. Bush, more and more isolated over Iraq and raked over the coals by the Hurricane Katrina fallout (August 2005), the Mark Foley scandal (the congressman accused of harassing pages) and the pre-election publication of Bob Woodward's book *State of Denial,* which portrayed a White House out of touch with reality.

Bush, concerned about his place in history, spent months trying to pave the way for another Republican victory. He urged his supporters to throw their weight behind the Iraq war as an essential element in the war on terror and criticized Democrats for their cowardly "cut and run" policy.

This time the tactic failed. The verdict was unmistakable. The Democrats took a majority in both Houses. Many Americans wanted the Iraqis to take responsibility for their country and felt that the U.S. should pull out of the quagmire. In an attempt to bring practical bipartisan sense to an increasingly polarized debate, the Iraq Study Group, led by a republican former secretary of state, James Baker, and a former Democratic congressman, Lee Hamilton, pronounced that the "situation in Iraq is grave and deteriorating" and made a number of recommendations, most importantly new diplomatic and political efforts in Iraq and the region, and a change in the primary mission of U.S. forces that would enable the United States to begin to withdraw its combat forces from Iraq responsibly."

Donald Rumsfeld, the architect of the war effort, was the first victim of a policy shift, resigning in December 2006. But the details of just how to withdraw remained to be worked out. They depended largely on Americans' level of tolerance and were negotiated fiercely by a president who did not want to lose face. Still hoping for victory, Bush called for a "surge" of 20,000 new troops in his State of the Union address. The buildup was introduced in spite of Democrat majorities because the administration was still militarily committed to a policy of victory.

The direst predictions made at the outset were now coming true: the international coalition was disintegrating, the United States was mired in a drawn-out occupation, and Iraq and the Middle East had been destabilized. It appeared American administrations could pay a high price for a long time to come as revelations continued to emerge about a war waged on false premises.

BIBLIOGRAPHY

The output of books on American history is enormous. The following are some titles that will be useful to the reader who wishes to delve further. The list includes some titles that the author recommends to his French-speaking readers.

Documents

The classic: Commager, Henry S., ed. *Documents of American History,* 2 vols. New York, Appleton-Century-Croft, 1963.

The invaluable: Boorstin, Daniel J., ed. *An American Primer.* New York, New American Library. 1968. Interesting analyses.

For visual documentation: Bowen, E. ed. *This Fabulous Century, 1870-1970,* 8 vols. New York, Time-Life, 1970; and Adams, James T., ed. *Album of American History,* 6 vols. New York, Scribner, 1969.

Les Presses de l'Université de Nancy in France published (1985-1994) their *Histoire documentaire des États-Unis* in 10 volumes. The collection, directed by Jean-Marie Bonnet and Bernard Vincent, comprises the following titles:

L'Amérique coloniale, 1607-1774 (Jean Béranger)
La Révolution américaine, 1775-1783 (Bernard Vincent)
Naissance de la République Fédérale, 1783-1828 (Élise Marienstras)
L'Union en peril : la démocratie et l'esclavage, 1829-1865 (Jean Heffer)
L'Âge doré, 1865-1896 (Jacques Portes)
L'Amérique, puissance mondiale, 1897-1929 (Yves-Henri Nouailhat)
De la crise à la victoire, 1929-1945 (Claude Fohlen)
L'Amérique triomphante, 1945-1960 (Marie-France Toinet)
Les Années soixante, 1961-1974 (Claude-Jean Bertrand)
Une Crise d'identité ? 1974-1993 (Pierre Mélandri)

General works

Artaud, Denise. *La Fin de l'innocence : les États-Unis de Wilson à Reagan.* Paris, A. Colin, 1985.

Bailyn, Bernard et al. *The Great Republic: A History of the United States,* 2 vols. Lexington, Heath, 1992.

Faragher, John M. et al. *Out of Many: A History of the American People.* Upper Saddle River, Prentice-Hall, 1997.

Fohlen, Claude. *Les États-Unis au xxe siècle.* Paris, Aubier, 1988.

——. *De Washington à Roosevelt : l'ascension d'une grande puissance,* 1776-1945. Paris, Nathan, 1992.

Foner, Eric and John A, Garrity, eds. *The Reader's Companion to American History.* Boston, Houghton Mifflin, 1991.

Gutman, Herbert G., ed. *Who Built America?* 2 vols. NewYork, Pantheon, 1989, 1992.

Heffer, Jean. *Les États-Unis de Truman à Bush.* Paris, A. Colin, 1991.

Henrietta, James A. et al. *America's History.* New York, Worth, 1993.

Kaspi, André. *Les Américains,* 2 vols. Paris, Seuil, 1986.

Mélandri, Pierre and Jacques Portes. *Histoire intérieure des États-Unis au xxe siècle.* Paris, Masson, 1991.

Nash, Gary et al. *The American People: Creating a Nation and a Society.* New York, Longman, 2004.

Vincent, Bernard, ed. *Histoire des États-Unis.* Paris, Flammarion, 1997.

Specialized works

Ambrose, Stephen E. *Eisenhower.* New York, Simon & Schuster, 1983.

Bailyn, Bernard. *The Peopling of British North America.* New York, Knopf, 1986.

Béranger, Jean, Y. Durand, and J. Meyer. *Pionniers et colons en Amérique du Nord.* Paris, A. Colin, 1974.

Brands, H.W. *The Reckless Decade: America in the 1890s.* New York, St. Martin's Press, 1995.

Carter, Dan T. *The Politics of Rage: George Wallace, the Origins of the New Conservatism, and the Transformation of American Politics.* New York, Simon & Schuster, 1995.

Cohen, Warren I., ed. *The Cambridge History of American Foreign Relations,* 4 vols. Cambridge University Press, 1993.

    Vol. I: Perkins, Bradford. *The Creation of a Republican Empire, 1776-1865.*

Vol. II: La Feber, Walter. *The American Search for Opportunity, 1865-1913*.
Vol. III: Iriye, Akira. *The Globalizing of America, 1913-1945*.
Vol. IV: Cohen, Warren I. *America in the Age of Soviet Power, 1945-1991*.
Coulon, Jocelyn. *L'Agression : les États-Unis, l'Irak et le monde*. Outremont, Athéna, 2004.
Dallek, Robert. *An Unfinished Life: John F. Kennedy, 1917-1963*. Boston, Little Brown, 2003.
———. *Flawed Giant: Lyndon Johnson and His Times, 1961-1973*. New York, Oxford, 1998.
Daniels, Roger. *Coming to America: A History of Immigrations and Ethnicity in American Life*. New York, Harper, 1991.
Evans, Sara M. *Born for Liberty: A History of American Women*. New York, Free Press, 1989.
Fohlen, Claude. *L'Amérique de Roosevelt*. Paris, Imprimerie nationale, 1982.
Fox, Richard W. and James T. Kloppenburg, eds. *A Companion to American Thought*. Cambridge, Blackwell, 1995.
Franklin, John Hope. *From Slavery to Freedom: A History of African Americans*. New York, McGraw-Hill, 2000.
Fromkin, David. *In the Time of the Americans: FDR, Truman, Eisenhower, Marshall, MacArthur. The Generation That Changed America's Role in the World*. New York, Vintage, 1995.
Fursenko, Aleksander and Timothy Naftali. *One Hell of a Gamble: Khruschev, Castro, and Kennedy, 1958-1964*. New York, Norton, 1997.
Graebner, William S. *The Age of Doubt: American Thought and Culture in the 1940s*. Boston, Twayne, 1991.
Hodgson, Godfrey. *America in Our Time: From World War II to Nixon*. New York, Vintage, 1976.
Johnson, Haynes. *The Best of Times: The Boom and Bust Years of America Before and After Everything Changed*. San Diego, Harcourt, 2002.
Kaspi, André. *Franklin Roosevelt*. Paris, Fayard, 1988.
———. *La Vie quotidienne aux États-Unis au temps de la prospérité, 1919-1929*. Paris, Hachette, 1980.
———. *États-Unis 68 : l'année des contestations*. Brussels, Complexe, 1988.
Kennedy, David M. *Freedom from Fear: The American People in Depression and War, 1929-1945*. New York, Oxford, 1999.
Kolchin, Peter. *American Slavery, 1619-1877*. New York, Hill and Wang, 1993.

Manchester, William. *The Glory and the Dream: A Narrative History of America,* 2 vols. New York, Little Brown, 1974.
McCullough, David. *Truman.* New York, Simon & Schuster, 1992.
McPherson, James M. *Battle Cry of Freedom: The Civil War Era.* New York, Oxford, 1988.
Mélandri, Pierre. *Reagan, une biographie totale.* Paris, Laffont, 1988.
Middlekauff, Robert. *The Glorious Cause: The American Revolution, 1763-1789.* New York, Oxford, 1982.
O'Neill, William L. *Coming Apart: An Informal History of America in the 1960s.* New York, Quadrangle, 1971.
Paterson, James T. *Grand Expectations: The United States, 1945-1974.* New York, Oxford, 1996.
Paterson, Thomas G. ed. *Major Problems in American Foreign Policy,* 2 vols. Lexington, Heath, 1989.
Perrett, Geoffrey. *Days of Sadness, Years of Triumph: The American People, 1939-1945.* Madison, University of Wisconsin Press, 1973.
Perry, Lewis. *Intellectual Life in America: A History.* Chicago, University of Chicago Press, 1989.
Portes, Jacques. *Les États-Unis au xxe siècle.* Paris, Colin, 1997.
——. *Les Américains et la guerre du Vietnam.* Brussels, Complexe, 1993.
Posner, Gerald. *Case Closed: Lee Harvey Oswald and the Assassination of JFK.* New York, Doubleday, 1993.
Rosenberg, Norman L. and Emily Rosenberg. *In Our Times: America Since World War II.* Upper Saddle River, Prentice-Hall, 1999.
Royot, Daniel, Jean-Loup Bourget and Jean-Pierre Martin. *Histoire de la culture américaine.* Paris, PUF, 1993.
Schrecker, Ellen. *Many Are the Crimes: McCarthyism in America.* Boston, Little Brown, 1998.
Seller, Maxime. *To Seek America: A History of Ethnic Life in the United States.* Englewood, Ozer, 1977.
Semidei, Manuela. *Kennedy et la révolution cubaine.* Paris, Julliard, 1972.
Toinet, Marie-France. *La Chasse aux sorcières : le Maccarthysme.* Brussels, Complexe, 1984.
Wood, Gordon S. *The Creation of the American Republic, 1776-1787.* Chapel Hill, University of North Carolina Press, 1969, 1998.

INDEX

abolitionism, 100–102, 109, 111, 113, 115, 119
abortion, 250, 251, 254, 265. *See also* women's rights
Abrams, Elliot, 273
Academy of Philadelphia, 37
Acadia, 22, 23
Adams, John, 45, 51, 57, 65, 72, 75, 77, 78, 79, 81, 86
Adams, John Quincy, 86, 87, 90, 91
Adams, Samuel, 51, 72
Adamson Act (1916), 171
Administration of Justice Act, 53
Afghanistan, 252, 260, 251, 272
AFL. *See* American Federation of Labor (AFL)
Africa, 2, 4, 21, 27, 31, 200, 209, 210
African Communities League, 185
Age of Reason, 36, 38
Agnew, Spiro, 241, 247
Agricultural Adjustment Act, 192, 196
agriculture, 27–28, 47, 80, 102–103, 110, 132, 142, 143, 156, 193, 205, 221, 248
Alabama, 2, 102, 119, 232, 233, 241
Alabama, ship, 128
Alabama, University of, 232
Alamo, battle, 95
Alaska, 161
Albany, N.Y., 39, 60, 80
Albany Congress, 40
Alger, Horatio, 149
Algonquin Indians, 7
Alien Act (1918), 184
Alien and Sedition Acts (1798), 78, 79, 81
Alliance, organization, 139
  Northern Alliance, 139
  Southern Alliance, 139
Alliance for Progress, 235
Al Qaeda, 272
Amalgamated Clothing Workers of America, 190, 195
American Civil Liberties Union, 208
American Communist Party, 221
American Constitution, 64, 67, 70–75, 78, 82, 117, 135, 136

Thirteenth Amendment, 134, 135
Fourteenth Amendment, 136
Fifteenth Amendment, 137
Eighteenth Amendment, 187, 188
Nineteenth Amendment, 176
Twenty-first Amendment, 188
American Federation of Labor (AFL), 153, 194
American Independent Party, 241
American Liberty League, 193
American Party (American Republican Party), 116
American Protective Association, 150
American Revolution, 26, 29, 37, 41, 45–63, 66, 71, 72, 73, 144. *See also* Revolutionary War
  deteriorating relations with Britain, 41–44
  root causes, 45–48
  immediate causes, 48–53
  revolt, 55–59
  war, 59–63
  surrender, 62
  peace, 63
American Sugar Refining Company, 147
American System of manufacturing, 106
American Temperance Society, 101
Ames, Nathaniel, 38
Anaconda Plan, 128
Andros, Sir Edmund, 19
Anglican Church, 6, 7, 15, 37. *See also* Church of England
Annapolis, Md., 70
Anti-Federalists, 71, 72
Anti-Imperialist League, 164
Antietam, battle, 126, 129
Appalachians, 44, 48, 62, 79
Appomatox, surrender at, 130
Arbuckle, Fatty, 187
Argentina, 251
Arizona, 174, 269
Arkansas, 2, 102, 121, 139, 208, 264, 266, 267
Armour, Philip, 148
Army of Northern Virginia, 129
Arnold, Benedict, 56
Articles of Confederation, 64, 66, 70

asiento, 23
Association, the, 55
Atlanta, Ga., 129, 130, 184
Atlantic, battle of the, 203
atomic bomb, 211, 212, 215, 219
Austria, 201
automobile, 182, 186, 189
Azerbaijan, 261

Baghdad, Iraq, 263, 273
Baker, James, 275
Bakke, Allan, 250
Bali, 274
Ball, George, 230, 231
Baltimore, Md., 8, 27, 60, 98, 103, 107, 112
Baltimore, Lord. *See* Cecilius Calvert
banking, 30, 68–69, 94–95, 171, 183, 192
Bank of the United States, 86, 91, 94–95, 106, 124
Baptists, 36, 37, 38, 104
Barbados, 18
Barre, Vt., 150
Batista, Fulgencio, 200
Bay of Pigs invasion, 226, 229, 235
Bay Psalm Book, 38
Beecher, Henry Ward, 113
Beecher, Lyman, 113
Beirut, Lebanon, 256
Bell, Alexander Graham, 144
Bell, John, 118
Bellamy, Edward, 132
Bentsen, Lloyd, 260
Berkeley, Sir William, 12
Berkeley Free Speech Movement (1964), 240
Berlin, Germany, 200, 210, 227, 229, 261
Berlin Wall, 227, 261
Bernstein, Carl, 245
Beveridge, Albert J., 163, 169
Bill of Rights (England, 1689), 20
bin Laden, Osama, 272
Birmingham, Ala., 233
Blackstone River, 106
Black Farmers' Alliance, 139
Black Muslims, the, 239
Black Panthers, 239
Blaine, James G., 157, 161
Board of Trade, London, 19, 32
Boland Amendment (1984), 257
Bolshevik revolution, 184, 219
Bonus Army, 191
Booth, John Wilkes, 134
Bosnia, 265
Boston, Mass., 13, 16, 24, 26, 30, 31, 51–57, 85, 86, 98, 99, 105, 108, 113, 150, 181, 224
   Boston Associates, 105
   Boston Massacre, 51

Boston Port Act, 53
Boston Tea Party, 52
Botha, Pieter, 244
Braddock, General Edward, 40
Bradford, William, 13
Bradley, Bill, 269
Brain Trust, the, 192
Brazil, 2, 3
Breckenridge, John C., 118
Briand-Kellogg Pact (1928), 199
brinkmanship, 219
Britain and the British, 2–19, 21–32, 34, 38, 39, 40–63, 67, 70, 76, 77, 83–86, 95, 98, 99, 102, 105, 106, 123, 127, 128, 132, 143, 159, 161, 172, 173, 174, 176, 177, 199, 201, 202, 203, 209, 210, 216, 217, 218, 224
Brooklyn Bridge, 150
Brown, John, 115, 119
Brown University, 37
Brown v. Board of Education of Topeka, 222
Bryan, William Jennings, 154
Brzezinski, Zbigniew, 252
Buchanan, James, 98, 116, 117, 119
Buchanan, Pat, 264
Buffalo, N.Y., 80
Bulge, battle of the, 210
Bull Run, battle of, 128
Bull Run, second battle of, 129
Bunker Hill, battle of, 57
Bureau of Freedmen, 136
Burgoyne, General John, 60, 61
Burlington & Missouri Rail Road Co., 146
Burr, Aaron, 79
Bush, George H.W., 254, 258, 259–265
Bush, George W., 263, 269–270, 271–275
Bush, Prescott, 260
Butterfield, Alexander, 245

Cabot, John, 4
Caboto, Giovanni, 4
Calhoun, John C., 91, 93, 110, 111, 117
California, 2, 96, 110, 111, 116, 141, 146, 240, 250, 253
California, University of, 250
California gold rush, 141
Calvert, Cecilius, 8
Calvert, Leonard, 8
Calvin, John, 5, 14
Cambodia, 242, 243, 244
Camp David Accord, 252, 253
Canada, 3, 40, 61, 85, 113, 128, 160, 266
canals, 80, 86, 145
Cape Breton Island, 23
capitalism, 105, 131, 156, 166, 181, 183, 186, 197, 215, 223

INDEX

Capone, Al, 187
Carmichael, Stokely, 239
Carnegie, Andrew, 145, 148–149
Carolina colony, 18
carpetbaggers, 137
Carter, Jimmy, 246, 248–252, 254, 255, 258
Carter Doctrine, 252
Cartier, Jacques, 3
Cascade Mountains, 140
Cass, Lewis, 97, 109
Castro, Fidel, 200, 219, 226–229, 232, 234, 235
Catholics and Catholicism, 5, 6, 8, 22, 33, 53, 98, 115, 116, 132, 184, 185, 225. *See also* Roman Catholic Church
CBS, 186, 231
Central America, 2, 161, 256
Central Intelligence Agency, 218, 219, 226, 227, 231, 232, 234, 245, 261, 262
Central Pacific Railroad, 145, 146
Challenger space shuttle, 257
Chamberlain, Neville, 201
Champlain, Lake, 60
Champlain, Samuel de, 3, 12
Chancellorsville, battle, 129
Chaplin, Charlie, 187
Charleston, S.C., 26, 31, 99, 119
Charlestown, Mass., 17
Charles I, King, 6, 8, 13, 17, 18
Charles II, King, 18, 19
Cheney, Dick, 269, 273
Chesapeake Bay, 6, 8, 9, 10, 16, 60, 85
Chicago, Ill., 99, 114, 133, 141, 146, 148, 149, 150, 152, 170, 185, 186, 187, 190, 195, 201, 232, 240, 241
Children's Bureau, 170
Chile, 244, 251
China, 2, 3, 164, 200, 201, 211, 218, 219, 237, 243, 251, 261, 266
Christian fundamentalism, 254
Churchill, Winston, 210, 211, 216
Church of England, 5, 13. *See also* Anglican Church
CIA. *See* Central Intelligence Agency
Civilian Conservation Corps, 192
Civil Rights Act (1866), 136
Civil Rights Act (1964), 236
civil rights movement, 176, 214, 222, 224, 231, 235, 236, 239
Civil War, 108, 119–130, 131, 133, 140, 141, 143, 150, 151, 161
 secession, 121
 resources for war, 121–122
 recruitment, 124–126
 emancipation, 125
 diplomacy, 127–128

 military operations, 128–130
 surrender, 130
 reconstruction, 133–139
Clark, William, 82
Clay, Henry, 90, 91, 94, 95, 111
Clayton Act, 171
Clémenceau, Georges, 177
Cleveland, Grover, 153, 161, 162
Cleveland, Ohio, 147
Clinton, Bill, 264–269, 271, 272
 impeachment, 268
Clinton, George, 75
Clinton, Henry, 62
Clinton, Hillary Rodham, 264, 265
CNN, 270
coal, 106, 143, 144, 148, 168
Cold War, 215–217, 218, 219, 221, 227, 235, 252, 253, 261
College of New Jersey (Princeton), 37
College of William and Mary, 37
Colombia, 172
colonization, 3–20
Colorado, 141, 260
Columbia University, 37, 240
Columbus, Christopher, 1, 2
Committee for Industrial Organizations, 195
Committee to Re-elect the President, 245
Common Sense, 57, 58
communism, 184, 199, 215, 217, 218, 226
Compagnie du Nord, 22
Compromise of 1850, 110
Concord, Mass., 45, 55, 56
Confederate States of America, 119–130, 133, 134
Congregationalist Church, 37
Congress of Industrial Organizations (CIO), 195
Congress of Racial Equality (CORE), 232
Connally, John, 233
Connecticut, 16, 32, 33, 269
conscription, 122, 124, 126, 174, 203, 206
Conservative Revolution, 266
Consolidated Tobacco Company, 166
Continental Army, 56, 60, 61
Contras, Nicaragua, 257, 258
Coolidge, Calvin, 184, 199
Copperheads, 122
Cornell University, 240
Cornwallis, Lord, 62
Cosmopolitan magazine, 169
cotton, 27, 66, 86, 99, 102, 106, 122, 123, 127, 139, 142
cotton gin, 27, 86, 102, 106
Coughlin, Father, 194, 200
Council Bluffs, Iowa, 146

cowboys, 141
Cox, Archibald, 245
Cox, James M., 182
Crawford, William H., 90
Creek Indians, 85
de Crèvecoeur, Hector St. John, 46
Cromwell, Oliver, 17
Cronkite, Walter, 231
Cuba, 114, 158, 159, 161–163, 200, 219, 223, 226–229, 248, 252, 253
Cuban missile crisis, 227–229, 235
Currency Act, 49
Custer, George, 141
Czechoslovakia, 201

Daley, Richard, 240
Dallas, Texas, 224, 231, 233
Darrow, Clarence, 185
Dartmouth College, 37
Davis, Jefferson, 119, 121, 123, 133
Dayton Accords, 265, 266
Da Nang, Vietnam, 237
Dean, John, 245
Declaration of Independence, 42, 56, 58, 59
Declaration of Rights (1774), 54
Declaration on the Causes and Necessity of Taking up Arms, 57
Declaratory Act, 50
Deere, John, 142
Delaware, 18, 19, 25, 32, 33, 90, 121
DeMille, Cecil B., 187
Democrat-Republican Party, 75
Democratic Party, 91, 98, 109, 111, 114, 115, 116, 117, 122, 156, 170, 180, 193, 196, 214, 236, 240, 243, 249, 273
  Northern Democrats, 114
  Southern Democrats, 130
  War Democrats, 122
  Peace Democrats, 122
Dempsey, Jack, 187
Depression, the. *See* Great Depression, the
Desert Storm, Operation, 263
Detroit, Mich., 185, 187, 205, 207, 239
Detroit Free Press, 202
Detroit Riot (1967), 239
Dewey, Admiral George, 162
Dewey, Thomas, 214
de Grasse, Admiral, 62
Dickenson, John, 66
Dien Bien Phu, 218
Dinwiddie, Lieutenant-Governor Robert, 39
District of Columbia, 256
Dobrynin, Anatoly, 229
Dole, Robert, 267, 269
Dominion of New England, 19

Dos Passos, John, 188
Douglas, Stephen A., 111, 114, 116, 117, 118
Douglass, Frederick, 101
Drake, Sir Francis, 5
Dred Scott v. Sandford, 117
Dreiser, Theodore, 188
Dubinsky, David, 195
Dukakis, Michael, 260
Dulles, Allen, 226
Dulles, John Foster, 217, 219
Dutch Reform Church, 37
Eastern Europe, 215, 261
East Florida, 49
East India Company, 52
Economic Opportunity Act, 235
education, 36, 37, 98, 100, 101, 108, 118, 219, 222, 234, 236, 250
Edwards, John, 274
Edwards, Jonathan, 38
Egypt, 218, 252
Eisenhower, Dwight D., 191, 205, 217–222, 225, 226, 229, 258
  Eisenhower Doctrine, 218
elections
  1788, 72
  1792, 75
  1796, 77
  1800, 78, 79
  1804, 82
  1808, 83
  1810, 85
  1812, 85
  1816, 86
  1820, 86
  1824, 90
  1826, 91
  1828, 91
  1832, 94
  1836, 95
  1840, 95
  1844, 96
  1848, 97, 109
  1852, 98, 113–114
  1854, 114
  1855, 115
  1856, 98, 115–116, 117
  1858, 118
  1860, 118, 119
  1864, 130
  1865, 134, 136
  1866, 136–137
  1868, 137
  1872, 152
  1876, 138
  1884, 157

INDEX

1890, 153
1892, 153
1896, 153–154, 155, 157
1904, 168
1908, 170
1910, 170
1912, 171
1916, 171
1920, 182, 198
1924, 184
1928, 184, 188
1932, 188, 191, 199
1934, 193
1936, 180, 194
1938, 180, 196
1940, 202
1944, 211
1946, 214
1948, 214–215
1952, 217
1960, 225–226
1964, 233, 237
1968, 238, 241
1976, 248–249
1980, 252, 253–254
1984, 256, 257
1986, 258
1988, 260
1992, 264
1994, 266
1996, 267
1998, 268
2000, 269
2002, 273
2004, 274
2006, 275
elections, southern, 1865, 134–135
Electoral College, 77, 86, 90, 92, 94, 95, 116, 118, 138, 153, 196, 241, 254, 260, 265, 270
Elizabeth I, Queen, 5, 6
Elkins Act (1903), 168
Ellsberg, Daniel, 245
El Salvador, 256
emancipation, 59, 66, 101, 122, 126, 129, 133, 139
Emancipation Proclamation, 126, 133
Emergency Banking Act, 192
England and the English. *See* Britain and the British
Enlightenment, the, 36, 38
Equal Rights Amendment (ERA), 251, 254
Era of Good Feelings, 86, 90
Erie Canal, 80
Ervin, Sam, 245
Espionage Act (1917), 174

Estonia, 261
Ethiopia, 251
Ethiopian Crisis (1935), 200
"evil empire" speech, 256
Exposition and Protest, 93

Fair Deal, 213
Fair Labor Standards Act (1938), 196
Falwell, Jerry, 250
Farragut, David G., 128
Father Knows Best, 222
Faulkner, William, 188
FBI. *See* Federal Bureau of Investigation
Federalist Papers, 72, 73
Federalist Party, 71–83, 86
Federal Bureau of Investigation, 221, 232, 234, 244, 245, 266
Federal Emergency Relief Administration, 192
Federal Farm Loan Act (1916), 171
Federal Reserve System, 171
Federal Trade Commission Act (1914), 171
feminism, 243, 265. *See also* women's rights
Ferdinand of Aragon, 2
Ferraro, Geraldine, 256
Fillmore, Millard, 98, 111, 116
films. *See* movies
Final Solution, the, 210
Fire-Eaters, 119
First Continental Congress, 53, 54, 55
First World War, 159, 164, 172, 175, 179, 191, 198, 200
Fitzgerald, F. Scott, 188
Florida, 2, 3, 19, 22, 23, 42, 49, 61, 62, 63, 76, 77, 85, 93, 119, 138, 150, 189, 270
Florida, ship, 128
Flowers, Gennifer, 267
Foley, Mark, 275
Force Bill (1832), 93
Ford, Gerald, 247, 248, 249, 254, 258
Ford Motors, 186, 190, 195, 205
Fortune magazine, 221
Fort Duquesne, 40
Fort Necessity, 39
Fort Sumter, S.C., 121, 130
Foster, Vincent, 267
"Four Freedoms" speech, 209
France and the French, 3, 4, 6, 12, 18, 19, 21, 22, 23, 26, 30, 39, 40, 42–46, 53, 57, 61–63, 76–82, 127, 143, 150, 159, 173, 174, 177, 199, 201, 202, 210, 218
Francis I, King (France), 3
Franco, Francisco, 79, 177, 200
Franklin, Benjamin, 36, 38, 70
Frederick II, King (Prussia), 40
Freedom Riders, 232

Free Soil Party, 97, 109, 113
Free Trade Area of the Americas (FTAA), 266
Fremont, John C., 116
French and Indian War, 39. *See also* Seven Years' War
French Canadians, 56, 150
French Indochina, 203
French Revolution, 63, 76
Fugitive Slave Act, 111, 113
Fulton, Mo., 216
fur trade, 22, 23, 45

Gaddafi, Muammar, 256
Gage, General Thomas, 55
Galatin, Albert, 81
Garfield, James A., 161
Garrison, William Lloyd, 101
Garvey, Marcus, 185–186
gay rights, 265, 274
Gazette of the United States, 78
General Electric, 144, 253
General Motors, 189, 213
Genêt, Edmond-Charles, 76
George, Henry, 132
George I, King, 34
George II, King, 34
George III, King, 48, 49, 56, 57, 58, 95
Georgia, 19, 27, 32, 33, 44, 54, 57, 62, 65, 90, 91, 102, 115, 119, 137, 138, 248, 249, 261
Germany and Germans, 19, 26, 46, 98, 99, 116, 150, 159, 173–178, 199, 200, 202, 203, 204, 208–212, 215, 227, 261
 East Germany, 217, 227
Gettysburg, battle, 128, 129
Gettysburg, Pa., 126
Giancana, Sam, 232
Gibraltar, 23, 42, 61, 62, 63
Gilbert, Humphrey, 5
Gilded Age, 132
Gilpatric, Roswell, 227
Gingrich, Newt, 266, 268
Glorious Revolution, 20, 32
Gloucester, Mass., 150
Goldwater, Barry, 235, 236, 237, 253, 257
Gompers, Samuel, 152
Good Neighbor policy, 199
Gorbachev, Mikhail, 257, 261
Gore, Al, Jr., 269, 270, 271
Gospel of Wealth, The, 148
Gould, Jay, 145, 152
Granges, the, 142, 143, 153
Grant, Ulysses S., 128, 129, 137
Great Awakening, 38, 39
Great Depression, the, 179, 184, 188–191, 200, 248

Great Lakes, 22, 62, 85
Great Peace of Montreal, 23
Great Plains, 140
Great Society, the, 235, 237, 242, 257
Greece and the Greeks, 150, 216
Green Party, 269
Grenada, 256
Grenville, Lord, 48, 49, 50
Guadalupe, 42, 96
Guam, 158, 164, 209
Gulf War I, 262–263, 264, 267
Gulf War II, 273–275
Guyana, 161
Guzman, Arbenz, 219

Haiti, 82, 159, 200, 265
Haldeman, H.R., 245
Hamilton, Alexander, 70, 72–79, 94, 143, 166, 255
Hamilton, Lee, 275
Hancock, John, 72
Hanna, Mark, 167
Hanoi, Vietnam, 237, 238
Harding, Warren G., 182, 183–184
Harlem, N.Y., 185
Harper's Ferry, Va., 119
Harriman, Averell, 145
Harrison, Benjamin, 161
Harrison, William H., 83, 84, 95
Hart, Gary, 260
Hartford. Conn., 16
Harvard University, 37
Hat Act (1732), 28
Havana, 162
Hawaii, 158, 161, 164, 203, 204
Hawkins, John, 5
Hay-Bunau-Varilla Treaty (1903), 172
Hayes, Rutherford B., 138
Haymarket Riot, 133, 152
Hayne, Robert, 93
Hays, Will, 187
Hays Code, 187
health care, 213, 236, 264, 265, 269
Hearst, William Randolph, *and* Hearst newspapers, 161, 199, 200
Helsinki Treaty, 248
Hemingway, Ernest, 188
Henry, Patrick, 45, 50
Henry the Navigator, 2
Henry VII, King, 5
Henry VIII, King, 5, 6
Hepburn Act (1906), 168, 169, 170
Hill, Anita, 264
Hill, James J., 145
Hillman, Sidney, 190, 194

INDEX

Hinckley, John, Jr., 255
Hiroshima, Japan, 212
Hiss, Alger, 219
Hitler, Adolf, 200, 201, 202, 203, 209, 210
Hoffman, Abbie, 240
Holland and the Dutch, 4, 6, 11, 12, 18, 19, 25, 26, 33, 37, 46, 61, 62
Hollywood, 186–197, 206. *See also* movies
Holocaust, the, 210
Homestead, Pa., 133, 149
Homestead Act (1862), 123, 142
Hong Kong, 209
Hooker, Thomas, 16
Hoover, Herbert, 184, 189–190, 191, 199
Hoover, J. Edgar, 232, 245
Hoovervilles, 179
House, Colonel Edward, 176, 178
House Select Committee on Assassinations (HSCA) (1979), 233–234
Houston, Sam, 95
Howe, Admiral Richard, , 60
Howe, General William, 60
Ho Chi Minh, 218, 238
Hudson Bay, 22, 23
Hudson River, 3, 12, 60
Huguenots, 18, 26, 46
Humphrey, Hubert, 240, 242
Hungarian Revolution (1956), 217
Huron Indians, 18
Hurricane Katrina, 275
Hussein, Saddam, 262–263, 266, 273
Huston Plan (1970), 245
Hutchinson, Anne, 15, 16

d'Iberville, Pierre Le Moyne, 22
Idaho, 140, 141, 266
Illinois, 80, 111, 114, 117, 118
immigration, 25, 26, 74, 80, 95, 115, 118, 132, 142, 144, 150, 167, 181, 185
indentured servants, 9, 10, 11, 13, 33, 35
Indiana, 80, 83, 118, 260
Indians. *See* native peoples
industrial development, 28–29, 31, 85, 105–108, 110, 132, 166, 189, 248
Industrial Revolution, 22, 102, 106, 143, 144
Industrial Workers of the World, 176
Intercourse Act (1790), 83
International Harvester, 195
International Ladies' Garment Workers' Union, 195
International Mercantile Company, 166
internment (Second World War), 208
Interstate Commerce Commission, 168
Intolerable Acts, 45, 53
Iowa, 114, 146, 165

Iran, 215, 218, 244, 251, 252, 257, 262, 263, 272
Iran-Contra affair, 257
Iran-Iraq war, 262
"Irangate" scandal. *See* Iran-Contra affair
Iranian revolution, 249
Iran hostage crisis, 251, 252, 255
Iraq, 257, 262, 262–263, 265, 266, 271, 272–276
Iraq Study Group, 275
Irish, 26, 46, 51, 78, 98, 99, 114, 115, 116, 132, 150, 224
"Iron Curtain" speech, 216
iron industry, 106
Iroquois Indians, 18, 22, 23, 40, 59
Isabelle of Castille, 2
isolationism, 159, 198, 202
Israel, 218, 240, 252
Issei (Japanese), 207
Italy and Italians, 1, 2, 150, 177, 199, 200, 203, 204, 210, 215
Iwo Jima, 210

J.P. Morgan and Company, 166
Jackson, Andrew, 85, 89, 90–96
Jackson, Jesse, 260
Jackson State University, 242
Jamestown, Va., 6, 7, 10, 12
James I, King, 6, 13
James II, King, 19
Japan, 199, 200, 203, 207, 209–212, 248, 251, 264
Japanese American Citizens League, 208
Jay, John, 72
Jay's Treaty, 77
Jefferson, Thomas, 58, 64, 73–79, 81–83, 85, 87, 89, 93, 123, 143, 160, 166
Jews, 33, 132, 150, 185, 210
Job Corps, 236
Johnson, Andrew, 134, 136, 137
impeachment, 137
Johnson, Lyndon B., 225, 233, 234, 235–241, 255
Jones, Paula, 266
Jordan, Hamilton, 249
Judiciary Act, 73, 81
de Jumonville, Joseph Coulon, 39
Jungle, The, 169, 170
Jupiter missile, 229

Kansas, 114–116, 117, 118, 140, 141, 153, 165
Kansas-Nebraska Act, 114, 116, 118
Kansas-Nebraska crisis, 114
Keating-Owen Act (1916), 172
Keaton, Buster, 187
Kennan, George, 215, 217
Kennedy, Edward, 254

Kennedy, John F., 223, 224–235, 255, 264
  assassination, 233–234
Kennedy, Joseph P., 224
Kennedy, Robert, 227, 232, 239–240
Kentucky, 78, 80, 85, 90, 111, 118, 121, 122
Kentucky militia, 85
Kent State University, 242
Kerner Commission, 239
Kerry, John, 274
Khrushchev, Nikita, 227, 229
Kidder, Peabody and Company, 166
King, Martin Luther, Jr., 225, 232, 239
  "I have a dream" speech, 233
King, Rufus, 86
King's College (Columbia), 37
Kissinger, Henry, 241, 242, 244, 248
Knights of Labor, 139, 152
Know-Nothings, 116, 117
Knox, Henry, 73
Korean War, 218, 219, 221
Kosovo, 266
Kuhn, Loeb and Company, 166
Kuwait, 262, 263
Ku Klux Klan, 138, 184–185, 250

labour unions, 107–108, 151–153, 167, 168, 174, 176, 181, 183, 190, 194–195, 197, 205, 220
Lachine, New France, 22
Lafayette, General, 62
Lake Shore and Michigan Southern Railroad, 108
Latin America, 158, 161, 199, 218
Lawrence, Kans., 115
Lawrence, Mass., 106, 108
League of Armed Neutrality, 62
League of Nations, 176, 178, 198, 199, 200
Lebanon, 218, 256
Lee, Richard Henry, 58
Lee, Robert E., 129
Lend-Lease program, 203
Lewinsky, Monica, 268
Lewis, John L., 194, 195, 205
Lewis, Meriwether, 82
Lewis, Sinclair, 188
Lewis and Clark Expedition, 82, 140
Lexington, Mass., 45, 56
Liberator, The, 101
Libya, 256
Lieberman, Joe, 269
Lincoln, Abraham, 117–128, 130, 133, 134, 169
Lincoln, Mary Todd, 122
Lincoln, USS, 273
Lindbergh, Charles, 187
Little Big Horn, battle, 141

Livingston, Robert, 268
Lloyd, Henry Demarest, 132
Lloyd George, David, 177
Locke, John, 36, 38
Lodge, Ambassador Henry Cabot, 231
Lodge, Senator Henry Cabot, 178
logging, 27, 29
London Company. *See* Virginia Company
Long, Huey, 194
Lords of Trade and Plantations, 19
Los Angeles, Ca., 205, 207, 255
Los Angeles Olympics, 255
Louisbourg, 23, 39, 40
Louisiana, 22, 42, 76, 82, 104, 119, 139, 143, 194
Louisiana Purchase, 82
Louis XVI, King, 61, 76
Lowell, Mass., 105, 106, 108
  Lowell Mill Girls, 106
Loyalists, 57, 58, 59, 60, 61, 62, 70
Lusitania, steamship, 173
Luther, Martin, 5
Lynn, Mass., 105
Lyon, Matthew, 78
MacArthur, General Douglas, 191, 209, 210, 218
Madison, James, 70, 71, 72, 74, 75, 78, 81, 83–88, 93
Madrid, Spain, 274
Mafia, 224
Mahan, Alfred, 158
Maine, 3, 19, 80, 87, 162, 201
Maine, USS, 162
Malcolm X, 239
Manchester, N.H., 106, 108
Manchuria, 199
Manhattan Project, 211
Manifest Destiny, 97, 114, 160
Manila, 162, 163
Mann-Elkins Act (1910), 170
manufacturing, 4, 28, 67, 221
Marbury v. Madison, 1803, 81
March of the Flag, 163
Marcos, Ferdinand, 244
Marshall, John, 81
Marshall Plan, 217
Martinique, 42
Maryland, 6, 8, 9, 10, 12, 15, 20, 27, 28, 32, 33, 39, 44, 57, 66, 70, 112, 121, 123
Mary II, Queen, 20
Mary Tudor, 5
Mason, George, 70
Massachusetts, 13, 15–17, 20, 23, 30, 32, 33, 37, 48, 49, 50, 51, 52, 53, 56, 57, 68, 72, 86, 93, 105, 107, 111, 150, 260, 274
Massachusetts Bay Company, 13
Massachusetts Government Act, 53

Mayflower Compact, 13
Maytag Company, 195
McCarthy, Eugene, 239
McCarthy, Joseph R., 220, 221
McCarthyism, 219–221, 224
McClellan, General George B., 128, 129
McClure's magazine, 169
McCormick, Cyrus, 142
McGovern, George, 244
McGrath, J. Howard, 219
McKinley, William, 153, 154, 155, 162, 164, 167
McNamara, Robert, 238
Meade, General George, 129
Meat Inspection Act (1906), 169
Medicaid, 236
Medicare, 236
Mellon, Andrew, 255
Memorial Day Massacre, 195
mercantile system, 11, 30, 34, 44
Meredith, James, 232
Methodist Church, 104
Mexican-American War, 96
Mexican Cession, 97
Mexico, 2, 95, 96, 97, 109, 110, 159, 160, 174, 207, 266
Miami, Fl., 226
Middle colonies, the, 21, 25, 26, 27, 30, 33, 37
Middle East, 177, 218, 252, 256, 275
Midway, battle of, 209
Milosevic, Slobodan, 266
mining, 141
Minnesota, 256
Mississippi, 77, 102, 119, 137
Mississippi R., 45, 48, 62, 82, 94, 128, 129, 140
Missouri, 87, 90, 114, 115, 117, 121, 123, 146
Missouri Compromise (1820), 87, 114, 117
Molasses Act, 30, 49
Molotov, Vyacheslav, 211
Mondale, Walter, 249, 256
Mongoose, Operation, 227–228, 229
Monroe, James, 86, 88
Monroe Doctrine, 87–88, 158, 160, 161, 169, 172, 199
Montana, 140, 141
Montesquieu, 38
Montevideo, 199
Montgomery, Ala., 119, 232
Montgomery Bus Boycott, 232
Montgomery, Richard, 56
Monticello, 87
Montreal, 3, 23, 40, 56, 240
Great Peace of Montreal, 23
Moody, John, 166
Morris, Gouverneur, 70
Morris, Robert, 67

Moscow Olympic Games, 252
Mossadegh, Mohammed, 218
Mott, Lucretia, 101
movies, 186–187, 206. *See also* Hollywood
mugwump, 157
Munsey's, 169
Mussolini, Benito, 200, 201, 210
My Lai Massacre, 243

Nader, Ralph, 269
NAFTA. *See* North American Free Trade Agreement
Nagasaki, Japan, 212
Nanking, Rape of, 200
Nantes, Edict of, 18
Napoleon, 82, 83
Napoleon III, 127
Nasser, Gamal Abdel, 218
National Association for the Advancement of Colored People, 186, 207
National Association of Manufacturers, 149, 265
national bank, 73, 74
national debt, 44, 69, 74, 81, 256, 265
National Industrial Recovery Act, 192, 196
National Labor Relations Act (1935), 195, 196
National Labor Union, 152
National Prohibition Act (1919), 187
National Republican Party, 91
National Security Council, 227, 272
Nation of Islam, 239
Native American Party, 116
native peoples, 1, 3, 7, 11, 12–16, 18, 22, 26, 31, 33, 35, 38, 39, 44, 45, 48, 49, 52, 59, 60, 61, 65, 80, 82, 83, 84, 85, 91, 94, 102, 140, 141, 156, 250
NATO. *See* North Atlantic Treaty Organization
navigation acts, 19, 46
NBC, 186
Nebraska, 114, 116, 118, 146, 165
Nelson, "Baby Face", 187
Neutrality Acts, 200
Nevada, 140, 141
Newfoundland, 4, 5, 23, 42, 62
Newport, R.I., 27, 31
Newton, Isaac, 36, 38
New Deal, the, 179–181, 191–197, 204, 214, 222, 242, 255, 257
  First New Deal, 192–193
  Second New Deal, 194–197
New England, 12–17, 19, 21, 22–27, 29, 30, 31, 37, 39, 44, 48, 60, 80, 83, 85, 86, 90, 99, 102, 105, 106, 150
New France, 22, 23, 25, 26, 39, 43
New Hampshire, 32, 33, 72, 113, 239

New Haven, Conn., 16
New Jersey, 18, 25, 32, 33, 37, 57
New Left, the, 240
New Lights, 38
New Mexico, 2, 97, 110, 111, 174
New Orleans, La., 77, 82, 85, 90, 99, 128
New Orleans, battle of, 85
New Right, 251
New Rochelle, N.Y., 26
New York City, 3, 24, 26, 27, 31, 33, 60, 62, 72, 73, 80, 81, 90, 98, 99, 108, 124, 149, 150, 184, 185, 187, 190, 248, 271
New York State, 6, 18, 19, 20, 25, 32, 39, 44, 57, 65, 72, 80, 90, 125, 191
New York Times, 190, 243, 244, 245
New York Tribune, 126
Nez Perce indians, 140
Ngo Dinh Diem, 218, 230, 231
Nguyen Van Thieu, 241
Nicaragua, 114, 251, 252, 257
Nine Years' War, 22–23
Nisei (Japanese-Americans), 207, 208
Nixon, Richard M., 219, 225, 226, 241, 242–246, 247, 249, 257, 258
Noriega, Manuel, 262
Normandy invasion, 210
North, Lieutenant Colonel Oliver, 257
North, Lord, 52, 60, 61
Northern colonies, 30, 31, 32, 33
Northern Securities Company, 168
Northwest Ordinance, 67
Northwest Territory, 67, 80
North American Free Trade Agreement, 266
North Atlantic Treaty Organization, 217, 261
North Carolina, 3, 6, 18, 27, 29, 32, 33, 102, 121, 274
North Korea, 272
Nova Scotia, 4, 23, 59
nullification theory, 78, 92, 93, 94
Nye Committee, 200

Office of War Information, 206
Ohio, 39, 80, 83, 90, 144, 147, 154
Ohio Valley, 39, 80
oil, 144, 215
Okinawa, 210
Oklahoma, 140
Old Hickory. *See* Jackson, Andrew
Old Lights, 38
Olive Branch Petition, 57
Olney, Richard, 161
Omaha, Neb., 146
O'Neill, Eugene, 188
O'Neill, Tip, 249
Open Door policy, 159, 164

Ordinance of 1785, 67
Oregon, 96, 140
Oregon Treaty (1846), 96
Orlando, Vittorio, 177
Ostend Manifesto, 114
Oswald, Lee Harvey, 233, 234
Otis, James, 45, 48

Paine, Thomas, 57, 58
Palestine and Palestinians, 252
Palmer, A. Mitchell, 184
Panama, 158, 164, 172, 252, 262
 Panama Canal, 172, 252
Panay, incident, 201
Panic of 1837, 95, 108
Panic of 1857, 108
Paris, France, 210, 240, 241, 242
Paris Peace Conference, 176–178, 181
Parker, Alton B., 168
Parks, Rosa, 232
Parliament (British), 11, 13, 15, 17, 18, 32, 48, 49, 50, 51, 52, 53, 55, 56
Parris, Pastor Samuel, 17
Patriots, 50, 52, 55, 56, 57, 59, 60, 61, 62, 65
Patriot missiles, 263
Patton, George, 191
Peace Corps, 235
Peace Moratorium, 242
Pearl Harbor, 161, 202, 203, 204, 207, 209
Penn, William, 18, 19, 32
Pennsylvania, 18, 19, 25, 26, 32, 33, 37, 39, 44, 65, 66, 72, 75, 80, 106, 125, 129, 133, 144, 149, 190
Pentagon Papers, 238, 243, 245
People's Party, 139, 153, 154
People's Party of Kansas, 153
Perle, Richard, 273
Perot, Ross, 265
Peru, 2
Petersburg, siege of, 129
Philadelphia, 18, 19, 24, 26, 27, 31, 37, 54, 56, 58, 60, 61, 62, 70, 71, 73, 80, 98, 99, 108, 144, 149, 152
Philadelphia Convention, 71
Philadelphia Exposition, 144
Philippines, 158, 159, 162, 163, 164, 209, 210, 244, 251
Philip II of Spain, 5
Phillips, David Graham, 169
Phips, Sir William, 23
Pierce, Franklin, 98, 113, 114, 115, 116
Pitt, William, 40
Pittsburgh, Pa., 40
Plains of Abraham, battle of, 40
Platt Amendment, 200

INDEX

Plessy v. Ferguson, 222
Plymouth, England, 13
Plymouth Colony, 12, 12–13, 13
Poindexter, Admiral John, 257
Poland and Poles, 150, 201, 210, 211, 212, 215
Polk, James K., 96, 97, 109
Polk Doctrine, 97, 160
Pontiac's Rebellion, 48
Poor Richard's Almanack, 38
population growth, 20, 22, 25–26, 41, 79, 89, 98, 99, 110, 144, 223, 253
Populists, 139. *See also* People's Party
Portugal, 2, 6
Port Royal, 23
Potsdam Conference, 211, 212
Powderly, Terence V., 152
Powell, General Colin, 267, 273
Presbyterian Church, 37
price revolution, 3
Princeton, N.J., 60
Princeton University, 37
Progressive Party (1912), 171
Progressive Party (1948), 214
progressivism, 155–178, 164–172
Prohibition, 184, 187
Promontory, Utah, 145, 146
Prophet, the, 84
proprietary colonies, 18, 32, 33
protectionism, 91
Protestants and Protestantism, 8, 22, 33, 98, 158, 185
Protestant Reformation, 3, 5, 6
Providence, R.I., 105, 106
Public Works Administration, 193
Puerto Rico, 158, 163, 164
Pulitzer, Joseph, 161
Pullman strike, 133
Pure Food and Drug Act, 169
Puritans, 5, 6, 12–17, 33, 35, 37, 46, 53, 185

Quakers, 18, 35, 37, 238
Quartering Act, 50, 53
Quayle, Dan, 260
Quebec, 3, 23, 40, 49, 53, 56, 60
Queen's College (Rutgers), 37

race relations, 179, 185–186, 197, 206–207, 214, 232–233, 239, 250
radio, 186
railroads, 107, 114, 118, 121, 123, 142, 143, 145, 146, 148, 150, 168, 191
Rainbow Coalition, 260
Raleigh, Sir Walter, 5
ranching, 141–142
Randolph, Edmund, 73

Ray, James Earl, 239
Reagan, Ronald, 246, 248, 249, 253–259, 261, 265, 271
Reaganomics, 255
Reconquista, 2
Red Scare, 184
Reformation, 3, 5, 6
reformism, 100, 113, 133, 167
Report on a National Bank (1790), 73
Report on Manufactures (1791), 73, 74
Report on Public Credit (1790), 73
Republican Party, 75, 76, 77, 78–80, 81, 85, 86, 90, 91, 101, 114, 116–117, 118, 122–123, 131, 136–138, 139, 154, 156, 170–171, 178, 183, 198, 214, 221, 236, 237, 254–255, 269, 273, 274, 275
Republic Steel, 195
Restoration, 18, 19
Revenue Act (1764), 49
Revolution. *See* American Revolution
Revolutionary War, 55–63. *See also* American Revolution
Rhode Island, 15, 16, 32, 33, 37, 62, 70, 105
Rhode Island College (Brown University), 37
Richmond, Va., 128, 129
Rochambeau, General, 62
Rockefeller, John D., 145, 147, 149
Rockefeller, Nelson, 247
Rockwell, Norman, 209
Rocky Mountains, 140
Roe v. Wade, 251
Rolfe, John, 7
Rolling Thunder, Operation, 237
Roman Catholic Church, 5, 98. *See also* Catholics and Catholicism
Roosevelt, Franklin Delano, 179–181, 191–197, 199–201, 202, 204, 205, 210, 211, 213, 255, 257
Roosevelt Recession, 196
Roosevelt, Theodore, 157, 158, 159, 162, 164, 167–172
Roosevelt's Rough Riders, 163
Roosevelt Corollary, the, 158, 169, 172, 199
Rosenberg, Ethel and Julius, 219
royal colonies, 20, 32, 33
Royal Proclamation (1763), 49, 50
Rubin, Jerry, 240
Ruby, Jack, 233
Ruby Ridge, Idaho, 266
Rumsfeld, Donald, 272, 273, 274, 275
Russia, 4, 42, 62, 159, 160, 161, 173, 174, 261. *See also* USSR
Rutgers University, 37
Ruth, Babe, 187

Saigon, Vietnam, 237, 238, 244
Saint-Jean-sur-Richelieu, Canada, 56
Salem, Mass., 15, 17, 27, 31
SALT I (Strategic Arms Limitation Treaty), 248
SALT II, 252, 253
Samoa, 158, 161, 164
Sandinistas, 251
Santo Domingo, 42, 159, 161
Saratoga, battle, 61, 62
Saudi Arabia, 262
Savannah, Ga., 130
scalawags, 137
Scheslinger, Arthur M., Jr., 247
Schwarzkopf, General Norman, 263
Scopes, John T., 185
Scopes Monkey Trial, 185
Scots, 17, 26, 46
Scott, General Winfield, 113, 128
Screen Actors Guild, 253
Scud missiles, 263
Seamen's Act (1915), 171
secession of the South, 109
Second Continental Congress, 56–58, 60, 61, 64–66, 68
Second World War, 181, 201–212, 224
   neutrality, 200–203
   Pearl Harbor, 203–204
   mobilization, 204
   war production, 205
   life in wartime, 206
   the armed forces, 206–207
   Japanese internment, 207–208
   women at war, 208
   military operations, 208–210
   war's end, 212
Security Council Resolution 1441, 273
Sedition Act (1798), 78
self-governing colonies, 32, 33
Seminole Indians, 93
Seneca Falls Convention, 101
September 11, 2001, 271, 272
Seven Years' War, 25, 27, 39–40, 46, 48
Seward, William Henry, 161
Shah of Iran, 218, 251
Share our Wealth, 194
Shays, Daniel, 68
Shays' Rebellion, 68, 70
Sheehan, Neil, 245
Sherman, William T., 129, 130
Sherman Antitrust Act (1890), 147, 168
Shiloh, battle, 128
shipbuilding, 24, 29
Shotwell, James T., 199
Sierra Nevada, 140
Sinclair, Upton, 169, 170, 193

Sirica, Judge John, 245
Sitting Bull, 141
Slater, Samuel, 105
slavery and slaves, 2, 9, 10, 14, 18, 21, 23, 25, 31, 33, 59, 60, 66, 67, 87, 95, 96, 97, 99, 100, 101, 102–104, 109–115, 117, 118, 119, 121, 122, 126, 131, 134, 135, 161. *See also* abolitionism; *See also* emancipation
"Slave Power", 110, 117
slave trade, 21, 25, 111
Smith, Al, 184
social Darwinism, 148, 151, 158
Social Security Act (1935), 195, 196
Somalia, 265
Somoza, Anastasio, 251
Sons of Liberty, 50, 51, 52
Southern Christian Leadership Conference (SCLC), 232
Southern colonies, 26, 27, 30, 32, 33, 36, 38
South Africa, 244, 251
South America, 87
South Carolina, 18, 23, 27, 29, 32, 33, 62, 65, 67, 93, 94, 102, 111, 115, 119, 121, 138
South Korea, 251
Soviet Union. *See* USSR
Spain and the Spanish, 2–7, 19, 22, 23, 39, 42, 61, 62, 63, 76, 77, 82, 87, 95, 114, 133, 150, 155, 158, 160, 161, 162, 163
   Spanish Civil War, 200
Spanish-American War, 133, 158, 160
Spanish Armada, 5
Spanish flu, 174
Spencer, Herbert, 148
Sputnik, 223
St. Kitts, 23
St. Lawrence R., 3, 22, 23, 42
St. Louis, Mo., 141
St. Pierre and Miquelon, 42
St. Leger, Barry, 60, 61
Stalin, Josef, 203, 210, 211, 215
Stalingrad, 209
Stamp Act, 44, 45, 50
Standard Oil, 147, 169
Standard Oil Trust, 166
Stanford, Leland, 145, 149
Stanton, Edwin, 137
Starr, Kenneth, 268
"Star Wars" (Strategic Defense Initiative), 256, 260
State of Denial, 275
Steffens, Lincoln, 169
Stephens, Alexander, 134
Stevenson, Adlai E., 224
Stimson, Henry, 205
Stimson Doctrine, 199

Stone, Oliver, 231, 234
Stowe, Harriet Beecher, 113
Strategic Arms Limitation Treaty. *See* SALT
Strong, Josiah, 158
Students for a Democratic Society, 240
Student Non-Violent Coordinating Committee (SNCC), 232
Suffolk Resolves, 55
Sugar Act, 44, 49, 50
Sulzberger, Ferdinand, 148
Sumner, Charles, 115
Supreme Court, 73, 76, 81, 94, 117, 137, 147, 176, 180, 183, 196, 201, 208, 222, 232, 235, 239, 245, 246, 250, 258, 264, 265, 266, 268, 270
Sussex, steamship, 173
Sweden and the Swedish, 6, 19
Swift, Gus, 148

Taft, William Howard, 157, 159, 170, 170–171
Taft-Hartley Act, 214
Taliban, 272
Talleyrand, 78
Talon, Jean, 25
Tampa, Fla., 150
Tarbell, Ida, 169
Tariff Act (1833), 93
Taylor, Zachary, 97, 109, 111
Tecumseh, 83, 84, 85
Tehran Conference, 210
Teller amendment, 162
temperance movement, 100–101, 116, 185, 188. *See also* prohibition
Tennessee, 80, 90, 102, 121, 129, 134, 136, 192
Tennessee Valley Authority, 192
Tenure of Office Act, 137
Tet Offensive, Vietnam, 238
Texas, 2, 95–96, 110, 111, 119, 137, 139, 141, 174, 225, 233, 260, 265, 266, 269
textile industry, 105–106, 148
Theory of the Leisure Class, 149
Thomas, Clarence, 264
Thoughts on Government, 65
Thurmond, Strom, 214
Tilden, Samuel J., 138
Tippecanoe, 84
tobacco, 2, 6–11, 13, 21, 24, 31, 32, 102, 148
Tobago, 63
Tokyo, Japan, 200, 210, 240
Toleration Act (1634), 8
Tonkin Gulf Resolution, 237
Treaty of Tordesillas, 2
Tower Commission (1987), 258
Townsend, Dr. Francis E., 193
Townshend, Charles, 51

Townshend Acts, 51, 52
trade, 29–32, 44, 47, 48, 55, 91, 105, 127
Treaty of Ghent (1814), 85
Treaty of Guadalupe Hidalgo (1848), 96
Treaty of Paris (1763), 42
Treaty of Paris (1783), 42, 62
Treaty of Paris (1898), 158, 163-164
Treaty of Ryswick (1697), 23
Treaty of San Lorenzo (1795), 77
Treaty of Utrecht (1713), 23, 39
Treaty of Versailles (1783), 63
Treaty of Versailles (1919), 178
Trenton, N.J., 60
Trent incident, 128
triangular trade, 31
Trilateral Commission, 251
Truman, Harry S., 211–218, 220, 257
  Truman Doctrine, 216, 217
Truth, Sojourner, 101
Tubman, Harriet, 101, 113
Tunisia, 274
Turkey, 4, 216, 227, 229
Turner, Frederick Jackson, 161
Tyler, John, 95, 96

U.S. Steel Corporation, 166, 195
UN. *See* United Nations
Uncle Tom's Cabin, 113
Underground Railroad, 113
Underwood Tariff, 171
Union Pacific Railroad, 145, 146
Union Party, 194
United Auto Workers, 195, 205
United Fruit Company, 219
United Mine Workers, 194
United Nations, 211, 216, 273
United States v. E.C. Knight Co., 147
Universal Negro Improvement Association, 185
urbanization, 26–27, 98–99, 132, 149
Uruguay, 251
USSR, 199, 201, 203, 206, 209, 211, 214, 215, 217, 218, 219, 226, 227, 237, 244, 248, 251, 252, 253, 256, 257, 261
Utah, 110, 111, 145, 146

Valley Forge, Pa., 61
Vance, Cyrus, 252
Vanderbilt, Cornelius, 145
Van Buren, Martin, 95, 97, 109
Veblen, Thorsten, 149
Venezuela, 161, 219
Vergennes, Comte de, 61
Vermont, 78, 80, 150
Verrazano, 3
Vicksburg, battle, 129

Vietnam, 229, 235, 236, 241, 252
  North Vietnam, 230, 237, 238, 244
  South Vietnam, 218, 242, 244
Vietnam War, 218, 229–231, 237–238, 240, 242–244, 264, 269
Viet Cong, 238
Virginia, 5–10, 12–15, 18, 27, 28, 32, 33, 39, 44, 50, 57, 62, 70, 72, 78, 86, 90, 95, 102, 119, 121, 128, 129, 130, 137, 250
Virginia Company, 6, 12
Volstead Act (1919), 187, 188

Wabash Valley, 84
Waco, Texas, 266
Wade-Davis Bill, 133
Wagner Act. *See* National Labor Relations Act (1935)
Walker, Admiral Sir Hovenden, 23
Walker, William, 114
Wallace, George, 241, 242, 244
Wallace, George C., 232
Wallace, Henry A., 213, 214
Wall Street bombing, 184
Walpole, Robert, 34
Waltham, Mass., 105
Warren, Earl, 222
Warren Commission (1964), 233–234
Warsaw Pact, 261
Wars of the Roses, 5
War Bonds, 175, 209
War Hawks, , 85
War Labor Board, 205
War of 1812, 83–88
War of the Austrian Succession, 39
War of the Spanish Succession, 23
War Powers Act, 204
War Powers Act (1973), 247
Washington, D.C., 74, 81, 92
  burning of, 85
Washington, George, 39, 56, 59, 60, 61, 62, 70, 72, 73, 75, 77, 86
Washington Post, 245
Washington state, 140
Watergate scandal, 244–246, 249
Weaver, James B., 153
Webster, Daniel, 111
Weinberger, Caspar, 256
Wells, H.G., 198

Westinghouse Company, 144, 195
Westmoreland, General William, 238
West Florida, 49
West Indies, 3, 10, 21, 24, 27, 29, 30, 31, 32, 42, 48, 49, 55, 61, 73, 76
West Virginia, 121, 144
Whig party (Britain), 34
Whig Party (U.S.A.), 95, 97, 100, 109, 111, 113, 114
Whiskey Rebellion, 75
Whitefield, George, 38
Whitewater scandal, 267
Whitney, Eli, 27, 106
William of Orange, KIng, 20
Willkie, Wendell, 202
Wilmot Proviso, 97
Wilson, Woodrow, 157, 159, 171–174, 176–178
  Wilson's New Freedom, 157
  Wilson reforms, the, 171–172
Winthrop, John, 13–14
Wisconsin, 117, 165, 220, 224
Wobblies, 176
Wolfe, General James, 40
Wolfowitz, Paul, 273
women's rights, 100, 101, 208. *See also* feminism
Woodward, Bob, 245, 275
Wool Act (1699), 28
Worcester, Mass., 106
Workingmen's Party, 108
World Court, 200
World Trade Center, 271
World Trade Organization (WTO), 266
World War I. *See* First World War
World War II. *See* Second World War
Wounded Knee, battle, 141
Wyoming, 141

XYZ Affair, 78

Yale University, 37, 260
Yalta Conference, 211, 212
Yippies, 240
York, Duke of, 18
Yorktown, 62
York (Toronto), 85

Zimmerman, Arthur, 174
  Zimmerman telegram, 174